ARGENTINA

A Global Studies Handbook

Other Titles in
ABC-CLIO's
**GLOBAL STUDIES: LATIN AMERICA
& THE CARIBBEAN**
Series

Brazil, Todd L. Edwards

Chile, Lisa M. Edwards

Costa Rica, Meg Tyler Mitchell and Scott Pentzer

Cuba, Ted A. Henken

Mexico, James D. Huck, Jr.

GLOBAL STUDIES: LATIN AMERICA
& THE CARIBBEAN

ARGENTINA

A Global Studies Handbook

Todd L. Edwards

A B C 🛥 C L I O

Santa Barbara, California   •   Denver, Colorado   •   Oxford, England

Copyright © 2008 by ABC-CLIO, Inc.

All rights reserved. No part of this publication may be reproduced,
stored in a retrieval system, or transmitted, in any form or by any
means, electronic, mechanical, photocopying, recording, or otherwise, except for the inclusion of brief quotations in a review, without
prior permission in writing from the publishers.

Library of Congress Cataloging-in-Publication Data

Edwards, Todd L.
  Argentina : a global studies handbook / Todd L. Edwards.
    p. cm. — (ABC-CLIO's global studies. Latin America and the
    Caribbean)
  Includes bibliographical references and index.
  ISBN 978-1-85109-986-3 (hard copy : alk. paper) —
  ISBN 978-1-85109-987-0 (ebook)

  1. Argentina—Handbooks, manuals, etc. I. Title.

  F2808.5.E39 2008
  982—dc22   2007031368

  12 11 10 09 08   1 2 3 4 5 6 7 8 9 10

Production Editor   Kristine Swift
Editorial Assistant   Sara Springer
Production Manager   Don Schmidt
Media Editor   Katherine Jackson
Media Resources Coordinator   Ellen Brenna Dougherty
Media Resources Manager   Caroline Price
File Management Coordinator   Paula Gerard

ABC-CLIO, Inc.
130 Cremona Drive, P.O. Box 1911
Santa Barbara, California 93116-1911

This book is also available on the World Wide Web as an ebook.
Visit www.abc-clio.com for details.

This book is printed on acid-free paper. ∞

Manufactured in the United States of America

Contents

Series Editor's Foreword

In a world in which borders are blurring and cultures are blending at a dizzying pace, becoming more globally aware and knowledgeable is imperative. This is especially true regarding one's immediate neighbors, where the links are most intense and most profound. For this very pragmatic reason, knowing more about Latin America is especially relevant to us in the United States. Yet outside of such a practical consideration, Latin America is a fascinating region of the world on its own terms, and it is worth the time and energy to get to know the region better simply as a matter of intellectual curiosity. By providing a readable and engaging introduction to a representative selection of the region's countries, this series hopes to engage readers and nurture their curiosity in the region and its people.

One thing that this series will make abundantly clear is that Latin America is not a homogeneous region. For example, its population is remarkably diverse. Indigenous peoples are spread throughout the region, even constituting the majority of populations in countries where the largest of the region's magnificent pre-Columbian civilizations were centered. Descendents of the Iberian European colonizers continue to dominate the region's political and economic landscape, although recently arrived immigrant populations from Europe and Asia have made significant inroads in the economic, political, and cultural life of the countries of the region. The centrality of Latin America to the Atlantic slave trade network brought hundreds of thousands of Africans to the region to labor in the plantations. The African cultural legacy is particularly relevant to modern Brazil and the Gulf-Caribbean countries. And the process of racial mixture, or miscegenation, that occurred freely and consistently over the past

500 years of the region's history, has created a unique mestizo identity that many modern Latin Americans embrace as their own. Therefore, one of the things about the region that makes it so intriguing is that it is so vastly different from one country to the next; and yet, at the same time, the countries of the region bear striking similarities. In addition to sharing a physical continent and space in the Western Hemisphere, the countries of Latin America also share a basic, common history that stretches from the colonial period through the present day. And the region is bound together in many ways by language and culture.

In terms of its geography, Latin America is a vast region, encompassing more than one-half of the entire Western Hemisphere; and its natural environment is one of the more diverse in the world, including some of the driest deserts in northern Chile to the lushest and most ecologically diverse rain forests of the Amazon River basin. It is also a region rich in natural resources, providing the world with many of its foodstuffs, energy and mineral resources, and other commodities.

A few basic statistics in this regard can help illuminate the importance of learning more about the region. Latin Americans constitute approximately 12 percent of the world's total population, and Latin American countries make up approximately 6.5 percent of the world's landmass. By some estimates, Spanish is the most spoken language in the Western world; and is second only to Mandarin Chinese among all linguistic groups worldwide. The vast majority of Spanish speakers reside in Latin America. Portuguese, the native language of Brazil, is among the world's top ten most spoken languages.

Among the developing world, Latin America as a region ranks consistently at the top in terms of most economic and social indicators in aggregate terms; but the region still struggles with chronic poverty and suffers from highly skewed patterns of income distribution. A consequence of this has been growing out-migration, with more Latin Americans each year making their way to better opportunities in other wealthier and more economically developed countries. Recent efforts to promote greater economic integration through regional free trade agreements throughout the Western Hemisphere also illustrate the growing importance of a greater knowledge and awareness of Latin America.

In terms of politics and governments, Latin America finds itself squarely in the traditions of Western liberal democracy. Most Latin Americans embrace the values of individual freedom and liberty and expect their political systems to reflect those values. Although this has not always been the reality for Latin American countries, as of late, it has been the norm. In fact, all of the countries of Latin America today, with the exception of Cuba, have governments that are democratically elected and all are actively engaged globally.

The specific volumes in this series introduce Mexico, Brazil, Chile, Costa Rica, Cuba, and Argentina. They represent all of the different subregions in Latin America; and they range from the smaller countries in terms of population, landmass, and economic wealth to the largest. The countries included in the series are varied in terms of their ethnic and class composition, with Cuba and Brazil containing large Afro-Latin American populations and Mexico representing a society shaped by a rich and vibrant indigenous culture. The inclusion of Cuba, which remains the region's stalwart socialist experiment, offers ideological variation in the series as well. Argentina, Brazil, Chile, and Mexico represent the region's top four economic regional powerhouses, whose places in the global economy are well established. These four countries are also the region's most influential actors in the international arena not only serving as leaders within the Latin American region but also exercising influence in the world's premier international bodies. On the other hand, Costa Rica and Cuba demonstrate the challenges and possibilities for the region's many less-influential global actors and smaller economies.

Finally, Latin American culture continues to seep into the mainstream of U.S. culture. People in the United States are enjoying the food, music, and popular culture of Latin America because of those items' availability and appeal. In fact, one might argue that the United States is becoming more Latin. And a great deal of convincing evidence indicates as much. The numbers of those who identify themselves as Hispanic or Latino in the United States are growing rapidly and disproportionately to other ethnic or racial groups. According to the 2000 census, the Hispanic population in the United States constitutes about 12.5 percent of the total U.S. population and is now the country's largest ethnic minority group. Even more striking is the incredible growth rate of the Hispanic population in the United States relative to the total population. In just twenty years, the Hispanic population more than doubled and went from constituting only 6 percent of total U.S. population to over 12 percent. If this trend continues, Hispanics will constitute a majority of the U.S. population in about fifty years. The fact that Hispanics in the United States maintain strong ties to their countries of origin and maintain an affinity for the culture and lifestyles common to the region makes Latin America all the more relevant to understand.

The volumes in this series provide a basic introduction to some of the countries and people of Latin America. In addition to providing a survey of a Latin American country's history, politics, economy, and culture, each volume provides an extensive reference section to help point readers to additional resources that will be useful in learning more about the country and even in planning trips to the country. But above all, the hope is that through this series, readers will come to better appreciate Latin America as a region and will want to learn more about the region and experience the richness that is Latin America.

James D. Huck, Jr.

Preface

While in graduate school in the early 1990s, I studied the history, politics, and economics of Argentina in considerable depth as I pursued a PhD in Latin American Studies. However, I was a Mexico specialist at the time and had not yet had the opportunity to visit Argentina. In fact, I did not visit Argentina until 1997. By that time, I had left the academic world and was employed by a large Spanish bank, which owned Banco Francés, one of Argentina's largest and most prestigious banks. I worked for the Spanish parent bank as an investment strategist based in New York City. As a result, I spent considerable time in the major Latin American countries and their respective financial capitals, including Argentina and Buenos Aires. At the time I began to visit Argentina, the country was quite popular among global investors, due largely to its economic reform program, which included a massive push to privatize state-owned industries, an opening of the economy to global trade and investment, and the well-known convertibility plan that pegged the Argentine peso to the U.S. dollar.

Without question, my years of specialization in Mexico colored my first visits to Argentina. For example, on my first flight to Buenos Aires, before landing, I was struck by the vastness of the pampa that surrounded the capital, not to mention its obvious fertility. For me, this was a huge contrast to the dry and mountainous terrain of Mexico. The land surrounding Buenos Aires is flat, often damp or wet, and relatively lush.

I also was immediately struck by the differences between the people of Argentina and the people of Mexico. Most importantly, Argentina quickly stands out to the visitor as a country made up of largely European people. This is in stark contrast to the mestizo population of Mexico (and other Spanish American countries such as Peru and Ecuador). Argentina also is noticeably different from its neighbor Brazil, which has a huge black and mulatto population. The European influence is also quite obvious as one travels from the international airport into the heart of downtown Buenos Aires. The city is beautiful, and its architecture and layout are reminiscent of many cities in Europe. The reasons that Buenos Aires has often been called the "Paris of South America" become immediately apparent.

I was struck on my first visits, as well, by the vibrancy of the city's culture, despite its reputation for political and economic instability. This vibrancy is apparent in numerous ways. For example, it is not uncommon to strike up a conversation with taxi drivers, discussing any number of topics from national politics to the latest Argentine films. Cab drivers are often well educated—from their perspective, of course, the fact that they are driving taxis underscores the employment problems of their country. Several times I have ridden in taxis driven by veterans of the Falklands War; these drivers did not hesitate to ask my view on the conflict or to expound on their own. Bookstores and cafés are numerous in the capital; and as in Paris, one sees a considerable number of people perusing the daily newspaper or a book over a cup of coffee. Discussions of politics are nearly unavoidable. In this sense, visitors are exposed immediately to the vibrancy of the city's "café culture." I quickly adapted to this culture and incorporated it into my business schedule when visiting this beautiful city. Quite often, in fact, my first meeting of the day would take place at a café—outside if the weather permitted—where business could be discussed in a leisurely fashion over breakfast. Notably, when this was not the case, it was uncommon to start the day's meetings before 9 a.m.—a schedule quite different from the daily grind in New York City, which, for me, started by 7 a.m.

The drive from the Buenos Aires international airport into the heart of the city also highlights many of the struggles Argentina faces in its quest for development. For example, the huge highway into the city illustrates the strides made in the provision of transportation infrastructure, but it also stands in stark contrast to the inadequate road system often visible on the periphery. Likewise, one cannot miss the shanty towns that have sprung up just off the main thoroughfares. These shanty towns underscore the deficit of affordable housing that the considerable portion of the country's population living in poverty must face. While evidence of poverty is unavoidable, so is evidence of wealth and economic development. For me, one of the biggest contrasts between Argentina and other countries in Latin America was the relative prosperity that seemed to characterize Buenos Aires and Argentina. There is no question that poverty is a problem; but compared to other countries I frequented in the region, things seemed to be quite a bit better.

I must admit that I may be somewhat biased regarding Buenos Aires, a reflection of my personal affinity for Argentina and, in particular, for its beautiful capital. Over time, this bias played out in my ability to choose to begin my business trips to South America in Buenos Aires. One must typically fly overnight from New York City to the main South American financial capitals—São Paulo, Rio de Janeiro, Santiago, and Buenos Aires, making early morning meetings the next day impossible or at least quite difficult. As a result, I would typically fly on Saturday nights to Buenos Aires, arriving by midday on Sunday. This gave me the afternoon to enjoy the sights—from a walk around the neighborhoods of San Telmo and Recoleta (with its famous Recoleta cemetery) to reading a newspaper or drinking a cup of coffee near the city's historic Plaza de Mayo to wandering around the lofts, restaurants, and shops of Puerto Madero. Bookstores, antique shops, cafés, and the like are abundant throughout the city. As in many European cities, and in contrast to many Latin American cities, this can all be done on foot, with little danger during the daylight hours. In turn, the evenings gave me an opportunity to test the city's culinary reputation, which never seemed to fail—whether I ate in one of the city's modest family-style restaurants featuring Italian fare and à la carte grilled meats or in one of its more upscale eateries.

My hope is that these impressions of Argentina convey my personal fascination with this interesting and complex nation—not to mention my affinity toward its typically warm and outgoing people. As an outsider, I was consistently made to feel at home in Argentina. Argentines also seemed to go out of their way to help me understand their country and its political and economic affairs.

I have been a student of the country for almost twenty years, and plan to continue as such for the rest of my life. This book is designed to be an introduction to Argentina for readers that are, for whatever reason, interested in this country. It is intended to serve as a "stand-alone" introduction to the country—no prior knowledge of Argentina is expected of readers. It is also designed to serve a wide variety of audiences—from high school and college students interested in researching and writing about Argentina to businesspeople planning a work-related trip to the country to interested travelers planning to visit the country. The idea for this book, then, is to provide an important foundation of knowledge for those interested in learning more about Argentina, whether this book is the only one consulted or it serves as a gateway into further, more detailed exploration.

The book is divided into two main parts—a narrative section and a reference section. The narrative section, interdisciplinary in nature, is divided into four chapters that reflect key subject areas: geography and history, the economy, government and politics, and society and culture.

Chapter One covers Argentina's geography and history. This chapter introduces readers to the country's fascinating history as well as to its immense and diverse landscape. The chapter is arranged chronologically, starting around the time Juan Díaz de Solís first entered the Río de la Plata in 1516 and ending with the current presidency of Néstor Kirchner. This discussion of Argentina's history should underscore the country's fascinating and unique nature.

Chapter Two is an examination of the Argentine economy. The first section follows a chronological order; the second section deals with a number of important contemporary issues relating to the economy. The Argentine economy is the second largest in Latin America, after Brazil. It is also a complex industrialized economy. However, as a developing nation, Argentina faces significant obstacles—most notably a large component of the population that lives in poverty. Chapter Two discusses these important issues and some of Argentina's efforts to overcome them.

The third chapter focuses on Argentina's government and politics. First, it covers the key issues in chronological order, starting with the country's colonial administration and finishing with its transition to democracy and the most recent democratically elected presidents. Chapter Three also deals in some depth with a number of topical issues facing the country and its political system. While this book recognizes that Argentina has experienced considerable political instability in the past, including extended periods of authoritarian rule, it also attempts to stress the positive nature of current political events. Most importantly, even in the face of the collapse of the de la Rúa government in December 2001, the country's democratic institutions have held up, leading to the legitimate election of Kirchner (and the absence of military involvement).

Chapter Four is an exploration of Argentine society and culture. This chapter breaks from the chronological mold of the first three chapters and is roughly divided between topics that relate to society and those more specifically associated with culture. For example, the chapter includes a good deal of content about the various groups that have come together to form the Argentine population—from Native Americans, Spanish settlers, and African slaves to later waves of immigrant populations. Together these groups have formed Argentina's unique population and culture. Chapter Four also covers issues such as Argentine customs, Argentina's unique "brand" of the Spanish language, and Argentine cuisine and music. While space is a constraint, the chapter also attempts to introduce readers to the country's rich traditions in the arts—from literature to film to fine art.

The chapters of the narrative section are followed by a reference section. The reference section starts with a timeline of Argentina's history—again from the time of "discovery" to the current presidency of Néstor Kirchner. That is followed by a section on famous figures of Argentine history, including heroes of independence, famous writers and musicians, key political figures, and internationally famous sports stars. That content is followed by a short section on significant people, places, and events used in the narrative section of the book, serving as a helpful aid to interested readers. Further reference materials are provided, including resources for further investigation and an annotated bibliography.

Many people have contributed to the production of this book. I would like to thank ABC-CLIO and its team of editors—especially Alex Mikaberidze—for all of the work that has gone into this project. I would also like to thank James D. Huck, Jr., the series editor, who invited me to be a part of this interesting project. I want to thank my former teachers and fellow students at Tulane University's Roger Thayer Stone Center for Latin American Studies. Specifically, I want to thank Richard Greenleaf, Roderic A. Camp, and Andrew Morrison, who provided guidance and inspiration during my graduate studies at Tulane. I also want to thank all of my Wall Street colleagues and clients who also provided inspiration to my career, as well as considerable insight into contemporary Argentina. Among them are John Purcell, Peter West, Amalia Estenssoro, Ernesto Gaba, Gloria Sorensen, and Gustavo Neffa. Last but not least, I would like to thank my wife, Laura Edwards, for all of the work she put into this book and for all of the patience she showed while I wrote it. It is to her that I dedicate this book.

Todd L. Edwards

Maps

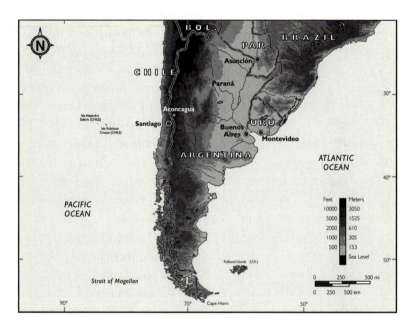

Topography of Argentina

Provinces of Argentina

Major Cities of Argentina

PART ONE
NARRATIVE SECTION

CHAPTER ONE
Geography and History

THE PHYSICAL SETTING

Argentina, officially named *La República Argentina,* covers an area of 1.7 million square miles. The country is bordered by the Atlantic Ocean on the east and by Chile (and the Andes Mountains) on the west; Bolivia is to the northwest, Paraguay to the north, and Brazil and Uruguay to the northeast. Spanning a good portion of the southern half of South America, Argentina is the eighth largest country in the world; and after Brazil, it is the second largest country in South America. The country is roughly one-third the size of the continental United States, or about the same size as Western Europe. From top to bottom, Argentina stretches 2,170 miles.

The official 2000 census places Argentina's population at 37 million people, the sixth most populous nation in the Americas (behind the United States, Brazil, Canada, Mexico, and Colombia). Greater Buenos Aires, which includes the federal capital and its surrounding suburbs, is by far the largest city in the country, with an estimated population of 17.3 million people. Nearly half of all Argentines live in the metropolitan area of Buenos Aires.

The country's environment is quite diverse, containing temperate and subtropical forests, fertile prairies (the pampas), snow-capped mountains, and Antarctic expanses. The Andes cordillera, a high mountain spine, forms the 3,195 mile border with Chile. The highest mountain in the dramatic mountain range is called Cerro Aconcagua, which reaches 22,835 feet. To put that in perspective, the highest mountain in the continental United States is Mount Whitney in

California, which reaches 14,494 feet in elevation, while Mount McKinley in Alaska reaches 20,320 feet. Despite this diversity, nearly all of the country lies in the temperate zone of the Southern Hemisphere.

Argentina, formally a federal republic, is divided into twenty-three provinces and one autonomous federal district. Geographically, the country is typically divided into four main zones: the Andes, the North, the pampas, and Patagonia.

The pampas region is the most important zone in the country—economically, politically, and demographically. The region is comprised of relatively flat but highly fertile plains that dominate the landscape between Córdoba, Santa Fe, Buenos Aires, and northern Patagonia. The pampas extend westward from the city of Buenos Aires in a radius of some 400 miles. The southern pampas, known as the *pampa humeda,* see considerable rainfall; the northern pampas, known as the *pampa seca,* are considerably drier. The pampa is Argentina's agricultural heartland. While Argentina originally focused on "colonial commodities" such as hides and tallow (supported by vast herds of wild horses and cattle), over time, those products were complemented and ultimately supplanted by the country's "mother industries": ranching and grain farming. The region contains the country's largest cities and industrial centers, such as Mar del Plata, Rosario, Córdoba, and Buenos Aires. The pampa contains 70 percent of Argentina's population and produces 80 percent of its agricultural output. Eighty-five percent of the country's industrial enterprises also are located in this region.

The North is typically subdivided into three distinct regions: the Andean North (roughly the provinces of Jujuy, Salta, Tucumán, Catamarca, and La Rioja), the Chaco (Formosa, Chaco, and Santiago del Estero), and Mesopotamia (Misiones, Corrientes, and Entre Ríos). Argentina's northwest and far west are dominated by the Andes (sharing the cold, arid high-country characteristics of Bolivia and Peru).

The northwest is where some of Argentina's oldest cities and towns are located. Traditionally, economic activity at the lower elevations has concentrated on cotton, sugar, and tobacco production, as well as sheep herding and cattle ranching. However, in more recent years, the northwest has been developing into a center for mining and energy production. The subtropical Chaco is flat; this region enjoys high rainfalls and forests and is drained by the Paraguay and Bermejo rivers. The principal economic pursuit in Chaco is logging, but cotton and tobacco are grown as well. Southeast of Chaco but west of Brazil is a region called Mesopotamia, as it is situated between two major rivers: the Paraná and the Uruguay. Much of this region's climate is tropical. Forested in the north, the region gradually turns to open grasslands in the south. Agriculture and the processing of agricultural products are the main economic activities of this region, including the production of *yerba mate,* a hot, caffeinated beverage quite popular in the country.

South of the Andean northwest lies the *Cuyo,* the most densely populated portion of the Andean region. Provinces in this region include Mendoza, San Juan, and San Luis (which, many point out, is more appropriately an extension of the pampas than part of the Andes Mountains) and part of La Pampa. This region also includes many of the first settlements dating to the early colonial era. Areas of the region utilizing irrigation have proven highly productive. Historically, the region has focused on wine production and ranching; but it has seen significant diversification in recent years, growing a broad array of agricultural commodities.

Five provinces make up Patagonia: Neuquén, Río Negro, Chubut, Santa Cruz, and Tierra del Fuego. A number of islands in the Atlantic, in addition to a portion of Antarctica, which Argentina claims, also are included in Patagonia. The region is sparsely populated, although it makes up nearly 25 percent of Argentina's territory. The northern parts of Patagonia are warm and dry, while the south is windy and very cold during the winter. In general terms, eastern Patagonia is wetter than western Patagonia. Agriculturally, the north is dedicated to fruit production and farming; farther south sheep herding gains in importance. The region contains some of Argentina's most important petroleum reserves. Tourism (and increasingly, ecotourism) is important to the region. The far west, of course, is dominated by the high Andes Mountains. Ushuaia, the capital of Tierra del Fuego, is the world's southernmost city.

ARGENTINA'S IGNOMINIOUS DISCOVERY

The first expedition to Argentina was led by Juan Díaz de Solís, who left Spain with three ships in 1515. The trip's original goal was to find a southern passage to the Pacific Ocean. First sailing along the Brazilian coast (discovered by the Portuguese on April 23, 1500), the group arrived in Argentina in January 1516 at a large estuary that would later be called the Rio de la Plata (the River Plate or Silver River). Following the custom of the time, the Spanish explorers documented their discovery and claimed the territory for their Crown. The trip ended in disaster, however, as Solís and a small group of his party were killed while trying to communicate with a party of native inhabitants. The group had landed somewhere on the coast of present-day Uruguay; further exploration would come later.

Three years later the Spanish sent the famous Portuguese sailor and explorer Ferdinão de Magalhâes, or Magellan, to search for the southern passage again and to delineate Spain's territorial claims. Having absorbed the message in Solís's disastrous visit, Magellan visited the Río de la Plata region only briefly before moving southward to winter on the Patagonian coast. (The name Patagonia came from Magellan and was most likely a reference to the big feet and large stature of the southern Indians he encountered, although Patagon was also a dog-headed monster in sixteenth century Spanish literature.) The next spring in 1520 the expedition succeeded

Ferdinand Magellan was a Portuguese explorer who, while leading the first European voyage to circumnavigate the globe, encountered Argentina and gave name to both Patagonia and the Straits of Magellan. (Library of Congress)

in passing through the straits (now named in Magellan's honor), claiming the southern lands for the Kingdom of Spain.

Conquistadors made two more attempts to claim parts of what is now Argentina. Sebastian Cabot made an attempt in 1526–1529, establishing a base of operations north of what is now Rosario. This mission was driven by rumors of great silver wealth in the interior. However, the silver remained beyond the reach of the lusting conquistadors. And during Cabot's absence, local Indians launched a surprise attack on the base, destroying the Spanish fort and leaving the survivors to find their way back to Spain.

The third attempt, motivated again by the dream of unlimited silver but this time supplemented by concerns about Portuguese claims to the Río de la Plata region, was made by Pedro de Mendoza. This expedition was larger, with some 1,500 men landing in 1536. This group optimistically named the estuary the Rio de la Plata. Landing on the southwest bank, the group named the settlement *Nuestra Señora del Buen Aire,* referring not to the area's pleasant climate (*buen aire*), but to an Italian patron saint popular among Mediterranean sailors.

The expedition met fierce resistance from the local indigenous residents, who attacked both the settlement and expeditionary parties with mounted warriors. The inability to conquer and integrate the local population into the colonial system ultimately doomed the expedition. With food supplies dwindling and few supplies remaining, the settlement was abandoned in 1537; the group splintered, although the leaders continued their push to explore. Some of the group deserted, ultimately getting help from the Guaraní Indians in present-day Paraguay. Those settlers eventually founded Asunción (now the capital of that country).

The failure of the third expedition brought significant consequences to the early development of Argentina. The Río de la Plata region seemed to have little to offer the Spanish conquistadors, who were looking for large native populations (to provide a labor force) and mineral wealth. Offering neither, the coastal region was ignored for a long time. Settlement of what is now Argentina took place in the northwest and Andean regions of the territory, with conquistadors coming east from Chile and south from Peru to found some of Argentina's oldest cities (for example, Mendoza in 1561, Santiago del Estero in 1533, and Córdoba in 1573). In general, those areas proved more hospitable and of more immediate utility to Spanish efforts in the New World.

At the end of the century the descendants of Mendoza's venture pushed again to settle the coast and establish Atlantic approaches to the territory. In some ways they were too late. The colonial trading system had already been established, with a primary focus on two regions that provided both treasure and large populations of Indians—Peru and Mexico. For Argentina, this established trade route was overland. The route ran from Lima to the agricultural communities in Argentina's northwest. The reverse trip from Spain sailed to Panama, crossed overland over the isthmus, sailed to Lima, and then traveled overland again to Argentina. And for the next 200 years, Lima and Panama prevented any permanent reopening of a legal port of entry at Buenos Aires. Thus,

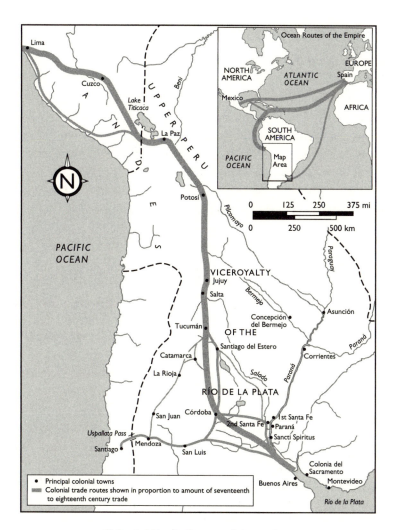

Colonial Trade Routes of Argentina

colonial Argentina existed as a sort of backwater, depending on and answering to the Viceroyalty of Peru; only toward the end of the colonial era did Buenos Aires emerge as an important center of the territory.

SPANISH EXPLORATION AND CONQUEST

Spain's conquest of the New World was little short of astounding, albeit disastrous for the native populations. Starting with Columbus's voyage in 1492, exploration and conquest quickened in the years to follow. In the early years, the Crown's main competitor was Portugal, which, in many respects, was more advanced in the process of exploration, having started its own overseas adventures nearly 100 years before Columbus's first voyage. Significantly, Portugal's Vasco de Gama had rounded Africa and opened the passage to India (1497–1499). Columbus died believing he had reached China and Japan; other explorers soon realized they were exploring not Asia, but two new continents. Amerigo Vespucci, an Italian seaman, came to the coast of Brazil; upon his return to Europe, a map was produced using the term *America* for the southern continent. Eventually, the name was applied to both North and South America. (The first such map was produced in 1538 by Gerardus Mercator.)

The Treaty of Tordesillas

The Treaty of Tordesillas, signed on June 4, 1494, divided the New World between Spain and Portugal (and was signed just two years after Columbus's initial voyage to the New World and before Portugal had ever discovered Brazil). The treaty settled an ongoing dispute between the two countries, which followed a series of Papal bulls issued by Pope Alexander VI that divided the New World between the two contending powers. The Portuguese argued against the pope's line of demarcation. In the new agreement, the line was moved to the west, giving Portugal access to the New World through a strip of land along the west coast of modern-day Brazil. Therefore, Spain could lay claim to much of the rest of the Americas.

The Spanish Crown was involved in two related projects in its New World explorations. The first was building a "mercantile" empire. In this process, the conquistadors were helping the Crown extend Spanish territories in the hope of finding riches, including precious minerals, crops, and people. In the mercantilist world of the time, this wealth was intended for the express benefit of the Crown. In turn, the Crown was motivated to spread its religion to the peoples of the New World. Obviously, for the conquistadors, the driving motivation was the acquisition of wealth, especially in the early years of contact, exploration, and subjugation (1492–1525). The Spaniards' experiences in Mexico and Peru with the Aztecs and Incas, respectively, gave the Spaniards an idea of what was to come. In both cases, small groups of conquistadors conquered vast populations of indigenous people. In return for the riches they obtained for the Crown, early conquerors earned titles of nobility.

A second issue is related: The conquerors were dependent on the labor of those they had conquered, given the very small size of their bands. These conquerors were not farmers, but rather soldiers, administrators, and masters. As a result, colonial organization and exploitation of any given area depended on concentrations of indigenous peoples for labor. This meant that until the 1700s, the Spanish focused on territories with the largest indigenous populations. That focus led to the two capitals of the Spanish Empire in the New World being located in Peru and Mexico. As mentioned, this was a strike against Argentina and contributed to the early colonial populations being centered in the north and northwest.

A NOTE ON THE INDIGENOUS POPULATION

In their "discovery" of what is now Argentina, Spanish explorers encountered lands that were already populated. The indigenous people of the New World were called *indios,* or

Indians, a name reflecting Columbus's mistaken notion that he had reached Asia, calling the lands *las indias,* or the indies.

At the time of discovery, Argentina contained a wide range of indigenous people who spoke a multitude of languages and who had numerous types of social organization. As mentioned, Argentina did not have dense populations of natives like the Aztecs or the Incas. In general, Argentina's Indians were divided between hunter-gatherers and agriculturists.

In Argentina's Mesopotamia region in northeastern Argentina, small agricultural communities developed over a large territory among peoples sharing a common language. These Guaraní settlements practiced swidden, or slash-and-burn, agriculture, living a semisedentary existence. To prepare a new location for planting and settlement, they set fires to clear the existing vegetation. As the land gave out over a period of time, they simply moved to another unoccupied area. The Guaraní lived in villages of several large buildings, which housed a number of families following the lead of a chief.

A number of distinct sedentary cultures in Argentina's northwest developed links of trade. Somewhere around 1480 Inca armies conquered the northwest, integrating populations collectively referred to as the Diaguitas into the Inca Empire. This population provided labor and other resources for the Inca Empire.

The Huarpes developed to the south in the Cuyo region, living in villages of some 50–100 residents. As agriculturists, they supported themselves by raising corn, beans, squash, and quinoa. They also herded llamas (suggesting a strong influence from the Incas).

The rest of Argentina was settled by nomadic hunter-gatherers. In Patagonia, the pampas, and the northern lowlands, at least ten separate Indian groups existed at the time the Spanish arrived. The Querendí and Serranos lived in eastern Buenos Aires, the Pampa controlled the central plain, and

Native Tehuelche women in Argentina, ca. 1898. (F. Leblanc/Getty Images)

the Tehuelche dominated an expanse stretching from Río Negro south to Patagonia. The fearsome Araucanians also spread from Chile into northern Patagonia and the pampas, conquering or absorbing previous inhabitants. By the eighteenth century, these Indians had adopted the horse and were constantly battling with Spanish settlers. Not until the national government—armed with modern Remington rifles—moved to eradicate these people did the mounted warriors of the pampas cease to be a significant component of the population.

Argentina's earliest towns were based where the Spanish could find settled, relatively populous Indian groups. These settlements occurred mostly in Argentina's Andes foothills, the site of Indian agricultural communities: the Guaraní of Paraguay, Corrientes, and Misiones; the Huarpes of the Cuyo; the Toconotés in Santiago del Estero; the Comechingones of the Córdoba hills, and the Diaguitas of Tucumán and the northwest.

While the arrival of the Spanish in Argentina resulted in extensive racial mixture, it also represented disaster for the indigenous way of life. The Spanish used two different systems to harness Indian labor in the northwest, the *encomienda* system and the *mita* (adopted from the Inca). Both disrupted the way of life of indigenous populations, and both largely disappeared by the mid- to late-sixteenth century as the indigenous populations suffered demographic catastrophe. As the Indians succumbed to European diseases such as smallpox, measles, and influenza, a huge portion of the indigenous population disappeared.

THE EARLY COMMUNITIES OF ARGENTINA

The early communities in Argentina's northwest were basically outposts of the Viceroyalty in Peru and were intended to further the Crown's goals. In short, their role was to supply the lucrative mining regions in Peru. As the indigenous population dwindled by the mid-1500s, the Spanish turned to slavery, purchasing both Indians and Africans. The first African slaves arrived around 1580. However, compared to countries such as Brazil, slavery was small in magnitude, reflecting the relatively minor scale of economic activities pursued at the time. By the 1600s, Argentina's north and northwest were dedicated largely to the production of agricultural products and cattle. These products were produced for local use and for sale to communities to the north.

Early towns in Argentina were fairly small, with creole, or locally born whites, sitting at the top of the social scale. Below the creoles was the rest of the population made up of many racial shades and economic levels. Slaves, along with free blacks, mestizos, mulattoes, and numerous other combinations, performed manual labor. Beyond the town were the villages of *encomienda* Indians, involved primarily in raising crops. Towns reflected the village layout in Spain, dominated by a central plaza with a church, municipal hall, and often a building for a Crown official. Perhaps with a few shops and warehouses, creole residences lay beyond. Compared to the wealth existing in Lima and Mexico City, Argentina's early towns were quite modest.

The 1600s witnessed significant conflict between the Spanish and the Indians in the northwest. The worst conflict occurred with the Diaguitas in the years between 1630 and 1637. The Spanish ultimately prevailed, but only by preventing the natives from planting their crops, which resulted in famine and disease. Ironically, the Spanish "won," but at the cost of a severe population decline, which resulted in a dramatic loss of labor. Some of the loss would be replaced by slaves and wage labor, but the northwest's economic ambitions were constrained for many years by an ongoing shortage of labor.

For a number of reasons, the Catholic Church had less influence in early colonial Argentina than in other parts of Spanish America (although it was still important for religious services, guidance, and education). This lack of influence reflected more than anything the region's relative isolation— only a small number of clergy would voyage as far as Argentina. The most important group was the Jesuits, who arrived in the 1580s and established their famous missions. Jesuit influence grew in early Argentina as the Jesuits produced sought-after products using Indian labor, assumed active roles in education, and acted as principal confessors in the territory.

The Jesuits did not go unchallenged, however, as settlers saw the Jesuits as competitors in the grab for land, labor, and access to markets. One of the most dramatic conflicts between Spanish settlers and the Jesuits took place in Asunción and Corrientes, in the so-called Comunero Revolt. The conflict involved attacks against the Jesuit missions. The Jesuits were eventually expelled from Argentina in the 1760s. The Comunero Revolt marked the beginning of the end for the Jesuit order in Argentina.

Buenos Aires in Early Colonial Argentina

The early years in the Colonial Americas were characterized by competing claims to territory, involving not only competition between Spain and Portugal but also attempts by European powers such as England and France to establish territories in the New World. The Río de la Plata region in particular saw a number of disagreements between Spain and Portugal over the territory on the eastern shores of the Rio de la Plata. Partly as a response to fears of Portuguese encroachment, the Spanish Crown authorized another attempt to create settlements in eastern Argentina. Spanish expeditions traveled east on the Paraná River in 1573, establishing the town of Santa Fe. In 1580 a fort was constructed near the site Pedro Mendoza had previously attempted to settle. This time being better supplied and defended, the site eventually became Buenos Aires. However, at least in early colonial times, growth was slow given a limited labor supply and a dearth of economic opportunities.

The principal industry was cattle ranching; the key question facing settlers was what to do with the cattle to make a profit. Mendoza had left behind a few horses and some cattle, which had multiplied into the thousands, creating huge herds of wild animals that thrived on the pampas. The settlers had two problems: Scarce labor made frequent roundups difficult; and more importantly, markets for the products were too far away to make economic sense.

Remember that distant Lima was the capital of the viceroyalty, and the Spanish Crown required all exports from the territory to pass through the capital; the result, given the impracticality of sending goods from Buenos Aires through Lima for export, was rapid growth in illegal trade. One of the earliest was the trade of illegal imports of silver, which was exchanged for manufactured goods from Europe. Much of this trade was controlled by Portuguese merchants residing in Buenos Aires.

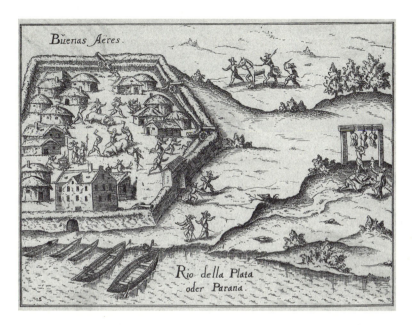

Illustration of the early settlement at Buenos Aires on the Río de la Plata. (Bettmann/Corbis)

The growth of this trade underscores a major point about Argentina's future orientation: Buenos Aires developed in good measure independently of the official colonial trading system, a fact that would resonate throughout the late colonial period and result in independence.

Several developments helped drive the continued growth of Buenos Aires. Contraband trade was one of the most important. The Crown created a customs office in 1622 to reduce contraband trade and to enforce the regulation to trade through Lima (which, of course, was being pushed particularly hard by those residing in Lima). However, given the shortage of inspectors, not to mention Spain's relative inability to provide the manufactured goods desired in Buenos Aires, the illegal trade continued.

The importance of international trade grew rapidly in the eighteenth century; one of the key components was the slave trade. Spain granted England the right to act as the sole supplier of slaves for all of Spain's territories in the Americas. In Buenos Aires, merchants attended to the sale of slaves and the transfer of slaves to the interior; at the time, most slaves left Buenos Aires for other parts of the viceroyalty. Note that by the end of the colonial era, slaves made up as much as 25–30 percent of the population in Argentina's main towns.

The British did not limit themselves to the slave trade, however. The ships used to transport slaves also contained manufactured goods, which the British exchanged for hides, tallow, and other local products. (Tallow, a hard fat derived from cattle, was used to make items such as food and soap.) The British also continued to trade for silver from Peru. This trade, beneficial for both Argentina and England, grew well into the nineteenth and twentieth centuries. Through the colonial era, silver maintained the top spot as an export, but ranching grew steadily as foreign demand for hides and tallow expanded.

The growing foreign demand for goods available in Buenos Aires, primarily those derived from cattle, led to some important changes in the eighteenth century. Most importantly, the era of open-country roundups came to an end as investors moved into the countryside and property rights were assigned to a privileged few. This led to the development of Argentina's large cattle ranches, called *estancias*. Another development was heightened conflict with indigenous populations; as ranchers moved farther from Buenos Aires to find wild cattle, battles with the Indians increased. In 1752, Buenos Aires officials organized a rural militia, the so-called *blandengues,* to fight the Indian threat.

The era also saw the beginnings of the gauchos, Argentina's famous cowboys. Over time, a number of people headed into the countryside to try to eke out a living from their hands; these people were often called *vagos,* or lost people. Typically, they slaughtered cattle for food and traded hides for the little merchandise they might need. By the eighteenth century, they were called gauchos and worked for wages during the *estancieros'* roundups. Over time, Buenos Aires tried to regulate this rural population, with only limited success.

THE BOURBON REFORMS

While Argentina was under the rule of the viceroyalty based in Lima and subject to all sorts of restrictions to trade, the Habsburgs, the royal family in Spain, were not able to enforce these limitations effectively. As mentioned, the result was that Buenos Aires developed in good part outside the officially sanctioned colonial system. Contraband trade was simply a way of life.

However, the War of the Spanish Succession, which took place from 1701 to 1714, changed things dramatically. The war left a new royal family on the throne, the Bourbons. For decades, the new royal family focused on consolidating its authority at home; as a result, the change had little immediate impact on Argentina. However, by 1750, the Crown began to focus on its overseas colonies, looking to invigorate their economies and tighten up colonial administration (not least of which was to increase their economic benefits to the Crown).

In Spanish America, the Bourbon Reforms focused on three main changes. First, the entire bureaucratic structure was tightened up, in essence to bring the colonies under more effective control. Second, existing industries were expanded while new activities also were developed. Again, these improvements were intended to bring benefits to the mother country as opposed to the colonies themselves. Third, military defenses were strengthened for the colonies and for the colonial trading system that connected the colonies and the mother country. In the Río de la Plata region, the Bourbons pursued a series of military actions against the Portuguese in the Banda Oriental (modern-day Uruguay). The military capture of Brazil's *Colônia do Sacramento* in 1762 and again in 1777 allowed Spain to better control trading in the region.

Most importantly for Argentina (and for the future predominance of Buenos Aires in Argentina), in 1776, the Bourbons split the Viceroyalty of Peru in two, creating the Viceroyalty of the Río de la Plata in the process. In effect, the move represented and strengthened the importance of this southern component of the Spanish Empire in South America. Buenos Aires served as the capital of the new viceroyalty, which contained the modern countries of Argentina, Uruguay, Paraguay, Bolivia, and Peru. The new viceroyalty was split from the Viceroyalty of New Granada, which consisted of modern Venezuela, Colombia, and Ecuador.

Notably, the Bourbons moved against the Jesuits at the same time, ultimately stripping the order of its privileged status because it was seen as a cause of lost revenue and a threat to royal authority. As part of a larger agreement at the time, Spain granted Portugal authority over the missions to the east of the Uruguay River. This allowed Brazilians to mount slave raids against the missions, with much of the surviving Guaraní Indian population sold into slavery. Spain ultimately expelled the Jesuits from its colonial territories in 1768.

Buenos Aires and the Bourbon Reforms

The creation of the new viceroyalty based in Buenos Aires led to the arrival of a host of new royal officers. The job of these officers was to inspect the colonies and their administration, focusing in particular on ensuring that the tax revenues due to the king were being collected. The creation of the viceroyalty also led to the growth of Buenos Aires as a major mercantile center of the Spanish Empire. The most important legal change was the enactment in 1778 of the *comercio libre,* or free trade, policy. By modern notions, this was certainly not a free trade agreement; but it did end the tortuous regulations requiring Buenos Aires to trade via Peru.

The free trade policy allowed trade between "approved" ports within the Spanish Empire as well as directly between those ports and Spain. In part, the measure was aimed at reducing contraband trade through Buenos Aires, as "legalized" trade would bring higher tax revenues to the Crown. In general, the policy worked as trade boomed. At the same time, the population grew and local industries sprouted.

With legal foreign trade, cattle ranching boomed. (It already was the main export before the change.) Before the reforms, 100,000 hides were exported per year from Buenos Aires; by 1776, the number had exploded to some 700,000 a year (Scobie, p. 61). New industries also were developing, such as a shoe industry. One of the most important areas of growth was the development of the beef industry; dried and salted beef were exported for use by slave populations in Brazil and Cuba.

The Crown's new policies contributed to the rapid growth in the population of Buenos Aires. From only around 12,000 in 1750, the population grew to as much as 50,000 in 1800; cities of the interior were growing as well, and Buenos Aires became an important market for the products produced in the interior. The era also saw a growing resentment in other regions at the increased importance of Buenos Aires. For example, Córdoba had been the cultural center of Argentina during the Habsburg era; the Bourbon Reforms signaled Córdoba's decline in relative importance. Merchants and the mining elite in Peru also complained about Buenos Aires's control of the silver trade.

Another important source of discontent concerned the Spaniards who controlled the colony. The combination of additional colonial officials and tightened control of the system underscored the downside of colonial status for local residents. As long as Argentina had remained a colonial backwater, royal control was limited and creoles managed many matters of defense, administration, and the like. The creation of the new viceroyalty changed that, with creoles reduced to minor, even subservient, roles. The resulting resentments grew and played an important role in the eventual push for independence from Spain.

The Bourbon Reforms and the ascendance of Buenos Aires coincided with a time of war in Europe, which led to disruptions in the contacts between Spain and its New World colonies, including the new Viceroyalty of the Río de la Plata. War between France and England, as well as the American Revolution, led England to restrict Atlantic trade; Spain, as an ally of France, would feel the effects. Buenos Aires had increasing difficulty obtaining the manufactured goods from Europe on which she depended. The French Revolution and the Napoleonic Wars would make matters worse. By 1800, merchants were calling for an end to the imperial trading system. The inability of Spain to meet the needs of its colonies was another important ingredient in the eventual collapse of the colonial system.

COLLAPSE OF COLONIAL AUTHORITY AND INDEPENDENCE

As mentioned previously, much of the period between 1776 and 1819 was marked by war in Europe and the disruption of the regular Spanish convoys to the New World. Besides making trade exceedingly difficult, it also made enforcement of Spanish colonial regulations nearly impossible. Increasingly, locals called for an easing of their ties to Spain as the Crown's policies became increasingly burdensome. Illegal trading activity increased. Portuguese and other merchants operated from Brazil's *Colônia do Sacramento,* while British ships entered Buenos Aires almost at will. Trade also increased between Buenos Aires and other port cities of the Spanish Empire.

While this activity was technically illegal, it presented colonial officials with a dilemma. The decline in legal trading opportunities signaled a decline in revenues (as the opportunity to levy tariffs declined). Given ongoing budget needs (such as funding the military, running government offices, etc.) officials tolerated this activity at first and ultimately supported it.

Trade outside the colonial system continued to expand in Buenos Aires. Importantly, tensions continued to grow between the port and the interior of Argentina. Potosí (an important region of the new viceroyalty that had once served Lima) resented the fact that the silver it sent to Buenos Aires served to enrich *porteños* (residents of Buenos Aires) and fund the bureaucracy, providing little benefit to the local economy. At the same time, more and more residents of Buenos Aires were pushing to make open trade permanent. (Those opposed to such measures represented the groups that benefited from the official trading system and its monopoly agreements.)

One major development in the events leading to independence occurred in 1806, when a British force attacked Buenos Aires (after having seized the Malvinas Islands, or Falklands, in the South Atlantic). Overpowering the Spanish militia, the English took control of the city while the viceroy from Spain,

British forces invade Buenos Aires, ca. 1807. (Bettmann/Corbis)

the Marquis de Sobremonte, fled. Two months later local residents retook the city; and with weapons seized from the British, they repelled a second attack in 1807. The locals' success had a profound effect in further eroding support for Spanish authority (after all, the viceroy had fled) and in building locals' belief in their own power. The viceroy was stripped of his rank and authority by the city's council, one of the first major steps away from colonial rule.

Several additional events accelerated the move to independence. First, the absence of Spanish authorities in Buenos Aires led to further calls for liberalization. Second, Napoleon invaded Spain in September 1807, leading the king of Spain, Charles IV, to abdicate in early 1808. Charles' son Ferdinand then assumed the throne, but was quickly replaced by Napoleon's brother Joseph Bonaparte as Napoleon gained control of Spain in 1808. The resulting breakdown in royal authority further encouraged locals to push for self-rule. Loyalists revolted; their defeat served as yet another victory for the city's council and those pushing for political liberty and an end to the colonial trade restrictions.

The Junta Central in Spain (independent and resisting Joseph Bonaparte) appointed a new viceroy, Viscount Balthasar de Cisneros, who faced an immediate fiscal crisis. Asking the local council for advice, once again *porteños* called for an end to colonial trading restrictions. By May 1810 news had reached Buenos Aires that Napoleon's forces had conquered all major Spanish cities The news gave local leaders leverage to push for more. The viceroy authorized a *cabildo abierto,* or open council, of 200 leading local citizens. The council, backed by the local militia, stripped the viceroy of his powers; and a new council took charge as a revolutionary *junta* on May 25, 1810. The junta did not openly break the link with Spain, but subsequent actions proved that it intended to control local government. Thus, May 25 symbolized separation from the empire. (Another date, July 9, 1816, represented the formal declaration of independence.)

Other regions of the viceroyalty rejected Buenos Aires's revolution—in particular, Peru, Asunción, and Montevideo. A fourth challenge came from Córdoba, but the junta's army managed to defeat that threat. While authorities tried to keep the territory together and under Buenos Aires's control, regional movements against central control gained unstoppable momentum. During this time, Buenos Aires lost the territories that make up much of modern-day Peru, Uruguay, Bolivia, and Paraguay. Likewise, threats from within the territory of modern-day Argentina continued. In fact, the struggle between regional leaders wanting autonomy and the government in Buenos Aires would become a driving issue in the tumultuous decades following independence.

UNITARIOS AND FEDERALISTS

The years following independence were marked by political instability and a constant threat from internal groups fighting for autonomy. Following military defeats and the loss of significant territory from the viceroyalty, the ruling triumvirate adopted a more defensive position. Led by Bernardo Rivadavia, rulers pushed for centralization of political control. A new leader, José Gervasio de Posadas, took over as "supreme dictator," following a first revolutionary congress. The government's main priority at the time was crushing royalist rebels and Spanish counterrevolutionaries.

While instability reigned, a second revolutionary congress was formed, meeting at San Miguel de Tucumán. The congress declared an end to slavery and then formally declared independence from Spain on July 9, 1816. It named Juan Martín de Pueyrredón to lead the country, called the United Provinces of the Río de la Plata. While internal rebellions continued, the counterrevolutionary threat was essentially dead. Pueyrredón focused on asserting the authority of Buenos Aires over the provinces; and a new constitution was written in 1819, giving Buenos Aires broad—albeit contentious—powers.

The country was split between two opposing factions. On one side were the *Unitarios,* who favored strong control of the territory by Buenos Aires. These people tended to be from Buenos Aires province and city. The *Unitarios* were opposed by the Federalists, mainly from the interior, who wanted local autonomy and a decentralized form of government. In general terms, the coast wanted free trade, while the interior demanded protection. In turn, *porteños* wanted to maintain Buenos Aires's domination over the remaining territories of the viceroyalty, while the interior demanded autonomy.

At this time, the country was rife with local militias, and skirmishes between the two opposing sides were frequent. Rivadavia, forced from power in 1812, led a new effort for central power and authority, exploiting infighting among the Federalists. The *Unitarios* pushed to control the port, as well as to force the Indians farther south in an effort to open up additional lands for ranching. Rivadavia remained the leading *Unitario* figure. He managed to push through a number of important liberal reforms and establish a national museum and a new university, among other things.

Rivadavia implemented two changes in the interior that would dramatically change the country. First, he enacted a sort of vagrancy law, which required rural dwellers (non-landowners, of course) to carry proof of employment. If this was not provided upon demand by authorities, the violator faced five years' service in the militia.

The second policy was called the Law of Emphyteusis (borrowed from an ancient Roman law fostering colonization). This law sought to regulate the private use of public lands. While ostensibly created to form small land holdings for crop farmers (and create a lease income for the government), with the ouster of Rivadavia, the law served to rapidly transfer huge amounts of public land to private owners. Numerous estimates suggest that some 21 million acres of public domain were transferred to a mere 500 individuals in the 1820s (certainly not what Rivadavia envisioned).

A new constitution was drafted in 1826 that declared the formation of a republic, dividing power between the congress and the president, and once again underscoring Buenos Aires's dominance over the provinces. Rivadavia was again elected president. Rebellion in the interior resumed, sparked by the new constitution and Buenos Aires's desire to control provincial territories. In a series of events, including misguided support for an attack on Brazilians in Montevideo and the resulting blockade of Buenos Aires, Rivadavia was forced to resign in 1827. The United Provinces fell, succumbing to rebel forces that captured the capital in 1829. The defeat of the *Unitarios* gave rise to the dictator Juan Manuel de Rosas, the central figure of Argentina's early post-colonial history.

JUAN MANUEL DE ROSAS (1829–1845)

Juan Manuel de Rosas is without question a leading figure in the history of emerging Argentina, although debate continues regarding the significance of his rule and the role it played in the country's development. Some scholars argue that Argentina owes its existence as a national unit to Rosas; others prefer to focus on his role in promoting authoritarianism and extremely large landholdings. Rosas came from an elite colonial family and became wealthy in his own right from his involvement in the *saladero* industry, which made cured, salted beef for export. As his wealth grew, Rosas became increasingly active in politics.

As suggested, the collapse of royal authority led to economic difficulties in the interior (not to mention serious quarrels with Buenos Aires) and the rise of caudillos, military strongmen who supported their own militias and used their armed forces as they saw fit. Rosas emerged as a caudillo from the province of Buenos Aires, switching from the *Unitarios* to oppose Rivadavia and the predominance of the city of Buenos Aires. In particular, Rosas argued that Buenos Aires had done little to protect provincial ranchers from Indian attacks;

as such, he became an ally of other caudillos of the interior.
Rosas was elected governor of the province of Buenos Aires in
1829, putting in place an authoritarian regime (and repressing political opponents). Once in power, Rosas extended the
power of the province over the rest of the country, helping to
build the country on the principle of federalism.

Rosas started his rule by negotiating treaties with the Indians, sending forces to fight those who would not come to the
table. He then began to attack his political rivals in other
provinces, destroying *Unitario* opponents in Córdoba, Entre
Rios, and Santa Fe. The ascendant Federalists then created
the *Confederación del Rio de la Plata*. Rosas, along with
Estanislao López and Juan Facundo Quiroga, emerged as the
dominant figures in the new state, representing Buenos Aires,
Santa Fe, and La Rioja, respectively.

With opposition effectively eliminated, by 1831, Rosas
turned his attentions to the province of Buenos Aires, using
his growing powers to promote ranching. Rosas enacted land
policies that allowed a privileged few to acquire huge tracts of
land. Rosas began to experience conflicts with other Federalists as his promotion of the port of Buenos Aires (and liberal
use of tariffs) impacted interior provinces negatively.

Rosas retired in 1832, but his supporters successfully
orchestrated his return to power in 1835. Rosas used the
opportunity to build a powerful dictatorial regime. Backed by
the army and his own police force (called the *mazorca*), Rosas
managed to hold power until 1852. His main rivals, Facundo
Quiroga and Estanislao López, died in 1835 and 1838, respectively, leaving Rosas the dominant political figure.

Rosas's domestic political rivals were fairly weak. In fact,
his real political challenges came from abroad as foreign
nations responded to his often punitive tariffs. The first challenge came from the French, who blockaded Buenos Aires in
1838, leading to economic crisis in the city. The *Unitarios*
seized the opportunity to fight Rosas, while Uruguay declared
war on Buenos Aires. A group of Buenos Aires ranchers also

revolted. However, Rosas triumphed, defeating his rivals in wars from 1839–1841.

Rosas attempted to make Buenos Aires the principal port, using the navy to patrol the Rio de la Plata and the Paraná River to ensure his policies were followed. Again, foreign merchants called for help from their respective governments. This time England joined France in blockading Buenos Aires, but Rosas survived. However, by 1848, Rosas's rivals were gaining strength. Domestic ranchers were turning against him, Montevideo had become a hotbed of opposition, and Brazil was increasingly unwilling to tolerate his meddling in her territories. At the same time, a more vocal opposition was growing in the so-called "generation of 1837," a group of intellectuals who were criticizing Rosas and calling for the transformation of the country. They argued that the Rosas dictatorship was backward and barbaric and that the country should focus on developing in a more European and urban direction.

The key figure in building resistance to Rosas was Justo José de Urquiza, a caudillo from the province of Entre Ríos.

Reacting to attempts by dictator Juan Manuel de Rosas to monopolize shipping routes, French ships blockade the city of Buenos Aires in a joint effort with the British in 1845. (Library of Congress)

As governor of the province and the region's wealthiest landowner, Urquiza resented Rosas's trade restrictions, which had a negative impact on Urquiza's business interests. His challenge to Rosas's reelection in 1851 turned into an armed conflict. This time the enemies of Rosas united behind Urquiza, with an army of Uruguayan, Brazilian, and Argentine troops rising to defeat the dictator. Rosas tried once again to defeat his enemies, but his defeat at the Battle of Caseros in 1852 represented the end of his long rule. (He lived out the rest of his life in exile in the United Kingdom.)

A NEW CONSTITUTION

After Rosas fell, the provinces sent delegations to San Nicolás in the province of Buenos Aires to attend a constitutional convention, which, among other things, endorsed liberal trade policies, promoted public education, and advocated the creation of a highly centralized government. The only problem was that both the city and province of Buenos Aires refused to participate, rejecting the agreement from San Nicolás and the new constitution. The new Argentine Confederation carried on without Buenos Aires, making Justo José de Urquiza the new president and naming Concepción del Uruguay (in the province of Entre Rios) the new capital. Buenos Aires continued to assert its autonomy.

Urquiza promoted the new Confederation, and Britain became the first major power to recognize its legitimacy in 1853. However, Buenos Aires's refusal to join cast doubts about the viability of the new country. Despite a military victory over Buenos Aires, the city and the province continued to reject the Confederation and its constitution. Bartolomé Mitre became the governor of Buenos Aires in 1860 and helped to organize rebellions against Urquiza. Urquiza led another attack on Buenos Aires; but this time at the Battle of Pavón, his forces were decimated. He retreated and ultimately resigned the presidency. Mitre and his allies pressed for political changes and managed to make some important modifications to the constitution of 1853. Mitre also pushed a broad effort to settle and exploit the southern and western territories of the country.

The dominance of Buenos Aires continued, and the majority of the revenues from foreign trade entered its coffers. However, the power of the federal government was growing. One major factor contributing to the power of the central government was the War of the Triple Alliance (1865–1870), pitting Paraguay against an alliance between Argentina, Brazil, and Uruguay. The war was a disaster for the losing Paraguay, which lost nearly half its population. For Argentina, several

The Paraguayan cavalry attacks the combined forces of Brazil, Argentina, and Uruguay during the War of the Triple Alliance, which began in 1865. (Library of Congress)

key developments occurred because of the war. First, the war allowed the government of Argentina to consolidate political control over the provinces. Second, the government used the war as an opportunity to modernize the army (which, in turn, became an active promoter of national unification). Finally, the government used the war as a reason to develop the country's infrastructure.

Mitre left the presidency in 1868, as called for by the constitution; his attempts to put his successor in place failed. Domingo Sarmiento won the presidency after a term as governor of San Juan province. Mitre ran for the presidency again in 1874, but lost to the opposition party *Partido Autonomista Nacional* (PAN) candidate, Nicolás Avellaneda of Tucumán province. Avellaneda's liberal presidency promoted Argentina's "Indian Wars," as General Julio Roca pushed to subdue the Indian population, exterminating those unwilling to cooperate (during the so-called Conquest of the Desert).

In 1880, the governor of Buenos Aires, Carlos Tejedor, lost the election for president to Roca, who had to put down a violent rebellion aimed at stopping him from ascending to the presidency. Roca's administration then federalized the city of Buenos Aires, signaling the end of the dominance of Buenos Aires province over the national government. Roca's presidency also represented the end of nearly seven decades of political turmoil, which stood in the way of national consolidation.

Roca and the "Generation of '80" (the group of landowners and politicians coming to power with Roca) were able to provide the stability needed to accelerate economic development. The so-called liberal age they ruled was one of unprecedented economic transformation as Argentina became a modern nation founded on agricultural exports (and imports of European capital, technology, labor, and businesspeople). Argentina's comparative advantage was based on the production of beef, mutton, wheat, and wool for the international markets.

THE LIBERAL ERA (1880–1916)

The period from 1880 to 1916, which saw tremendous growth in the Argentine economy, is referred to as the "golden age." (Some date the end of this economic period as 1914.) Economic growth was based on providing agricultural products to the economies of the North Atlantic—as suggested, Argentina's "comparative advantage." Two specific technological advances greatly helped Argentina in the process: First, the steamship enabled quicker and more predictable travel than sailing ships; second, the development of chilling factories, called *frigorificos,* allowed more efficient transportation of meats.

Despite the tremendous fertility of the pampas, Argentina lacked capital. England filled the gap, stepping in to invest in railroads, packing houses, docks, and the like. English firms also handled much of the banking, insurance, and shipping involved in Argentina's agroeconomy.

Argentina's economic growth was impressive during this period. From the 1860s until 1914, the economy grew about 5 percent a year, one of the highest sustained rates of growth ever seen in the world. The downside, of course, was that Argentina's growth depended largely on demand from elsewhere in the world. Likewise, the country was highly dependent on foreign capital to sustain growth—in particular, English capital. Finally, growth was uneven; rapid growth in Buenos Aires and the Pampas region contrasted with stagnation in parts of the interior. As a result, the long-standing battle between the port and the interior continued. Likewise, the distribution of wealth was uneven; rich *estancieros* built European-style chalets, while workers barely scraped by. Notably, Argentina did not develop a land-based peasantry as seen in other Latin American countries such as Mexico and Brazil; as such, land reform never assumed the importance it did in other countries, despite the fact that land was owned in huge tracts by a limited few.

Racial "Whitening"

Argentina's nineteenth-century elite worried about the racial makeup of the country and wanted to Europeanize the population, in particular by encouraging mass immigration from Europe. Domingo Sarmiento, for example, was pleased to see that African banners at Carnival were steadily being replaced by banners representing European clubs. Importantly, whereas slaves, free people of color, and mestizos made up a significant portion of the population in the colonial era, mass European immigration would completely change Argentina's racial and cultural makeup.

In addition to a shortage of capital, Argentina lacked labor. This problem was solved by mass immigration from southern Europe, especially Italy and to a lesser extent Spain. It is estimated that between 1857 and 1930, Argentina received net immigration of 3.5 million people (46 percent Italian, 32 percent Spanish). This accounted for some 60 percent of Argentina's population growth. Immigration had a larger impact on Argentina than any other country in the Americas. In fact, by 1914 it is estimated that 30 percent of the population was foreign-born (versus 13 percent in the United States at the same time).

This period saw the first attempts to organize workers, as manual laborers represented some 60 percent of Buenos Aires's labor force. Early efforts were influenced by European trends, particularly given the large number of foreign laborers. As strikes increased, the government issued the *Ley de Residencia,* a part of the overall effort to control labor, which gave the government the right to deport foreigners who were deemed a threat. Importantly, organized labor became an important political factor relatively early in Argentina's history and remained so through the middle of the twentieth century.

Importantly, Argentina's rapid development was characterized by an ongoing attempt to define and understand the "national character." Mass immigration contributed to the lack of consensus of what it meant to be Argentine. In the nineteenth century, this effort included criticism of Rosas and the caudillos he represented. The liberals leading the charge against Rosas argued against the "primitive" influence of the rough, cattle-oriented society of the interior, preferring to promote the cosmopolitan European influence of Buenos Aires. The twentieth century saw a backlash against the liberals, with writers such as Ricardo Rojas arguing that Indians and a love of the soil represented the true nature of Argentina. These figures would point to the poem *Martín Fierro* (discussed in detail in the chapter on society and culture), which praised the gaucho culture, as the source of the true nature of Argentines.

The late nineteenth century was characterized by the political dominance of the so-called Generation of 1880, a group of leaders who typically came from the landowning class. They operated a system characterized by *acuerdo* (or agreement)—in essence, informal agreements among the powerful elite of the executive branch.

However, increasingly, this leadership was challenged by the emerging middle class, which demanded to participate in public affairs. Three specific groups of people stood out: recently prosperous landowners, old landowning families not participating in the boom, and members of the growing middle class excluded from political power.

Together these three groups formed the Radical Party in 1890, a party that would play a very significant role in twentieth-century Argentine politics. The Radicals were led by Hipólito Yrigoyen, who pushed the group's efforts to enter the political system. Yrigoyen pushed for "intransigence"—in essence, the refusal to vote or participate in public life until free elections were guaranteed.

A moderate group of the old (and corrupt) political machine won power in 1911, with the victory of Roque Sáenz Peña in presidential elections. Sáenz Peña proposed electoral reform as a way to save the old conservative party. In 1912, Argentina adopted reforms that included universal male suffrage, secret ballots, and mandatory voting. This was, in part, an effort to co-opt these groups of disaffected Argentines, as the real threat to the ruling oligarchy was seen to be organized labor. However, the Radicals seized the opportunity, shrewdly voicing concern for the working classes in an attempt to garner votes. As a result, Radical leader Hipólito Yrigoyen succeeded in winning the presidential elections in 1916.

THE DECLINE OF THE LIBERAL ERA (1916–1930)

Crisis hit Argentina in 1917–1919 as Argentine workers took to the streets and organized strikes. These protests and strikes were part of a movement throughout the Western world to improve the lot of wage earners. Although President Yrigoyen purposely appealed to urban workers, the growing labor unrest proved troublesome for his government. The strikes coincided with World War I in Europe, whose economic dislocation caused economic crisis in Argentina, with layoffs, falling wages, and rising prices. Strikes were on the rise; the terrible economic conditions only made matters worse.

The events climaxed in January 1919, in what is known as the *Semana Trágica* (or Tragic Week), in which a police move against workers eventually caused mass rioting, leading to thousands of deaths and injuries. The Radicals immediately changed their policies toward labor, becoming aggressively antiworker. In a series of strikes in Patagonia, Yrigoyen brought in the military, which violently crushed the strikes and executed scores of workers and labor leaders. Ironically, the Radical government became decidedly conservative.

While economic conditions improved in the 1920s, the conservatives' efforts to co-opt the Radicals seemed to be failing, as efforts to join the political system appeared from all sides.

The Radicals, in turn, adopted some of the same mechanisms of machine politics to keep the conservatives from power. Another Radical, Marcelo T. de Alvear, won the presidency in 1922. Yrigoyen then returned to the presidency in 1928. However, the Great Depression hit Argentina late in the decade, exposing weaknesses in the political system.

THE MILITARY REMOVES YRIGOYEN

Political tensions were aggravated by the global crash of 1929, although Argentina was not hit as early or as hard as other countries in Latin America. However, conservatives would not prove generous in their response to the experiment of sharing political power; on September 6, 1930, a group of military officers and civilian elites removed Yrigoyen from power, arguing that his government was illegitimate. By 1930, in part a result of growing professionalization of the officer corps, the military had concluded that there was no democratic solution to the country's growing political turmoil. They decided to change the rules of the game completely and remove the Radicals from power, hoping to return to the old system.

There was division within in the military, however, as one faction recommended a return to the old system of oligarchic rule while another wanted to establish a semicorporatist state similar to those seen in European countries at the time, such as Portugal and Italy. The latter group argued that democracy was simply not a viable system for Argentina. In a corporatist system, legislators would represent functional (i.e., corporate) interests, such as workers, ranchers, and industrialists. In that faction's view, leaders could stop the chaotic class-oriented politics that had overtaken the country.

The more moderate faction of the military triumphed initially, creating a coalition of parties dubbed *the Concordancia*. In a gesture of conciliation, a number of civilians were added to the military leadership. The political scenario grew increasingly chaotic, however, as newly enfranchised parties refused to play by the old rules; the working class, in particular, continued to make demands on the government. The military watched the growing chaos with less and less tolerance.

War was raging in Europe at the time; and for a long while, it looked as if the Axis powers—Germany, Italy, and Japan—were winning. Argentina's military leaders believed their own country needed strong rule similar to that of the Axis powers. Argentina's military identified corrupt and bumbling civilian leaders as the country's main impediment to further development.

While Brazil sided with the Allies in 1942, Argentina attempted to remain neutral, hoping to continue to trade with the Allies (especially England) without joining the U.S.-led

Military college students and citizens parade through the streets of Buenos Aires to celebrate the fall of President Hipólito Yrigoyen on September 17, 1930. (Bettmann/Corbis)

military efforts. Plots against civilian government by the Argentine military grew, but they took a year and a half to come to fruition. On September 6, 1930, hard-liners took the initiative. The *Grupo de Oficiales Unidos* (GOU) ultimately toppled the government and seized power. Its members argued that they were simply responding to popular demand. They were not far off, as large crowds turned out to cheer the military procession.

Opposed to the moderates who preceded them, this group was intent on completely remaking Argentina's society and political structure. The GOU dissolved congress in 1943, with a few prominent military leaders proudly proclaiming that now "there are no political parties, but only Argentines." This was dubbed the "Revolution of 1943." In 1944, the military decreed an end to all political parties. At the time, demands by workers continued; Juan Perón would become the decisive player in the next chapter of Argentine politics.

JUAN DOMINGO PERÓN AND THE RISE OF POPULISM

Juan Perón, a colonel in the army who was from a middle-class background, was an active participant in the GOU movement. Initially, he was given a fairly minor government role as minister of labor. However, he used this position to become more powerful, courting the working classes to build a base of support. Perón recognized the potential political strength of the working classes and capitalized on it. He was then named minister of war—before becoming vice-president in 1943. A hero to the lower classes, Perón won the 1946 presidential election with 54 percent of the vote.

Perón furthered the hard-line GOU's corporatist plans, organizing Argentina by functional groups—ranchers, farmers, workers, etc. The government, led by Perón, acted as the final judge in disputes between groups. The government instituted a five-year economic plan and, in the process, created a

---

Evita

Eva Perón, affectionately known as Evita, was loved by millions of Argentines. Juan Perón grew to rely heavily on his wife, Eva Duarte (later Perón). A savvy politician in her own right, Evita used her work with the poor to build her status as one of Argentina's most famous people. Setting up her own foundation in 1948, Evita personally dispensed cash and other benefits to the working poor. Evita's death from cancer in July 1952 generated a massive public display of grief. In many ways, Evita became a larger figure in death than in life, becoming the symbol holding together Peronist stalwarts.

---

powerful new state monopoly that controlled the export of Argentina's main products. (These changes made Argentina the most state-directed economy in Latin America at the time.)

Perón differed from the GOU in one very important aspect. Whereas the GOU began by assuming it could stop popular demands, Perón made urban workers his most significant political constituency. Following a nationalist and populist strategy, Perón promised workers the benefits they had long been denied. One of his standard political techniques was to encourage workers to strike, then come in and settle affairs in favor of the workers. While the working class loved the policies of Perón, one clear goal of Perón's government was to remove labor's ability to act autonomously.

Real wages increased by some 25 percent between 1946 and 1950 under Perón's watch. The losers in this process were capitalists (primarily landowners) as Perón used the trade monopoly to transfer income from the rural sectors to urban supporters. Perón's nationalist policies were also quite dramatic; in the best-known example, he nationalized the British-owned railways in 1948. A true coup, the move satisfied nearly all members of his populist alliance: workers,

Eva Perón, wife of President Juan Perón, greets the crowds from the balcony of the Government House in Buenos Aires. (Keystone/ Getty Images)

the military, nationalists, and the middle class. In 1947, Perón paid off the entire foreign debt, issuing a "declaration of economic independence."

Perón soon ran into economic problems, which were created in part by his own policies. For example, in setting artificially low prices for certain agricultural products (to keep food costs low in urban areas), the government simultaneously discouraged the growth of agricultural exports. Inflation was also rising rapidly. Perón called for a standard "orthodox stabilization program," tightening credit, reducing government spending, and imposing strict limits on wages and prices. Perón wanted to fix the economy as quickly as possible so he could return to his ambitious social program.

Perón managed to get the Constitution of 1853 amended to allow his reelection; and in 1952, he was reelected with 67 percent of the vote. The Peronist party was officially founded.

One significant defeat for Perón was his attempt to nominate his wife, Eva, as the vice-presidential candidate; this the military flatly refused.

The austerity program seemed to be working, and Perón and his economic team put together another five-year economic plan. (This one was notably less nationalistic and populist than the first; Perón actively courted foreign investors this time.) However, Perón's political strategy became more radical; and after 1949, he tried to control the military. An attempted coup took place in 1952—it had become increasingly clear that the military was losing patience with Perón.

While economic policy remained relatively orthodox, Peronist rhetoric grew increasingly militaristic; and civil unrest returned to Argentina. In 1953, a group of Peronists wrecked the Jockey Club (a headquarters for Argentine elites). Then the Peronists mistakenly took on the Church, legalizing divorce and taking control of parochial schools. Anti-Church demonstrations were organized, and several well-known Buenos Aires cathedrals were damaged by crowds. The Vatican responded by excommunicating Perón and his cabinet.

Events unfolded quickly in the final days of the Perón era. In June 1955, some 100,000 middle-class protesters took to the streets of Buenos Aires. This was followed a few days later by a counterdemonstration by thousands of Peronist workers. Scores of military officers mutinied, sending warplanes to bomb the Peronist workers in the Plaza de Mayo, killing 156 people (with hundreds more injured).

By taking on the Church, Perón gave the military the excuse it needed to oust him from power. Within weeks of the violence, General Eduardo Lonardi launched the so-called *Revolución Libertadora* to end the Peronist regime. In September 1955, military officers gave Perón an ultimatum: Resign now or face civil war. Perón gave in and was escorted by a Paraguayan gunboat to a long asylum abroad. Once again, the military intervened to solve a national political and social crisis. However, Perón (and the Peronist movement he created) would remain on the national stage for years to come.

MILITARY STEWARDSHIP

One interesting historical question centers on what happened to the multitude of Perón supporters. Where were all of the workers, and how could such a small group of officers engineer Perón's rapid downfall? The simple answer seems to be that Perón chose to leave rather than face nearly inevitable violence. However, Perón—and especially Peronism—would by no means disappear from politics in Argentina.

The new military president was General Eduardo Lonardi, a relatively moderate figure. Divisions within the military were significant, and general officers had a hard time formulating unified and coherent policies. The disagreements centered on how to deal with labor, whether Peronism should be repressed, and how much power to give to civilians. Lonardi tried to accommodate labor and win its support for the regime. However, strikes continued, encouraging military hard-liners to adopt a tougher stance.

Hard-liners within the military deposed Lonardi in November 1955 and placed Pedro Aramburu in his stead. The aggressive anti-Peronists now had the chance to purge the system of Peronism, outlawing the party and going as far as making Peronist propaganda illegal. The military rulers thought they could destroy Peronism during a short period of military rule. Aramburu even went so far as to have Evita Perón's embalmed body removed from its resting place at a union headquarters, making it "disappear." He thought this would deny the Peronists of a powerful symbol of resistance, an act that would make him a target of the left in the future.

The Peronists organized and fought back in the summer of 1956. A pro-Peronist revolt took place within the military. Authorities responded harshly and executed some forty leaders. While Perón had, at times, resorted to authoritarian measures to control opposition, such as closing newspapers, under Aramburu, the military increased the use of violence; Aramburu wanted to change the political system completely. Still, the idea was not to hold power indefinitely; rather, the military planned to remove the Peronists and hand power back to "acceptable" civilians.

The anti-Peronist civilian politicians were divided. In 1956, the Radicals split into two distinct groups (one more dramatically anti-Perón than the other). The first elections since Perón's overthrow were held in July 1957, with the two Radical factions winning roughly equivalent seats to a constitutional assembly. Presidential elections were held in 1958, with Arturo Frondizi, head of one of the Radical factions, winning. To increase his chances of winning, Frondizi apparently made a secret pact with the Peronists. In effect, Frondizi traded Peronist votes for a promise to allow Peronist candidates to run in future elections.

Like other Latin American presidents at the time (such as Juscelino Kubitchek in Brazil), Frondizi had big ideas for developing the economy, wanting simultaneously to accelerate industrialization and stimulate agricultural production. Financing for his plan was to come from foreign investors. For the plan to work, the country required more moderate consumption. However, Frondizi faced a balance-of-payments crisis. He responded by implementing a major devaluation of the currency, putting controls on credit, cutting government spending, limiting wages, and firing redundant public employees. Frondizi was in a tough situation economically. Likewise, his political base also was questionable—the military in particular was suspicious of the deal he had cut with the Peronists to win the election.

Ultimately, Frondizi lost political support, as opponents would not forgive the harsh economic austerity or his "sellout" to foreign investors. In 1960, the opposition Radical faction won more congressional seats than Frondizi's wing, while Peronists cast blank protest ballots. Frondizi made good on his deal with the Peronists, allowing them to participate in the March 1962 elections. The result was political disaster, with the Peronists defeating all other parties. The military responded by forcing Frondizi to annul the Peronist victories. Frondizi made a last-ditch attempt to work with the other wing of the Radicals, but this failed.

On March 29, 1962, tanks rolled into the streets of Buenos Aires and forced Frondizi from the presidency. The Senate president, José María Guido, acted as president for the remaining year and a half of Frondizi's term; but the military was clearly running the country. The military remained deeply divided, eventually calling for new elections in July 1963. A Radical faction won, and Arturo Illia was named president. The Peronists opposed Illia, mainly because they had been excluded from the elections. They concocted a "battle plan" that included strikes and workplace takeovers. The Peronists were again allowed to run in congressional elections in 1965, making a strong showing. From exile in Spain, Perón sent his new wife, Isabel, to negotiate between feuding Peronist factions. However, as the economy worsened, the military stepped in, removing Illia from office in June 1966.

BUREAUCRATIC AUTHORITARIANISM

The military deemed the Radical presidencies incapable of ruling Argentina; in particular, the military was concerned about the inability to deal with the Peronist masses. The coup in 1966 represented a much sharper break with the past than any coup since 1946. This time there would be no pretense of civilian rule. This military regime also was one of the most repressive. General Juan Carlos Onganía was named president and declared the onset of "the Argentine Revolution." The new regime, a so-called bureaucratic authoritarian regime, attempted to attack the causes of Argentina's problems rather than the symptoms. Onganía shut down congress, ousted opponents, and set about to control Argentine society.

Like other bureaucratic authoritarian regimes of the time, military leaders in Argentina forged alliances with both technocrats and foreign investors. The plan also depended on suppressing labor; real wages would drop while foreign capital would contribute to economic growth. Onganía implemented a two-year wage freeze in 1967; and while he tried to "divide and conquer" organized labor, opposition labor exploded in 1969. In May 1969, the military responded to a series of work stoppages, strikes, and rioting in Córdoba. In the chaotic environment known as the *Cordobazo,* military forces killed as many as sixty people, with hundreds wounded. The violence shook the country, and protests spread. Onganía lasted only one more year, his credibility shattered.

Another disturbing trend at the time was the explosive growth in political violence; the government used torture and executions, while an increasingly radicalized left resorted to kidnappings and assassinations. However, this time around repressed groups were fighting back. Numerous revolutionary groups formed at the time, and a number of high-profile kidnappings were carried out. In 1970, leftists kidnapped ex-president Aramburu, the architect of the 1956 Peronist executions, and killed him. Politics had turned into near civil war in Argentina.

Roberto Levinston, more moderate than Onganía, was named president in 1971. Facing exploding inflation, he was removed by military coup and replaced by Alejandro Lanusse. Lanusse decided to take a huge gamble as he attempted to achieve political accord in the country: He decided to let "the old man," Juan Perón, return to the political stage in Argentina. Elections were announced for March 1973, with Héctor Cámpora nominated as a stand-in for Perón until he could return to Argentina. The political violence continued to escalate, with guerrillas targeting high-ranking military officials. Cámpora won the election, and many began to think that the only solution to the political chaos and near civil war was Perón's return. In essence, many believed that only the populist Perón could solve the growing leftist threat.

PERÓN'S RETURN TO POWER

Upon winning the election, Héctor Cámpora attempted to reverse economic policy quickly. In particular, he aimed to increase labor's share of national income until it returned to the levels seen before Perón's ouster. This would require considerable political cooperation from the various national interest groups, and Cámpora worked hard to sign a *Pacto Social* with labor. (He worked simultaneously with groups such as ranchers and farmers to reach similar agreements.)

Argentina's guerrilla groups rejected the Peronist regime, however, and continued to destabilize Argentine politics. This situation was considerably more difficult for Perón, who was now 77 years old and in failing health. Elections were scheduled for September, and this time Perón succeeded in nominating his wife, Isabel, for the vice-presidency. Together they won the election with 62 percent of the vote, and Perón proceeded to take on the revolutionary left. At first, many believed they had been correct in thinking Perón was the only one capable of taking on the left; as it would turn out, however, this was not to be the case.

Economic troubles resurfaced, in part due to the Organization of the Petroleum Exporting Countries (OPEC) oil price increase of 1974. In turn, Perón counteracted his stabilization program by granting huge wage increases. Then in July 1974, Juan Perón died in office, making his wife, Isabel, whom Perón met when she was a nightclub dancer in Panama, president. As events turned out, Isabel was incapable of meeting the tremendous challenges facing Argentina.

Isabel Perón's brief rule was tumultuous, to say the least, characterized by a number of reversals in economic policy. The economy went from bad to worse, with inflation running as high as 335 percent in 1975. Argentina was forced to implement yet another stabilization program to receive financial aid from the International Monetary Fund (IMF). The left continued its violent attacks, with a number of high-profile assassinations. The currency was falling daily. At this point, the president was incapable of commanding, but her term lasted until 1977. The military seemed willing to let her serve her term, in part to avoid responsibility for the economic disaster. Others speculate that the military was willing to let the economy collapse so that there could be little criticism when it finally did intervene. In 1976, the military finally stepped in, briefly placing Isabel Perón under house arrest and removing democratically elected officials from the government.

MILITARY RULE

The armed forces again imposed a bureaucratic authoritarian regime, instituting a far-reaching program called the Process of National Reorganization, or *El Processo* for short. The *Processo* was designed to fight two specific problems: rampant inflation and the guerrilla menace. Under the leadership of General Jorge Videla, the military government began the so-called dirty war, a vicious campaign to wipe out enemies on the left. Arrests of "subversives" began to grow in number. All told, as many as 20,000 people were tortured, were executed, or disappeared. (Many of the latter were simply thrown into the sea from military planes.) Those abducted, typically by "off-duty" forces, were rarely seen or heard from again. Those arrested consisted of true revolutionaries and people merely sympathetic to the cause, as well as a considerable number of unlucky innocent bystanders.

The revolutionaries were quite organized, using robberies and kidnappings to build up a war chest of some $150 million. Their strikes and targeted executions created considerable fear among the middle class. And while the revolutionaries were typically middle class themselves, their stated goal was to overthrow the government and install a socialist regime. For the revolutionaries, there was no turning back—it was a war to the finish.

Mothers of the Plaza de Mayo

These mothers and wives of those who disappeared organized regular protests in Buenos Aires's main square, the Plaza de Mayo. At first, they were simply trying to get information on the disappeared; but they were given bogus answers by military officials. In protest, the first group gathered in silent vigil in April 1977, cursed by passersby and threatened by military officers. From then on, they gathered each Thursday in protest, as they do to this day. The group played a significant role in questioning the excesses of the military rule and ultimately helped to bring down the dictatorship. The mothers then continued their fight to bring military leaders to justice; the process has been a long one, and efforts continue today.

The generals pursued an all-out war against the revolutionaries, using the "disappearances" as a conscious strategy to instill terror among their enemies. The generals won, but at a tremendous cost to the nation. Besides thousands being killed, Argentina became a pariah state along with Chile and South Africa.

Without a doubt, there was public support for the war against the revolutionaries, especially from the middle classes. Argentines had watched their economy implode under Isabel Perón and had seen an explosion in political violence. The generals aimed to turn things around; their "coup to end all coups" set out to reorder Argentine society. After some initial economic successes, however, the generals' situation deteriorated dramatically in the early 1980s. Inflation surpassed 100 percent in 1981, at the same time the economy fell into recession. The military presidency passed from Videla to Roberto Viola in 1981, then to General Leopoldo Galtieri in 1982, the commander-in-chief of the army. Ironically, Galtieri would make a military blunder that would bring down the military dictatorship. In the end, the generals would be forced from power not because of human rights abuse, labor agitation, tremendous national debt, or inflation, but because of a disastrous war with Great Britain over the Falklands.

THE FALKLANDS WAR

Known as the Malvinas in Argentina, the Falkland Islands were seized by Great Britain in 1833. Argentina claimed the islands, and the United Nations had passed a number of resolutions urging their return to Argentina. In 1982, Argentina guessed (incorrectly) that England would not defend the isolated and desolate islands, which supported only 1,800 inhabitants (and 600,000 sheep). Argentina also mistakenly assumed that the United States would support its invasion. On April 2, 1982, Argentine forces invaded and quickly overcame the small royal marine garrison stationed on the islands. Britain responded immediately, sending thousands of troops to take on the Argentines.

Argentine soldiers carry military supplies during the ill-fated Falklands War, April 13, 1982. (Daniel Garcia/AFP/Getty Images)

Historians continue to debate the logic of Galtieri's disastrous decision to invade the Falklands. Why did he make such a foolish move? The answer seems to be that the general thought a quick victory would redeem the credibility of the regime, whose popularity was plummeting. In the short term, Galtieri was right, as Argentines exploded in demonstrations of patriotism and support for the war. However, a British victory was swift, as their better-trained and better-armed forces quickly forced the Argentines to surrender. Prior to attacking the Argentine forces, a British submarine sank the Argentine battleship *General Belgrano,* killing more than 360 Argentine sailors. Argentina responded, sinking a British ship, killing 256 of its sailors. In the end, British marines faced very little resistance on land, forcing Argentina to a quick surrender.

The nation was shocked by the rapid collapse and surrender of its numerically superior armed forces. General Galtieri made a strategic blunder, starting a war he could not win. The massive outpouring of Argentine patriotism rapidly turned into demonstrations against the government. Galtieri was soundly criticized internally, and he ultimately resigned in disgrace. Galtieri was then succeeded by Reynaldo Bignone, who promised a return to civilian government by 1984. Ironically, this fatal blunder of the military contributed in good measure to the restored legitimacy of civilian government.

TRANSITION TO DEMOCRACY

Once again Argentina's economy was in dire straits, hardly an auspicious environment to attempt a return to civilian rule. Inflation was running at about 200 percent per year, and the government was forced into default on its foreign debt. Radical candidate Raúl Alfonsín won the presidential election in 1983 with 52 percent of the vote. In addition to the difficult economy, the Radical government faced the extremely difficult issue of how to go about prosecuting those who had committed human rights violations, including murder, during the dirty war. The central questions centered on who should be prosecuted and how far down the chain of command the prosecution should go. A final issue facing Alfonsín was political; it was far from clear whether the Radicals could maintain a viable political base to lead the country out of the mess it was in.

As far as prosecuting human rights violations, Alfonsín appointed a commission to investigate dirty war crimes. The commission documented 8,906 deaths or disappearances, and nine top military figures were charged with crimes. Of those men, five were convicted and sent to prison. Three of the four originally acquitted were later tried and convicted in military trials and sent to prison. Still, the question remained of how far down the chain of command the government should pursue prosecution; a major military revolt in 1987 forced the hand of congress on the issue, and it exempted all officers below the rank of general. In general terms, the prosecution phase bogged down, with all sides complaining about the process.

The economy proved unmanageable as well. The country obtained help from the IMF in return for yet another austerity program, but this generally failed, with inflation reaching some 700 percent in 1985. For a time, a price freeze seemed to help; but this too failed. And by 1989, prices were rising at the astronomical rate of 100 percent per month while the economy as a whole was shrinking. As the crisis deepened, food riots took place. Alfonsín responded to the economic despair and political volatility by announcing that he would leave office six months early.

Carlos Saúl Menem, a Peronist, took Alfonsín's place in July 1989 amid the gloomy environment, facing hyperinflation, economic stagnation, and default on the country's foreign debt. Immediately, Menem's economic team announced an aggressive new austerity plan. The government shocked Argentines in January 1990 with the announcement that private savings accounts would be exchanged for government-issued ten-year bonds. While the overall policy package caused a recession, it also brought an end to Argentina's hyperinflation.

Ironically, Menem, a Peronist, would steer a course to lead Argentina in the opposite direction of the populism of its Peronist past. Most importantly, Menem and his economic team designed a huge privatization program to sell off government-owned corporations, privatizing the state-owned airline, electric utilities, phone company, and the like. The culmination of this program was the sale of YPF, the state-owned oil company, which had long served as a symbol of Argentine nationalism.

A new economy minister was appointed in 1991, economist Domingo Cavallo, who pushed even harder for market-oriented economic reforms. Cavallo's main contribution was the so-called convertibility law, which established a one-to-one exchange rate between the Argentine peso and the U.S. dollar. (In theory, convertibility also limited government spending to its revenues, but this part of the program was largely ignored; and deficits grew over time.)

Convertibility seemed to work, winning Argentina credibility in the international markets after years of chaos. This credibility served to attract tremendous inflows of international capital in the form of direct investments as well as portfolio (stock and bond) investments. In the process, Cavallo also managed to restructure Argentina's foreign debt. Inflation fell from nearly 5,000 percent in 1989 to less than 4 percent in 1994. In the meantime, growth had returned; many at the time were beginning to speak of Argentina's new "economic miracle."

Some early costs were associated with the new economic program, however. Most importantly, the privatization drive took a large toll on the labor force as unnecessary workers were fired. Unemployment rose from about 6.5 percent in 1991 to more than 12 percent in 1994; strikes and protests rose as a result. In addition, convertibility led to an increasing overvaluation of the country's peso, which drove ever-larger external trade deficits (and eventually contributed to whole-sale economic collapse).

Menem was able to get the constitution changed to allow his own reelection in exchange for agreeing to shorten the presidential term to four years. Menem won the May 1995 election with 49.8 percent of the vote. The Radicals won a puny 17.1 percent of the vote. Despite the victory, there were growing complaints about Menem and his administration. Specifically, charges of high-level corruption were growing; in addition, there were complaints about Menem's authoritarian style of leadership.

Mercosur

Mercosur, or the *Mercado Común del Sur,* is a regional trade agreement between Argentina, Brazil, Paraguay, and Uruguay. It was created in 1991 with the Treaty of Asunción (known as *Mercosul* in Brazil). Other countries, such as Chile and Venezuela, have since joined in different capacities. The idea behind Mercosur was to create a common market between the four countries, over time eliminating such trade barriers as import duties. The goal was to promote closer economic relations between the countries and to support expanded economic activity.

The creation of Mercosur initially led to heightened trade and foreign investment in Argentina, particularly noticeable in the automobile industry. However, Brazil's devaluation in 1999 led to growing concerns about Argentina's lack of competitiveness. Mercosur was clearly weakened by Argentina's economic collapse in 2001. Fortunately, while disputes continue over trade policies within Mercosur, it has remained a viable platform. Looking forward, bigger issues such as political integration, as seen within the European Union, remain largely wishful thinking.

MENEM'S DEPARTURE AND THE COLLAPSE OF THE PESO

While the public was fed up with the corruption and high unemployment associated with the Menem administration, there were no apparent political alternatives. The Radicals had seen a steady decline in popularity; and FREPASO, a center-left coalition, was organizationally weak. However, the two parties joined in 1997 for the October congressional elections. The Alliance (officially called the *Alianza para Trabajo, Justicia y Educación*) maintained support for the existing economic model, but criticized rampant corruption and the unacceptably high rate of unemployment. The coalition made significant headway, taking away control of the lower house from the Peronists.

Around this same time, Menem began floating the idea of yet again changing the constitution to allow him to run for a third term. However, negative public opinion led him to abandon the project. The Alliance, having learned of their new-found political capabilities, put up a candidate for the presidency, Fernando de la Rúa, a Radical who had competed with Alfonsín for the presidential nomination in 1983. The political strategy remained the same: maintain support for the general economic model (based on convertibility) and focus criticism on high unemployment and high-level corruption. De la Rúa faced Eduardo Duhalde, but the Peronists were greatly divided by infighting between the Menem and Duhalde factions of their party. The Alliance rallied for the support of those groups most negatively impacted by Menem's policies. New trials for officers of the dirty war helped the Alliance, given Menem's pardons to some convicted abusers.

De la Rúa won the election on October 25, 1999, and took power in December 1999. A number of events immediately and negatively impacted his administration. To start with, de la Rúa had to obtain medical treatment for a condition that many thought was quite serious in the first days of his administration. This complication delayed aggressive movement on much-needed reforms and, unfortunately, contributed to a public perception of presidential weakness.

Argentina's economic conditions continued to worsen. The economy remained mired in recession, and unemployment stayed stubbornly high. (Estimates put it above 15 percent.) Argentina also experienced the growing impact of international economic shock. Its neighbor Brazil had already succumbed to the financial crises that had plagued developing Asia and Russia. After repeated runs on its currency, Brazil devalued in early 1999. This devaluation negatively impacted trading conditions between the two countries, quite seriously for Argentina. Specifically, Argentina's trade deficits ballooned, putting severe pressure on its obviously overvalued currency.

The de la Rúa government forged ahead with its agenda, focusing early on labor regulations. The government's proposals passed; but then it was revealed that government officials had bribed a number of senators to obtain their votes, significantly undermining the credibility of the new government. De la Rúa also faced a serious fiscal crisis. Once again the country worked with the IMF, putting in place austerity measures to cut spending and increase revenues in exchange for financial aid. Fears of debt default were growing domestically and internationally—ongoing capital flight was the result.

The Alliance proved fragile in this atmosphere of economic crisis. The vice-president, Carlos Álvarez, resigned in October 2000 to protest the austerity measures. As head of FREPASO, he had played a key role in attracting votes from the left. The remaining members of FREPASO then abandoned the Alliance in March 2001, leaving the government with only Radical support. The president's popularity was falling rapidly.

De la Rúa brought in Domingo Cavallo to deal with the economic crisis and the failing convertibility plan. Given the overvaluation of the currency (especially in relation to the now supercompetitive Brazilian currency), trade deficits soared, Argentine industry languished, and bankruptcies rose. The foreign debt had grown to some $130–$140 billion by 2001, and more and more government resources were being used to pay the interest on the debt.

Devaluation did not seem to be an option, as real incomes dropped precipitously, people feared a return of hyperinflation, and much debt was denominated in dollars. Protests grew. One type of protest proved quite effective: Middle-class housewives took to the streets banging on pots and pans to protest their economic difficulties. Cavallo tinkered with the convertibility plan but then resigned amid the mounting protests.

The protests climaxed in December 2001 as rioters looted supermarkets around the country, reminiscent of the IMF food riots a decade earlier. A massive march on the *Casa Rosada*

Demonstrators at the Casa Rosada *on December 29, 2001, amid riots in protest of President Fernando de la Rúa and the crumbling economy. (AP/Daniel Luna)*

(the Argentine White House; the term refers to its reddish hue) led to violent clashes with police, and the government called for a state of siege. This caused a spontaneous, massive movement of people to the Plaza de Mayo, the so-called night of the saucepans in which some 35 people were killed in violent clashes. President de la Rúa escaped the rioting surrounding the *Casa Rosada* by helicopter, resigning the presidency.

Political chaos reigned for two weeks, during which time congress selected three separate interim presidents in rapid succession. The fourth president was Eduardo Duhalde, the Peronist candidate for the 1999 presidential election who lost the election to de la Rua. In January 2002, Duhalde froze bank accounts to stop capital flight. Depositors lost as much as 40 percent of their frozen assets when the link between the Argentine peso and the dollar was broken and bank accounts were "pesified" (turned into pesos).

The stance of the United States and the IMF surprised and angered many Argentines who had endured years of economic hardship. The U.S. secretary of the treasury, Paul O'Neill, said it was up to Argentines to solve the problems they had created (despite the fact that Argentina had worked closely with the IMF for years and had, for some time, been a "poster child" for Washington Consensus economic policies).

NÉSTOR KIRCHNER

Néstor Kirchner won the presidential election after Duhalde's caretaker presidency. Kirchner can claim some credit for the speed and strength of Argentina's recovery from the debt default and devaluation of 2001 and 2002, having taken over the presidency in extremely difficult times. Imposing relatively tight fiscal and monetary policies, Kirchner and his team stabilized prices and the exchange rate. The government also was helped by strong international commodity prices, a more competitive currency, and a great deal of spare capacity in the economy.

Kirchner entered the presidency with a weak mandate; he was the fourth choice of his own Peronist party, and he received just 22 percent of the vote. However, his mandate was strengthened by midterm congressional elections in which his allies beat candidates representing Duhalde's wing of the Peronist party. Likewise, his popularity grew as a function of his success in restructuring Argentina's debts.

Following the elections, Kirchner shook up his cabinet, adding a number of left-leaning ministers. Many observers feared that economic policy would move in a more populist direction. Likewise, Argentina had serious problems with its relationship with foreign investors, especially foreign-owned utilities. During the height of the 2001–2002 financial crisis, the government converted the utilities' dollar-denominated tariffs into devalued peso rates. Likewise, the government froze these tariffs—and has kept them frozen, despite significant inflation in the economy. The government offered overall tariff increases of 20 percent, but most firms rejected the offer.

While this aggressive stance boosted Kirchner's popularity at home, it certainly did not help the economy, as the lack of economic profit led affected companies to underinvest. Kirchner also showed signs of developing a closer friendship with Venezuela's Hugo Chávez, an avowed populist and self-appointed enemy of the United States, Time will tell whether this was simply political posturing or if the country will move significantly leftward in public policy.

CRISTINA FERNÁNDEZ DE KIRCHNER

Following her recent victory, Cristina Fernández de Kirchner is now Argentina's second woman president (and the only one elected to the nation's highest office). Her victory follows a prominent career as a legislator and most recently as the nation's "first lady." While there are many theories regarding why her husband, Nestor Kirchner, opted out of the presidency, only time will tell what role the ex-president plays in his wife's administration, the direction of the new president's policies, and the success Argentina has in sustaining a healthy economy.

References

Brown, Jonathan C. *A Brief History of Argentina.* New York: Facts on File, Inc., 2003.

De la Balze, Felipe A. M. *Remaking the Argentine Economy.* New York: Council on Foreign Relations Press, 1995.

Díaz Alejandro, Carlos F. *Essays on the Economic History of the Argentine Republic.* New Haven, CT: Yale University Press, 1970.

Donghi, Tulio Halperín. *Politics, Economics and Society in Argentina in the Revolutionary Period.* Cambridge: Cambridge University Press, 1975.

Erro, Davide G. *Resolving the Argentine Paradox: Politics and Development, 1966–1992.* Boulder, CO: Lynne Rienner Publishers, 1993.

Gallo, Ezequiel. "Argentina: Society and Politics, 1880–1916," in Leslie Bethell (ed.), *The Cambridge History of Latin America, Vol. V.* Cambridge: Cambridge University Press, 1984: 359–392.

Lewis, Colin M. *Argentina: A Short History.* Oxford: Oneworld Publications, 2002.

Lewis, Daniel K. *The History of Argentina.* Westport, CT: Greenwood Press, 2001.

Lewis, Paul W. *The Crisis of Argentine Capitalism.* Chapel Hill: University of North Carolina Press, 1990.

Rock, David. *Argentina, 1516–1987: From Spanish Colonization to Alfonsin.* Berkeley: University of California Press, 1987.

Rock, David. "Argentina, 1930–1946," in Leslie Bethell (ed.), *The Cambridge History of Latin America, Vol. VIII.* Cambridge: Cambridge University Press, 1984: 3–72.

Rock, David. "Argentina from the First World War to the Revolution of 1930," in Leslie Bethell (ed.), *The Cambridge History of Latin America, Vol. V.* Cambridge: Cambridge University Press, 1984: 393–418.

Romero, Luis Alberto. *A History of Argentina in the 20th Century.* University Park: Pennsylvania State University Press, 2002.

Scobie, James R. *Argentina: A City and a Nation,* 2nd ed. New York: Oxford University Press, 1971.

Skidmore, Thomas E., and Peter H. Smith. *Modern Latin America,* 5th ed. Oxford: Oxford University Press, 2001.

Torre, Juan Carlos. "Argentina Since 1946," in Leslie Bethell (ed.), *The Cambridge History of Latin America, Vol. VIII.* Cambridge: Cambridge University Press, 1984: 73–194.

CHAPTER TWO

The Argentine Economy

INTRODUCTION

As this text's introductory review of Argentine history underscores, Argentina's economic history has been troubled, to
say the least. The country is blessed with abundant natural
resources and has an educated and literate society. Its export-
oriented agricultural sector is booming (thanks to the recent
devaluation and robust global commodities prices), and the
country's industrial base is relatively diversified. However,
historically, Argentina's economic performance has been
volatile and ultimately unsatisfactory.

As will be discussed in more detail, at the turn of the twentieth century, during the country's so-called golden age,
Argentina boasted one of the world's highest gross domestic
products (GDPs) per capita and, in fact, was largely on par
with that of the United States. Unfortunately, a series of economic and political crises caused Argentina to lose relative
ground. It is now classified as a middle-income country, with
significant pockets of poverty throughout the country. Any
discussion of Argentine economic history must address this
question: Why did the early promise of rapid economic
growth seen in the late nineteenth and early twentieth centuries fail to consolidate and lead to sustained economic
development? The question is particularly challenging since
this is not the case of a poor country failing to find the means
to achieve growth and development (thereby remaining
poor). Rather, Argentina is a case of a relatively rich country
that failed to find the means to maintain its position among
the rich countries of the world.

Despite the country's decline, most notably in the second half of the twentieth century, Argentina remains one of the most developed countries in South America. Rankings typically put the country as one of the twenty-five largest economies in the world. Its 2006 total GDP was just over $200 billion at the official exchange rate, leading to GDP per capita of about $15,000 (see CIA Factbook for economic statistics). It is estimated that GDP grew about 8.5 percent in 2006, leading to average economic growth between 2003 and 2006 of 9 percent, a considerable achievement. Inflation came in around 10 percent for 2006. While the post-crisis recovery numbers have been impressive, certain indicators serve as reminders of why Argentina remains a developing nation. For example, by some measures, as much as 31 percent of the population remains below the poverty line. Likewise, unemployment remains stubbornly high (over 10 percent).

Looking at GDP by sector, roughly 10 percent is represented by agriculture, 36 percent by industry, and 54 percent

Cargo ships navigate the Buenos Aires harbor and oil complex, February 1981. (Jean Guichard/Sygma/Corbis)

by services. Among the country's main industries are food processing, motor vehicles, consumer durables, textiles, chemicals and petrochemicals, printing, metallurgy, and steel. Argentina's main trading partner is Brazil. Other important partners include the United States, Chile, and the European Union. China is growing in importance, as well as becoming a destination for the country's exports.

This chapter will review Argentina's economic history, starting with a brief discussion of the economy in the colonial era and the early, somewhat turbulent years following independence. Then discussion will move to Argentina's "great transformation"—an analysis of the years typically known as the golden age from 1870 to 1914. The golden age was followed by a more difficult period, corresponding to the two World Wars and the interwar years marked by the Great Depression. The next phase of Argentina's economic progression, effectively starting after the Second World War, was a period of active industrialization, which helped transform the nature of the economy, but also ended in a series of economic crises (and often violent political struggles).

The initial steps to wholesale economic reform came after the transition from military to civilian rule in 1983, although two military dictatorships made much of their intentions to remake the Argentine economy. The efforts of the Alfonsín presidency and the early efforts of the Menem presidency had little success in returning the economy to growth and ending high inflation. However, Menem and his economy minister, Domingo Cavallo, successfully ended the years of high inflation with the convertibility plan. They also were able to produce economic growth, at least until the late 1990s. However, the convertibility plan ended in disaster as Argentina devalued its currency, endured a harsh recession, and brought about the biggest debt default in history (in 2001–2002). Fortunately, the economy has returned to growth, producing yearly rates of growth approximating 10 percent a year in the last several years. However, given the depth of the crisis, a number of significant economic problems must still be addressed.

Before turning to Argentina's economic history, a few comments about economic growth and development will be helpful. The historical analysis will follow with a detailed discussion of the contemporary economy and its main challenges.

GROWTH AND DEVELOPMENT

GDP is simply a way to measure the total market value of a country's goods and services. To correct for the impact of inflation, economists also measure real GDP, which identifies the true economic output of an economy, correcting for changes in prices. One way to compare global economies is to look at the absolute size of real GDP; some might even argue the bigger the GDP, the better.

However, identifying the size of an economy masks important details. Most importantly, a nation's people can become better off only if their country's real GDP grows faster than its population grows. In fact, many economists define modern economic growth as the long-term growth in average real GDP per person. Qualitatively, modern economic growth involves the systematic application of scientific and technical knowledge to economic pursuits in the process of developing and transforming agriculture, industry, and commerce.

While this description of modern economic growth is important, focusing specifically on growth may cause you to miss important qualitative components of the economic development process. In fact, many have argued that this focus largely overlooks a big part of today's world, where modern economic growth is absent. In general, there has been a shift over time in analysis from a pure focus on growth to a more general focus on development. This shift includes qualitative assessments and value judgments. For example, more qualitative assessments of development often include explicit calls for the elimination of poverty and the alleviation of income inequality. As you examine the Argentine economy more closely, keep in mind that the concepts of growth and development are not mutually exclusive—modern societies typically strive for growth, equity, and an overall improvement in the standard of living.

THE HISTORICAL SETTING: ARGENTINA'S COLONIAL ECONOMY

As discussed in Chapter One, the territory constituting modern-day Argentina was, in essence, a backwater in Spain's New World colonial empire. Possessing no meaningful source of labor and no obvious mineral wealth—as the Spanish encountered in Peru and Mexico—Argentina was, in effect, relegated to second-class status. Clearly, the port of Buenos Aires was an important asset, but it played little more than a smuggling role throughout most of the colonial era— no dynamic economy developed in the Río de la Plata region. The economy's development in the colonial era had more to do with shipping leather goods, cotton, rice, and wheat north to the mining regions of Upper Peru. Only with the colonial restructuring in 1776 and the creation of a new viceroyalty, with its capital in Buenos Aires, did the port and the surrounding coast enter into a phase of more rapid economic development.

The early neglect of the coast occurred because the area was deemed inhospitable, not least of which was due to hostile Indian populations. As a result, Argentina's interior regions were conquered and settled first. By the time settlers returned to the coast, it was essentially too late. The Spanish Crown had already established the "official" trade route for this part of the empire, a torturous route leading from Argentina's northwestern agricultural communities through the Andes Mountains to Peru. In turn, for the next 200 years, the key commercial centers (related to Argentina) were based in Peru and Panama; and they managed to prevent any efforts to open Buenos Aires as a legal point of entry. Remember, Spain monopolized the trade routes to and from the colonies, using annual fleets to carry goods. Colonists were forbidden from trading with other European countries and were denied the opportunity to trade with other ports in Spanish America.

Given Argentina's role as an economic backwater in the early colonial era, scholars have often referred to the 1600s as Argentina's "lost century." The economy of the interior was characterized by crop raising, small industries, and modest trade. However, the coast was developing, based on smuggling as well as the production of cows, horses, and mules. The *encomienda* system was quickly replaced by the *estancia* (large rural estate) as the means to exploit the rural economy. The Crown sold or granted these large extensions of land to private owners. At the time, the land did not contain much of anything that was of immediate economic value. On the coast, the land contained wild horses and cattle (the result of a few horses and cows left behind during early explorations). In the interior, the land contained sheep, grazing and crop lands, and Indian villages.

Probably the most important development to take place in the late seventeenth century into the eighteenth century was the growth of the coast—specifically the port of Buenos Aires—in part reflecting the port's growing success in supplying hides for export. Over time, the Spanish mercantilist system, with its excessively long trade routes and convoyed fleets, became increasingly stretched. This reflected Spain's declining economic and political power, as well as the emergence of Britain and France as world powers. The system was ultimately abandoned in 1778 with the Decree of Free Trade, one of the factors setting the stage for Buenos Aires's rapid economic development.

In essence, this laid a new economic foundation for Argentina, which was accompanied in 1776 by the creation of a new administrative subdivision of the Spanish empire, the Viceroyalty of the Río de la Plata with its headquarters in

Illustration of the coastal fort at Buenos Aires, ca. 1820. (Hulton-Deutsch Collection/Corbis)

the city of Buenos Aires. The change reflected both a shift in commercial policy as well as a response to strategic concerns (for example, increasing Portuguese activity on the other side of the Rio de la Plata). As discussed, for Buenos Aires, a significant piece of the shift in economic policy was the Crown's move to allow exchange between any port in Spain and the overseas ports of the colony; likewise, Spain moved to open up trade between ports in the colony. The result was growth in population and wealth in the new viceregal capital of Buenos Aires.

The rapid growth of the port city and surrounding areas underscored a growing divide between the region and the interior. The relatively wealthy coast was interested in international trade, exchanging its agricultural products for goods from abroad. The interior, on the other hand, wanted internal markets for its small industries and farms. Another highly significant development reflecting Buenos Aires's rapid growth was a growing resentment of Spanish economic and political control—it was in Buenos Aires that demands for independence grew among the creole elite.

BUENOS AIRES AND
THE RURAL ECONOMY

Livestock represented the foundation of the economy of the pampas, providing the principal products and exports for roughly three centuries. The economy progressed over time, from the hunting of wild cattle and horses for their hides (1600–1750) to the growth of herds of semitamed animals (1700–1850) to production of salted meats and fats by the meat-salting plants called *saladeros* (1800–1890) to the extensive raising of sheep (1840–1900). In the process, the divide between the coast and the interior widened, with the coast effectively winning the competition. By the nineteenth century, Buenos Aires monopolized all trade and its hides, meat, and wool helped establish patterns of landownership, the distribution of the population, and political developments, as well as social and cultural patterns.

Importantly, the overwhelming focus on livestock did not occur in Argentina's interior. Rather, livestock industries grew in tandem with other economic pursuits, such as crop raising and textile production, which produced goods bound for Peru. The coast reflected different circumstances—it was far from Peru, had a scarcity of labor, and was blessed with large herds of wild cattle and horses. As a result, on the coast, commercial and grazing interests won out over small industries and the growing of crops.

In the early colonial period, the principal good was the hides of wild animals; no real attempt was made to salt or dry the meat for export. Gradually, there was a shift in focus from wild animals and leather to semitamed animals, which could be driven with relatively little manpower. As the cattle were trained to stay in designated areas, more thorough preparation of products was possible. For example, hides were dried and sent to towns, while intestines and fatty portions were boiled to extract tallow, which was used in foodstuffs as well as in the production of lubricants, soap, candles, etc.

(Together hides and tallow represented the quintessential "colonial products.")

The development of the livestock industry also drove a change in landownership patterns. Most importantly, as production grew, ownership of the land replaced the early ownership of semitamed herds. In general, the livestock industries supported a pattern of large landholdings. For the rest of the rural population that did not have the resources or connections to acquire land, the developing economy led to a fairly transient lifestyle.

THE *SALADERO*

As mentioned, the early economic interest in livestock focused on hides; quite often animals that were not consumed were left to rot. The next step in the development of

Huge drying racks covered in hides sit out in the heat of the sun to dry, ca. late nineteenth century. (Hulton-Deutsch Collection/Corbis)

the livestock industry depended on finding ways to use the rest of the animal. The next major development, while significant, did not begin to have a meaningful impact until the beginning of the nineteenth century; this was the introduction of the *saladero,* which allowed a more comprehensive exploitation of the whole animal.

The development of the *saladero* generally coincided with Argentina's movement toward independence; in fact, the increasing dominance of the coast and its towns was very much related to the increased production of salted meat. Historically, salted meat was used extensively in the eighteenth century on board sailing ships as well as on slave plantations (where it formed an important part of slaves' diets). While the first *saladero* was built in Uruguay, *saladeros* were quickly introduced in Argentina as well. This development represented the introduction of a basic factory system into Argentina's rudimentary pastoral economy.

The first *saladero* in Buenos Aires appeared in 1810, but the earlier arrival of the *saladeros* on the Uruguayan shore had already attracted further economic activity to the coastal region. Importantly, the combination of the *estancia* and the *saladero* strengthened the interests of groups calling for open trade—these groups wanted access to world markets in order to exchange the products of the pampas for European goods (especially manufactures).

However, prior to independence, Spain continued to try to control trade in the Río de la Plata region (despite the fact that Spain could supply only about one-fourth of the goods destined for Buenos Aires, which reflected Spain's inability to keep up with Britain and continental Europe in the industrial revolution). Groups of merchants in Argentina, typically creoles, requested further liberalization of trade—the level of irritation with the Crown continued to grow at the same time. As described in the previous chapter, growing frustration with the ineffective colonial structures and a desire to trade directly with England and continental Europe led to petitions for more liberal trade, then to appeals for increased local autonomy, and finally to the struggle for national independence.

The end of the colonial era followed a series of struggles in Europe, which culminated in the French invasion and occupation of most of Spain (1808–1813). During this period, any remaining notion that the Spanish Crown was "protecting" trade in the Río de la Plata region was eliminated—hides and fats piled up, while economic activity stagnated. The British played an important role in the process, preventing communications between Spain and her colonies, restricting trade in Buenos Aires, and sending troops to lay claim to Buenos Aires and Montevideo. The British also were quick to seize the economic opportunity, flooding the region with her superior goods (for example, hardware and textiles) while also offering substantially more attractive terms for hides and tallow.

INDEPENDENCE AND ENTRY INTO THE WORLD ECONOMY

Once Napoleon invaded the Iberian Peninsula, Spain and England became allies and the British strategy in the Río de la Plata region became somewhat more subtle. Rather than additional attempts at military conquest, the British strategy turned to trade, with British merchants peddling their textiles, ironware, and china in the region. Independence, in effect, came on May 25, 1810. The viceroy and *cabildo* surrendered authority to a creole junta on that day. While the creoles were initially to rule in the name of the Crown, subsequent acts demonstrated that this was a move to independence. A second date—July 9, 1816—marks a second independence day, reflecting the formal Declaration of Independence of Argentina.

In a sense, the economics and politics of the time converged. The opening of Buenos Aires to world trade, both official and unofficial, coincided with the creole seizure of political power in 1810. That move strengthened an outward orientation toward global markets that could absorb the output of the pampas and supply manufactured goods and foodstuffs in exchange. It also marked a decline in crop farming and local industries in the interior, leading to a long struggle between Buenos Aires (and the coast) and the provinces of the interior. In a sense, it is somewhat surprising that the two components of the territory stayed together, rather than splitting apart like other portions of the viceroyalty (not to mention Spanish America in general). The coast depended on its exports and had little to offer the interior. In turn, the interior, no longer propped up by artificial colonial supports or able to depend on the markets of Peru, had little to offer the coast.

The process was exacerbated by the unfolding of the industrial revolution, in which England, much of continental Europe, and the United States had a head start. Soon products from around the world—from English textiles to American flour to Brazilian sugar—replaced high-cost inferior products from Argentina's interior. As the two halves of Argentina diverged, it was the *saladero* that cemented the economic supremacy of Argentina's coast.

ARGENTINA'S POST-INDEPENDENCE ECONOMY

By the 1820s, ever larger investments of local capital were being poured into the *saladeros*. The importance of these early factories to Argentina's early economic development is illustrated by the rise of Juan Manuel de Rosas, who essentially ruled as the country's dictator for two decades. Rosas did not actively take part in the country's independence movement, but he and other cattle barons used independence and open trade as an opportunity to build their wealth and power. (In many ways, Rosas's rise to power symbolizes the rise to power of the coastal livestock interests.) Over time,

Juan Manuel de Rosas dominated political and social affairs through-
out the territory that became Argentina for 30 years during the
mid-nineteenth century. (Hulton Archive/Getty Images)

Rosas made large sums of money in the *saladero* industry;
and growing control of both cattle and ports supported his
growing political power. Rosas eventually won the governor-
ship of the province of Buenos Aires; and by 1835, he became
the de facto leader of Argentina.

The divergence of economic interests was not as simple as the coast wanting free trade and the interior wanting protection. For example, political elites from Buenos Aires wanted the port city to control the viceregal territory, while the interior wanted more political autonomy. Conservatives in Buenos Aires wanted to maintain the existing economy, increasing profits simply by expanding the *estanciero* and *saladero*. Liberals, on the other hand, wanted to push the farming of crops, immigration, and new technology to modernize the country and its economy. The interior lost any outlet to the world, other than Buenos Aires, after independence—as such, its struggle included attempts to control authority in Buenos Aires and to reduce Buenos Aires's dominion. Before Rosas consolidated his control over the Argentine territory, these crosscurrents of political and economic interests drove a multitude of juntas, triumvirates, congresses, and directories.

In this environment of political instability, the landowning elite and cattle interests of the coast represented a powerful interest group that was able to consolidate its wealth and political standing in the post-independence expansion of international trade. In general, the group supported a continuation of the economic status quo, such as the continued expansion of large landholdings. The group was typically against immigration and the expansion of crop farming.

In general, the creole governments of Buenos Aires supported the cattle interests. In turn, the power of the cattlemen can be seen in the issue of landownership. At the time, a conflict occurred between the interests of the grazing economy and those involved in crop farming. Liberals favored land surveys and a subdivision of the lands surrounding Buenos Aires. They also proposed granting small lots to immigrants, among other things. A key liberal at the time was Bernardino Rivadavia, who was Argentina's president briefly in the 1820s. His vision was to replace the gaucho with immigrant peasant farmers and to cover the pampas with crops. In essence, he wanted to create a democracy of small landholders (not unlike the United States). However, Rivadavia and other liberals lost the battle with *estancia* and *saladero* interests, as public lands continued to be grazed and private lands were controlled by relatively few cattlemen.

Rivadavia was eventually overthrown, and title to public lands moved from the state to private hands. The figures are staggering. For example, it is estimated that in the 1820s, some 21 million acres were transferred from the state to some 500 well-connected individuals. The process of concentrating landownership continued with the rise of Rosas— by sales as well as outright gifts (which were typically directed to political supporters). Rosas also made additional lands available by expanding the frontier and confiscating lands of his opponents.

Rosas continued to expand his political control, building allies in other provinces and gaining control of the customs house in Buenos Aires. As such, he controlled the flow of imports and exports for the country, as well as the revenues gained from customs duties.

Rosas's policies continued to favor exports of salted meat and hides as well as imports of consumer goods. Needless to say, these policies were not supportive of the industries and agriculture of the interior. Politically, Rosas was able to block efforts to give other groups and areas any say in the country's direction. Despite the damage being done to the interior and the limitations of a coastal economy made up of little more than animals, *estancias, saladeros,* and ports, change was effectively blocked. (As a result of Rosas's authoritarian tactics, many of the country's liberal leaders left the country.)

Eventually, Rosas was driven from power by a coalition of forces led by Justo José de Urquiza (in 1852). The "jury is still out" concerning Rosas and his contribution to Argentine history. He is often described as a tyrant, a representative of the country's "dark ages" who was finally defeated by more progressive elements. And with regard to the economy, he clearly supported a rudimentary system based on land and animals, opposing efforts to foster immigration, diversify agriculture, or support local industries. On the other hand, Rosas did put an end to the period of political chaos following independence and held together the core of the viceroyalty's territory. This helped build a foundation for Argentina's nationhood. However, it also came at a significant cost, as it promoted large landholdings and authoritarianism.

THE RISE OF SHEEP RAISING (AND THE TRANSITION TO THE GOLDEN AGE)

The fall of Rosas occurred at the same time other major changes were taking place in the coastal economy. The coast was moving away from the *estancia* and *saladero* and heading rapidly in the direction of sheep raising, which soon became one of the principal economic pursuits in the coastal region. This shift encouraged immigration and led to increasing rural populations, not to mention further territorial expansion and improved livestock care. Over time, better breeds of sheep were introduced by immigrants (often English, Irish, and Scottish) who brought with them experience, capital, and improved techniques. In the decades following 1850, sheep raising dominated the coastal economy in the same way the *saladero* did after independence. Wool exports rose accordingly, leading them to contribute some 50–60 percent of the country's exports by the 1880s. This rapid growth reflected the growing demand in Europe for wool, arising from the industrial revolution. (Carpet and weaving factories demanded increasing supplies of wool and sheep's tallow.)

Land values rose, and the cattle industry moved west and south to the frontier; new groups were attracted to the pampas in the process. Shepherds, unlike the nomadic gauchos and *estancia* peons, could settle the land; and the dream of landownership stimulated immigration and further growth of sheep raising.

The 1850s and 1860s were characterized by civil strife and involvement in the Paraguayan War. Together these events contributed to a weakening of frontier defenses against Indian populations. However, the ascent of the sheep industry continued to push cattle to the frontiers. The heightened need for protection led to a significant military campaign in the 1870s, virtually destroying the Araucanian Indians in Patagonia. Significantly, with this campaign, another 100 million acres of land were added to the grazing economy.

The economy developed not only through the addition of new lands but also through better use of existing lands. For example, semitamed cattle began to be taken by middlemen, who fattened the cattle for the *saladeros* (and for local consumption). Wells were dug, and a rudimentary type of fencing began to be used. The open range did not truly die until the late nineteenth century, when the value of cattle spiked due to the frozen meat trade; however, both cattlemen and sheepherders began to use brittle iron strands and later flexible steel wire to enclose their animals. Fencing became commonplace by the 1880s.

The combination of fencing and better use of land contributed to a renewed emphasis on farming around Buenos Aires; over time, cultivation added to grazing and began to provide alfalfa pastures that greatly contributed to the pampas' output. Another key development was the role sheep played in attracting foreign capital to the region, both to buy land as well as to invest in improvements such as railroads and packing plants. The first major rail line was completed in Argentina in 1870, but the most significant expansion of the country's railroad network took place in the 1880s in the sheep-raising areas of Buenos Aires. (The British built and managed the three most important rail lines.)

Sheep raising also significantly influenced the early days of meat packing. The British, already involved in transporting mutton from Australia, moved on to Argentina by the 1880s. At the time, plants in Buenos Aires were better able to handle mutton than the larger beef carcasses. (As a result, for the next two decades, the expansion of meat shipments to Europe was based on mutton.) Another important transition was taking place as the economy moved from its focus on the *estancia* and the *saladero* to a more modern *estancia* that was developing in the late nineteenth century.

The sheep economy caused, or at least strengthened, many important changes, such as attracting immigrants and foreign capital and encouraging the settlement of the pampas. Sheep raising also encouraged breeding, crop growing, the building of railroads, and the growth of meat packing plants. In effect, the foundation was laid for an explosion of beef and wheat production in the twentieth century.

ARGENTINA'S GOLDEN AGE (1870–1914)

Backtracking a bit, it is important to reiterate that Argentina's transformation began during the Rosas years—or as some would say, the "Rosas Tyranny." Rosas secured the primacy of the province of Buenos Aires under a sort of loose federal system. Trade was concentrated in the hands of city merchants, while upriver provinces were forbidden from direct commercial contact with the rest of the world. Rosas continued the special relationship with the British, secured the frontier, and opened vast new lands for exploitation. While land was not yet the main economic resource, the extension and security of the frontier meant that cattle and sheep multiplied and that animals became the key resource and a means to increase one's wealth.

By the 1840s, the wool cycle had begun—the first "modern" commodity boom in Argentina's history. Higher-quality breeds multiplied, and the valuable wool production helped drive cattle to the frontier (since it was raised for less valuable "colonial" products such as hides and tallow). In effect, the stage was set for the next phase of expansion and Argentina's so-called golden age.

The pace of railway building gathered steam in the 1870s, built for the most part on British capital. Trade increased and government finances improved; by the beginning of the decade, wool had displaced hides as the main export. A key point regarding the changing economy is that producers' ability to shift to changes in the demand for wool and hides reflected a relatively flexible economy and group of producers. It also reflected growing attention to the science of land management.

By 1870, the coast had become the economic center of the country and Buenos Aires its leading city. The boom of the 1880s followed a number of events that helped transform the state and the market. For example, a new commercial code was set in 1859, a system of national schools was created in 1870, an immigration law was created in 1876, and the first national census was taken in 1869. For the most part, the great transformation occurred during and after the 1880s. Immigration spiked and population quadrupled from about 2 million to 8 million between 1869 and 1914, with immigration accounting for about half this number. The huge flow of immigrants is significant for many reasons. Besides the substantial increase in population, immigrants represented an important contribution to progress, as they were often skilled and literate (helping to boost productivity). It can also be argued that the huge flows of immigration highlight the attractive material conditions and the tremendous economic opportunities available in Argentina at the time.

The last quarter of the nineteenth century saw tremendous growth in the industries related to sheep, as well as in the production and export of cereals—an exponential growth in commercial agriculture. Land under cultivation also experienced phenomenal growth. A number of factors supported the boom and should be mentioned briefly.

First, as mentioned previously, the agricultural sector exhibited an important flexibility to produce a greater quantity of goods that yielded greater returns; upgrading to exports of wool and cereal is a good example. Likewise, the significant investments in infrastructure—from railways to ports—led to more efficient transportation. (A large proportion came from foreign investment.) The country also experienced relative monetary stability between the late nineteenth century and the 1940s, enhancing confidence and increasing investment.

Technological innovations also contributed to the boom. Cheap barbed wire fencing and windmills as well as the introduction of alfalfa increased the capacity of the country's cattle ranges. New methods of processing and shipping meat over long distances under refrigeration opened huge markets, stimulating the construction of refrigerated packing houses and refrigerated steamships. (By 1905, Argentina surpassed the United States as the principal exporter of beef and mutton to the British market.)

Another key factor was political: the internal political conflicts that had characterized the country until 1880 had

A barbed wire fence and wooden gate enclose the pampas near La Esperanza, Argentina. (Paul A. Souders/Corbis)

essentially come to a halt—relative political stability was supportive of economic expansion. Finally, industrialization in Europe and the United States contributed to global demand for raw materials.

Baring Crisis of 1889–1890

The Baring Crisis was an important exception to the rule of relatively stable, prosperous times for the economy. In the 1880s, much of the productive investments (rails, estate improvements, etc.) needed several years to come to fruition. In other words, the payoff to such investments was longer-term and came only after projects were completed and additional commodities were delivered to market. Much of this was financed with foreign borrowing that, until the new projects matured and generated their own inflows of export earnings, required a nearly continuous inflow of new money to provide the foreign exchange needed to finance existing debt.

Due to the need for ongoing credit flows from abroad, confidence was essential to sustain flows until projects matured. However, a wave of speculation and corruption damaged foreign confidence and caused a sharp contraction in flows. For a time, this confidence was restored; but it was not to last.

In the second half of the decade, landowners began investing increasing amounts of overseas money in land speculation rather than in the development of existing mortgaged estates (thereby extending the final payoffs via exports and resulting foreign exchange). Also, a considerable sum of foreign capital was lost to corruption. In a manner not dissimilar to the crisis of 2001–2002, the process unraveled quickly.

Foreign investors and creditors lost confidence that they would be repaid, and the flow of new funds declined precipitously; confidence ultimately disappeared completely as investments faltered, deposits were withdrawn from banks, gold was hoarded, the currency plummeted, and inflation spiked. The regime collapsed as asset values plunged, and the economy fell into recession. In the process, the Argentine

(Continued)

Baring Crisis of 1889–1890 *(continued)*

government nearly brought down the British investment bank Baring Brothers, causing chaos and financial pain in London.

Recovery eventually ensued as the incoming regime reached an agreement with creditors based on its ability to pay and the government returned to fiscal discipline and implemented currency and banking reforms. A number of other measures were required, such as turning a number of enterprises over to creditors. Exports also recovered—by the mid-1890s, investments of the 1880s came on stream and the country was helped by a favorable global commodities market; debt service was even resumed sooner than specified in the agreement with foreign creditors.

In the same manner that wool had replaced older colonial products such as hides and tallow, around the turn of the century, cereals (namely, wheat and corn) had become dynamic commodities. Then by the 1920s, stock raising began to test cereals. In sum, the entire nineteenth century was characterized by the expansion of exports, a process that accelerated dramatically in the last quarter of the century and continued until the First World War. (By the twentieth century, the production of manufactured products also began to expand rapidly.)

While the "golden age" was characterized by dramatic export expansion, the rate of growth in industrial nations largely determined increases in demand for commodity exports; in other words, growth was largely a function of demand in other countries, not in Argentina. This underlying vulnerability would become more apparent during the First World War. Still, at this point, Argentina remained one of the wealthiest nations in the world, helped by the dramatic expansion in commodity exports and by a relatively sparse population.

STALLED PROGRESS (1914–1930)

As mentioned previously, the "golden age" was characterized by the rapid expansion in commodity exports (and important improvements in living standards). Some industrial growth also occurred during this process. Processing plants for exports, food packing plants, textile factories, and factories for construction materials are important examples. However, the "golden age" of export growth broke down with the onset of World War I as global commodities markets became unstable and Argentina's exports suffered.

The outbreak of war also brought financial difficulties, even crisis, to the region; but recovery ensued relatively quickly as exports began to recover. Perhaps most important to understanding the impact of the war on the economy is that the changes taking place in the global economy provoked a number of policy responses that would drive structural change in Argentina. Notably, the First World War uncovered the economy's external vulnerability. (This recognition of external vulnerability was reinforced in 1929–1930 with the global financial crash and ensuing Great Depression.)

The immediate impact of the war's onset was a reversal of capital and credit flows; Argentina's domestic capital market was in no position to replace them. As a result, there were sharp disruptions to the credit and payments system, negative effects on production and employment, numerous bankruptcies, and even a fiscal crisis as state funding depended on borrowing and import tariffs. Over time, conditions improved as prices and demand for commodities strengthened due to the war; but the immediate adjustment was harsh. The lack of access to imported goods during the war did result in some domestic production of substitutes—as a result, many analysts have identified the war as a positive stimulus for industrial production. The 1920s saw some modest protection, but there was little in the way of a coherent industrial policy. However, the period set the stage for a major reevaluation of economic policies following the shock of 1929 and the onset of the Great Depression.

In sum, the trauma of the adjustment in the early war years combined with the shock of the worldwide depression sparked widespread debate about the nation's direction as well as calls for greater state action (i.e., intervention) in the economy. The Great Depression brought significant changes to the global economy, including declining economic activity in the developed world, a decline in the volume and value of world trade, high interest rates, and a sharp decline in the real prices of commodities. While Argentina was less vulnerable than other commodity exporters, it was still hurt by the shock. The initial response by the Argentine government was contractionary; however, by the mid-1930s, government spending started to increase.

The 1930s saw large-scale public investment in rail and road construction, the formation of a central bank, growth of agencies supporting commodity prices, and the like. The size of Argentina's state sector grew, and there was more intervention in the market. However, government action at this point remained fairly limited and pragmatic in nature—importantly, intervention had not become ideological, as it soon would. At this point, there continued to be strong concern about the fiscal and external accounts; and these remained broadly in balance as a result.

However, two issues deserve mention. First, the 1930s marked a turning point in politics, starting with a military coup in 1930 that was followed by a period notable for electoral fraud—this represented a break in the democratic system. The resulting political and social conflict would impact the country for decades. In turn, Argentina was increasingly isolating itself from the global economy; while perhaps an understandable reaction to the shocks of the era, the interaction between growing state intervention, political instability, and economic isolation would take a tremendous toll on the economy over time.

By the middle of the 1930s, industry was becoming the leading sector in the economy and was undergoing some important structural changes in the process. Traditional industrial pursuits such as food and beverage witnessed growth, but newer sectors turned out to be more dynamic. (These included sectors such as motor vehicles, textiles, and electrical appliances.) By this time, the real value of agricultural output had become relatively steady, while the value of industrial output grew quite quickly.

To conclude, the shock of World War I (reinforced by the difficulties of the Great Depression) provoked a shift in policy orientation, prompting the state to take a more active role in the economy. In general, the country witnessed a shift from orthodoxy to pragmatism. But a generalized concern with underlying economic fundamentals (fiscal balance, inflation, and the balance of payments) remained in place. Unfortunately, as the country began a more conscious

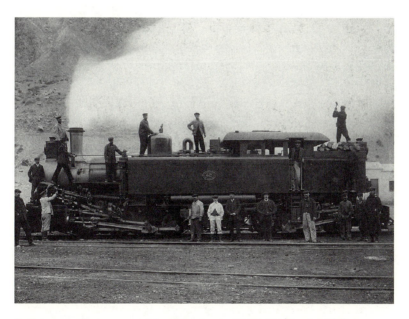

Railway workers pose with an engine in 1925. (A. Streich/Hulton Archive/Getty Images)

strategy of industrialization, this concern with sound economic fundamentals seemed to fade.

THE MOVE TO INDUSTRIALIZATION

Argentina's export-led growth helped build the economic infrastructure that led to industrial growth. Export earnings helped finance the firms supplying the domestic market, while also helping to finance important imports such as labor, technology, and capital goods.

In general terms, from the 1880s to the 1940s, there was little evidence of rapid growth in industrial production; rather, industrial output grew at largely the same rate as the economy as a whole. Firms remained relatively small—considerably smaller than their agroexport counterparts. Industrial entrepreneurs were often immigrants (or of immigrant origin). By the late 1890s, a number of industrial firms were starting to branch out, expanding into multiple activities in different sectors of the economy (such as meat packing, banking, and oil refining). These financial-industrial groups, which have been quite common throughout Latin America, are called *grupos economicos,* or economic groups.

The outbreak of World War II in 1939 had an immediate negative impact on Argentina. While a similar negative impact had occurred in 1914, the economy had since become more diversified and the government more qualified to craft a policy response. However, the ability to respond appropriately to the shock of the war was constrained by domestic politics—the regime at the time seemed incapable of reform, at the very time threats from labor and the nationalist military establishment mounted. The result of this policy standstill in an environment of economic crisis was a military coup in 1943. Many scholars see this event as a crossroads for Argentina: The failure to solve the problems of the 1940s in a democratic fashion foreshadowed the disappointing economic performance and political conflict to come in the years ahead.

PERÓN AND THE ECONOMY

The group of officers that took power in 1943 wanted to remake Argentina's entire political structure; they were also among the most nationalistic members of the officer corps. At the time, the two main political actors were the military and labor. The decisive new player would be Juan Perón, who courted labor and the lower classes. His tremendous popularity allowed him to win the presidency in 1946.

A five-year economic plan was created soon after Perón's victory, along with the powerful foreign trade institute that was given monopoly powers over the export of agricultural crops. At this point, Argentina began to push the most state-directed economic policy seen thus far in Latin America. The Perón government carried out a huge redistribution of national income, which at least in the short run benefited lower-income segments of society. Perón also laid the foundations of a welfare state and solidified the strategy of state-led development.

Perón followed a nationalist and populist path. As a populist, he promised workers the wages they had been denied previously. Between 1946 and 1950, labor's share of national income rose by 25 percent. The losers were primarily the owners of capital—and, most importantly, landowners, who were consistently shortchanged by the foreign trade institute (which bought their goods at low prices, sold them internationally at higher prices, and funneled the profits to urban and industrial projects). The strategy seemed quite effective, at least at the beginning, as the economy showed strong levels of growth.

Perón-the-nationalist also promised to reduce the role of foreigners in the economy. In one of his most symbolic moves, he nationalized the British-owned railways in 1948. He also nationalized some French dock facilities, as well as the main telephone company (controlled by the U.S. company ITT). While owners were compensated, the move was indicative of the more antagonistic stance the government would adopt vis-à-vis foreign investors. In the same vein, in 1947, Perón paid off the entire foreign debt, announcing to the country a "Declaration of Economic Independence."

Another direction of state policy was to promote public-private partnerships (the *sociedad mixta*), which, at the time, were typically joint ventures between British firms and the Argentine state. These mixed corporations reflected ideologies popular in the 1940s and were designed to harmonize the interests of producers, consumers, and the government. The strategy of development adopted by Argentina, similar to other countries in Latin America, was called import substitution industrialization (ISI).

Other countries in Latin America and the rest of the world experienced state intervention in infrastructure development, the productive sectors, and the like. However, at the time, a major difference between many of these countries and Argentina centered on the issue of funding—this issue was simply not addressed realistically by Argentina. Notably, the country began to use "inflation taxation" as the easy way out. (This typically occurs when the government prints money to pay the state's bills.) As a result, after the mid-1940s, Argentina witnessed a sustained divergence between its rates of inflation and the lower rates of inflation in the rest of the world.

From the 1940s until nearly the end of the century, Argentina displayed relatively high fiscal deficits, government indebtedness, and relatively high inflation. Many scholars have argued that excessive intervention and fiscal laxness were not the only causes of the eventual failure of state-led growth. Another problem Argentina faced at the time was a relatively poorly trained administrative apparatus; in many ways, the state was unprepared to implement complex, sustainable economic policies that depended on massive state intervention. Corruption exacerbated this problem as well.

Import Substitution Industrialization

For approximately fifty years, Latin America pursued a strategy of development called import substitution industrialization, or ISI—and Argentina was one of the leaders. As the name implies, the idea was to replace previously imported industrial goods with goods produced domestically. The strategy was inward-looking and was supported by Raul Prebisch, the head of the United Nations Economic Commission for Latin America (ECLA).

The strategy relied on exchange rate and trade restrictions, such as multiple exchange rates, import licenses, quotas, protective tariffs, and export taxes. The goal was to limit trade and reserve the domestic market for local producers, providing a protected "training ground" for domestic industry with the hope that it would eventually compete internationally. Unfortunately, the policy typically led to inefficient firms and high-cost industrial substitutes. In general, local industry failed to become internationally competitive, and Latin Americans were forced to pay high prices for poor-quality goods produced domestically.

Likewise, by de-emphasizing exports, the countries lacked foreign exchange to pay for much-needed imports. While ISI did play a meaningful role in stimulating the economic development of the region, by the 1980s, ISI was exhausted. During the 1980s and 1990s, Latin American countries were forced to introduce a host of reforms to open their economies, reduce the size of government, and improve efficiency.

Perón's early economic successes quickly ran into growing problems. In 1949, inflation jumped to 31 percent. This was hardly surprising since Perón was pursuing a strategy of demand expansion through wage increases when employment was already high and plants were near full capacity. Likewise, with imports controlled, stronger purchasing power siphoned off exports and triggered inflation.

In 1949, the country also ran its first foreign trade deficit since the war; and a drought that hit agricultural exports exacerbated the problem. Also, the so-called terms of trade were beginning to work against Argentina: World prices for her exports were falling, while prices for imports (namely, manufactured imports) were rising. Perón's own economic policies were making the problems worse. For example, in paying artificially low prices to farmers (partly to keep urban food costs low), the government created a disincentive to investment in and production of agricultural exports. The idea was to sell products at high external prices and buy at low internal prices and then funnel the proceeds to benefit industrialization via subsidies, cheap foreign exchange, investments, etc.

As the economy worsened, Perón responded with an orthodox stabilization program, tightening credit, cutting government spending, and putting strict limits on wages and prices. Perón wanted to get the economy back on track so he could return to his social agenda. The plan seemed to be working, and Perón and his team put together another five-year plan after his reelection in 1953. This plan was markedly less nationalist and populist than the first one; the nationalist Perón even called for increased foreign investment, signing a deal with Standard Oil of California in 1954.

Perón asked workers to accept a two-year wage freeze, and agriculture was no longer the direct target it was before. In fact, an export drive became a key feature of the new stance. Perón knew that he needed a quick return to growth since economic stagnation fostered a zero-sum game in which one class could win only at another's expense. Ironically, in the end, economic policies became more orthodox while Peronist political rhetoric grew more strident and radical. As Perón's political enemies grew, military conspirators stepped in; and in September 1955, Perón left Argentina for political asylum in Spain.

It must be noted that Perón and the military leaders who helped him to power played a large role in Argentina's growing isolationism. One telling example was the country's decision in 1947 not to participate in the General Agreement on Tariffs and Trade (GATT). GATT was part of the Bretton Woods agreement, which was created after World War II to help redefine the post-war international economic order. (The IMF and the World Bank also were created in this agreement.) In essence, the idea was to help harmonize world trade and strengthen the world financial system.

By adopting an aggressive, nationalistic stance, Argentina argued that the measures favored the interests of the United States and other advanced nations. At the time, Argentina was still a member of the twenty most economically advanced nations in the world; amazingly, Argentina was the

Participants of the United Nations Monetary and Financial Conference meet in Bretton Woods, New Hampshire, in 1944. The result was an agreement between forty-five countries to ensure worldwide financial stability after World War II. (Library of Congress)

only country of the twenty to reject the new system and to actively provoke a divide between rich and poor countries (despite the fact that it fit into the former).

MILITARY STEWARDSHIP

Obviously, Perón's economic measures were insufficient to save his regime. The military stepped in and began to look for ways to open the economy and stimulate foreign investment and trade. There was also a promise to reduce the scope of the interventionist state. However, shutting down state corporations and ending developmentalism did not happen. More than anything, powerful interest groups opposed these acts. For example, the military refused to hand over its industrial empire. Manufacturers, meanwhile, had become accustomed—some would say, addicted—to their subsidies, such as privileged access to credit and cheap foreign exchange. State-led development had laid down deep roots.

However, the next several decades were marked by profound economic failure—from the 1950s through the 1980s, very little real growth took place in the Argentine economy. Rather, there was more of an ongoing process of reallocation among competing groups and sectors. Lack of fiscal discipline, inflation, and balance-of-payments crises became nearly permanent features of the economy. The period was marked by expansionist policies alternating with stabilization plans, with regime changes often driving the reversals in policy. Other reversals centered on exports versus domestic production and capital inflows versus economic nationalism. A vicious cycle developed in which policy inconsistency fed political instability and political instability encouraged policy reversal.

The new president following Perón's ouster in 1955 was Eduardo Lonardi, who was quickly replaced by Pedro Aramburu, a hard-liner who moved to purge the system of Peronism. (In 1970, he was kidnapped and murdered by guerrillas in retribution for the execution of Peronist plotters within the military.) The military then held a presidential election in 1958, which Arturo Frondizi won. In many ways, Frondizi was similar to a number of reformers in Latin America at the time, a good example being Juscelino Kubitchek in Brazil. Frondizi's plan was to kick-start growth in Argentina by accelerating industrialization and stimulating agricultural production (the latter to increase export earnings and foreign exchange). Financing for industry was to come from abroad, and widespread state intervention was to be reduced. In a nutshell, investment was to be preferred over consumption.

Frondizi faced a balance-of-payments crisis early on; and on the advice of foreign creditors, he put in place an "orthodox shock." This included a huge devaluation, extremely tight credit, sharp reductions in public spending, tough wage limits, reductions in public employees, and the like. These were difficult conditions in which to start a major economic development program. The military forced a change in Frondizi's economic team, replacing it with free-market advocates of IMF policies. Frondizi was then locked in to "shock treatment."

While opposition to Frondizi's tough policies mounted— from both labor and business—there were some successes (for example, growth from 1960–1961, a decline in inflation, improved industrial production, and major improvement in domestic oil production). However, political opposition to Frondizi grew—most importantly for his political fate, from the military. On March 29, 1962, the army removed him from power.

After an acting president stood in for a year and a half, Radical Arturo Illia assumed the presidency in 1963. At least at the start, economic conditions were favorable; but the new team began to target expansion early on, granting wage increases while at the same time putting price controls in place. With these policies, Argentina entered the go phase of its seemingly endless stop-and-go cycles (in which it alternated between expansion and contraction).

Despite the government's generous wage increases, the Peronists drew up "battle plans" to oppose Illia, including strikes and shop takeovers. Allowed once again to take part in elections, the Peronists did well in the elections of 1965. Hard-liners in the military grew increasingly alarmed, especially since the economy started to sour—by this time, the budget deficit was large and inflation was on the rise. In June 1966, the military intervened and removed yet another Radical president from office.

BUREAUCRATIC AUTHORITARIANISM I

The military coup in 1966 represented the most dramatic break with the past since the coup of 1943; General Juan Carlos Onganía proclaimed "The Argentine Revolution" and a new kind of military regime, a "bureaucratic authoritarian" regime. The new regime claimed it would attack the root causes of Argentina's problems, rather than just the symptoms.

The military moved in and quickly ousted civilian politicians, forging alliances with technocrats and foreign investors. Foreign capital was needed to support economic growth. Domestic labor was repressed (in part, since increased investment would be based on reduced wages). Onganía put in place yet another stabilization program. He also implemented a two-year wage freeze in 1967.

Remember that this was a time of growing violence and protests that often resulted in violence. The worst of the protests was the so-called *Cordobazo* (named for the city in which the protest took place, Córdoba), in which police opened fire on protesters, killing protesters and innocent bystanders. With his credibility ruined, Onganía lasted only another year. The political violence also was escalating, with kidnappings and assassinations perpetrated by the radical left. Civil war was at hand.

Inflation was on the rise in 1971. A new president, Alejandro Lanusse (the brains behind Onganía's ouster eight months

Bureaucratic Authoritarianism

Argentina was by no means alone in Latin America when it imposed a bureaucratic authoritarian regime in 1966. Ruling elites in a number of countries imposed highly repressive regimes, typically through military coups (Brazil in 1964 and Chile in 1973). In these regimes, the most important decisions were made (or at least subject to veto) by the top ranks of the military. Typically, the leadership came in with a plan to stimulate investment to overcome economic stagnation. To succeed, the leaders deemed it necessary to dismantle (or even crush) the power of the working class. In each of these regimes, the government assumed control over decisions concerning labor's most important interests: wages, working conditions, and the right to organize.

Typically, the heavy hand toward labor reflected conditions that existed when the regimes took power. In particular, inflation and balance-of-payments deficits required unpopular anti-inflation policies. Since this usually caused recession and a drop in real wages, the militaries often saw themselves as the only political actor with the power to implement such tough policies.

Bureaucratic-authoritarian regimes shared a few common characteristics in Latin America. First, public office was typically given to people with highly bureaucratized careers, often to members of the military, civil servants, or corporate officers. A second important characteristic was the regimes' exclusion of the working class from politics and their control of the popular sector. A third characteristic was the reduction (and often near-elimination) of political activities. Finally, these regimes typically sought to push economic growth by building ties with the international economy, such as seeking foreign direct investment. Ironically, despite the rhetoric of economic reform and rationality, Argentina's military regimes failed in dramatically changing the structure of the economy and in markedly improving economic conditions.

earlier), followed a brief stint by Roberto Levinston. Lanusse pursued a relatively moderate nationalist course in economic policy, allowing budget deficits to rise. As a result, inflation also began rising, hitting 58.5 percent in 1972. It has been argued that Lanusse had no real plan for the economy; rather, his goals were political—he wanted to reach a new political accord. His major political gamble was to let "the old man," Juan Domingo Perón, return to Argentine politics as perhaps the only person who could save the country from civil war.

PERÓN'S RETURN

As discussed in the history chapter, the return of Perón would be tumultuous and short-lived. The politics of Perón's return will be discussed in the next chapter, but the economics are fairly clear—the return of Perón and the Peronists to power did very little to stop Argentina's disastrous stop-and-go cycles.

Perón was preceded briefly by Peronist stand-in Héctor Cámpora, who upon assuming office, pushed an aggressive new policy stance that called for stabilizing prices and increasing labor's share of national income to where it had been in the earlier Peronist era (requiring a great deal of coop-eration from the various national interest groups). Perón shortly won a new presidential election, with his second wife Isabel running as vice-president.

It appeared as though Cámpora's economic program was effective initially; but like a number of past programs, problems surfaced quickly. In 1974, OPEC dramatically increased the price of oil; and while Argentina imported only some 16 percent of its oil at the time, the shock hurt the bal-ance of payments as the import bill increased. Perón also agreed to some large year-end bonuses for workers, under-mining his own attempts at stabilizing the economy. Whether Perón at age seventy-seven could have worked his magic was never known, as he died in July 1974, leaving his ill-prepared wife Isabel Perón as president.

Isabel's policies were far from consistent. After mounting a campaign against large wage increases for union workers, she gave in after a series of massive strikes and granted the raises. By this point, the economy was out of control, with inflation

Workers take to the streets of Buenos Aires in January 1976 to demand salary increases. (Diego Goldberg/Sygma/Corbis)

reaching as high as 335 percent. Once again, Argentina was forced to get help from the IMF and implement an unpopular stabilization plan. Political violence escalated, and the currency lost value daily. As president, Isabel Perón lost all control of the government and the economy. As the situation neared the "point of no return," the military stepped in and placed Isabel under house arrest.

BUREAUCRATIC AUTHORITARIANISM II

Yet another authoritarian regime came to power in 1976. While some in the military argued that a successful national security state was impossible in Argentina, another group argued that a better-organized and more determined effort could succeed—for them, it was Onganía and not military authoritarianism that failed from 1966–1973. This text has briefly discussed the repressive tactics adopted by the military in the years between 1976 and 1983, and the following chapter on politics and government will discuss those topics in even more detail. But what were the economic objectives and policies of the second bureaucratic-authoritarian regime?

The new regime was run by General Jorge Videla, who was not content with Onganía's efforts to restore business confidence and accelerate industrialization with the help of foreign capital. Videla wanted to transform the economy and drastically reorient Argentine society—this was to be a new free-market economy, ending the inefficiencies associated with a closed development model. Thus, state corporations would be sold, tariffs would be reduced, and the private sector would have to learn quickly how to compete.

In addition to a stabilization plan, the government intended to follow market-based reforms. First, tariffs would be reduced, inviting foreign competition and forcing greater efficiency and productivity. Capital markets also were to be opened up, allowing supply and demand to determine interest rates (after having been controlled and subsidized by the government). Finally, the public sector deficit would be reduced by cutting wages, increasing taxes, and selling large numbers of state enterprises.

The economy minister was José Martínez de Hoz (a so-called neoliberal). He designed the plan to force business owners to adapt to competition, ending their reliance on government subsidies. There was considerable progress at first—the deficit was reduced, and subsidization of businesses dropped. Likewise, inflation fell and the balance of payments was positive for four years (1976–1979).

However, very little progress was made selling public enterprises. (The military in particular resisted selling firms they had long controlled, while there also was a notable scarcity of buyers.) The fiscal gap was not closed either. External indebtedness was careening out of control, just as international interest rates were on the rise. The outlook was deteriorating quickly.

General Roberto Viola succeeded Videla in late March 1981; complaints about economic policies rose, as did calls for the dismissal of the economy minister and a return to the old "business-as-usual" policies. Conditions continued to deteriorate due to a global recession that hit Argentina in 1981— Argentina's GDP fell by 6 percent that year. The exchange rate had become overvalued, and Viola announced a series of large devaluations. He also suspended the tariff reduction program, reintroduced export taxes and import licensing, and cut government spending. Bankruptcies rose and foreign debt spiked alarmingly (reaching some $45 billion by the time the military left at the end of 1983). Ultimately, the military government failed to control government spending, leaving a legacy of unsustainable indebtedness, an even more cumbersome state sector, and capital flight.

Military colleagues grew dissatisfied and replaced Viola with army commander Leopoldo Galtieri at the end of 1981. To everyone's surprise, Galtieri launched an invasion of the Falkland Islands on April 2, 1982—a huge mistake the military would soon regret. In essence, the move was a desperate gamble to regain political popularity; its complete failure underscored the incompetence of the armed forces and its leaders. After a swift and humiliating defeat at the hands of the British, Galtieri was replaced and the military announced its intention to hand power back to civilian leaders; once again an authoritarian experiment ended in political and economic crisis.

To conclude, despite the tough rhetoric, the military government failed to close the fiscal gap; government expenditures remained a pernicious problem. Likewise, external indebtedness had grown out of control at a time when international interest rates were on the rise. The main causes of the economic crisis in the early 1980s were internal; and to a large extent, this was the failure of the military regime to control government expenditures. The main tasks of the subsequent civilian government would be to reconstruct democratic government as well as build up civil society after years of brutal, violent repression. Economic reactivation also was deemed important, but this goal would prove more elusive.

THE ECONOMY AND THE TRANSITION TO DEMOCRACY

Clearly, the Falkland Islands invasion was based on the military leadership's desire to improve its dwindling popularity; and one of the core reasons for its declining popularity was the atrocious state of the economy. The economy continued to deteriorate in 1982; inflation reached some 200 percent, and workers lost approximately 25 percent of their purchasing power. The government also went into de facto default on its foreign debt. This was, to say the least, a challenging environment in which to manage a transition back to civilian democratic rule.

Raúl Alfonsín (who had battled for human rights during the brutal military regime) won the presidential election in 1983. At least two major issues faced the new democratic leader: how to go about prosecuting military and police officers responsible for the atrocities of the "dirty war" and how to improve the horrendous state of the economy. The next chapter on politics and government will discuss the former topic, as it represents one of the more complicated political issues in the transition from military to civilian rule. The state of the economy will be discussed briefly next.

Alfonsín inherited a high-inflation economy that was in the fourth year of a sharp recession. Equally daunting was the foreign debt, which approached a record $46 billion and required more money to service than the country's sickly economy could afford. In an attempt to build political support, Alfonsín ran a loose populist monetary policy, leading to a surge in inflation (and flight from the peso). Early tentative efforts to restore order failed; and by 1985, prices were rising at the astronomical annual rate of 1,000 percent, while payments on the debt constituted 60 percent of the earnings received on exports.

Alfonsín and the Radicals were forced to seek help from the IMF; and in September 1984, they secured a standby loan that came with fairly standard conditions: tighter monetary policy, reduction in public sector subsidies, controls on wage increases, and a gradual phasing out of price controls. Few believed the administration would deliver, and ultimately it did not.

In June 1985, Alfonsín announced a "battle plan" that was to be a "war on inflation." This was the famous *Plan Austral,* or Austral Plan, a heterodox blend of policies that was intended to fight inflation without incurring the negative growth impact of typical orthodox policies. Specifically, this meant an end to printing money to pay public debt, as well as raising taxes and the prices of services. It also called for a new currency, the austral. Finally, the plan called for a freeze on prices and wages. Argentina's creditors were impressed, and they agreed to renegotiate Argentina's massive foreign debt. The Argentine public also was enthusiastic about the plan.

Despite early success, the plan began to unwind as inflation returned and debt payments were increasingly hard to make (especially since the goal was to promote growth). A second shock was administered; but it, too, failed. Other attempts were made to stabilize the economy, but to no avail; the Alfonsín administration never regained control of the economy and thus lost its credibility.

Presidential elections were scheduled for May 1989, which was noteworthy as the first time since 1928 that one civilian had been elected president to replace another (let alone a candidate from the opposition). However, the economic chaos dampened any political pride. Taking advantage of the economic chaos, candidate Carlos Menem rallied the lower classes, promising to rescue them (as Juan Perón had done long ago).

Menem won the election, but it was by no means clear at the time whether he and the Peronists could govern the chaotic nation effectively. He would inherit a severe economic crisis; poverty was on the rise, inflation was out of control,

Money is printed in Argentina in 1989 in response to heavy inflation, despite efforts like Raúl Alfonsín's 1985 Austral Plan to ease the nation's economic problems. (Diego Goldberg/Sygma/Corbis)

and the foreign debt remained massive (and Argentines continued to send their own capital abroad).

The crisis worsened, with food riots breaking out across the country (hard to believe given Argentina's status as a "breadbasket" country in South America). Amid the chaos, Alfonsín announced that he would resign the presidency six months early, handing power to Carlos Menem under terrible circumstances.

THE REFORM ADMINISTRATION OF CARLOS MENEM

By the late 1980s, the Argentine public had had enough of the status quo, which equated to high inflation, poor-quality and high-priced goods, run-down public utilities, and extremely weak (if not negative) rates of economic growth. These conditions contributed to Menem's victory and his ability to push aggressive market-friendly reforms, including opening up the economy to trade and foreign investment, privatizing an enormous proportion of state assets, and deregulating the economy. While the story ends in crisis, it is important to understand that Argentina became an international success story during much of the 1990s—perhaps best reflected by the huge amounts of foreign capital that were attracted to the country.

Menem began his term by seeking assistance from all sectors of Argentine society, wisely assuming a nonconfrontational approach (a move atypical for a Peronist). He also invited members of the business community as well as the conservative opposition to accept positions in his cabinet. Menem appointed an economy minister who quickly announced an austerity plan; as part of the process, Menem shocked the country by announcing that private savings accounts would be exchanged for ten-year bonds. (In essence, this represented a confiscation of the population's savings.) The package induced recession, but it also helped end hyperinflation.

In an about-face for a Peronist president, Menem and his economic team unleashed a massive privatization program, selling off huge state-owned telephone, airline, and electric utility companies. (In general, the approach of the Menem government was "neoliberal" economic reform; i.e., opening the economy and rationalizing the state.) The climax of Menem's privatization program was the sale of the state-owned oil company (YPF), which was, as in a number of Latin American countries, a symbol of nationalist pride.

Menem appointed a new economy minister (his fourth) in 1991, an appointment that would prove highly significant to the continuation of liberal reforms. The new minister, Domingo Cavallo, would deepen market-oriented reforms, push for additional privatizations, and (perhaps most importantly) create the new convertibility law. That law established a one-to-one exchange rate between the Argentine peso and the U.S. dollar. (In theory, the law also limited public expenditures to revenues; but this part of the program

Argentina's finance minister Domingo Cavallo introduced the "convertibility law," fixing the peso to dollar exchange rate at one-to-one in an attempt to stop inflation and repair Argentina's economy. (Manny Ceneta/AFP/Getty Images)

was conveniently ignored, especially in Menem's later years.)

While convertibility is a somewhat complex economic policy, its key concept was that currency in circulation was limited to dollar reserves and other foreign reserves held by the central bank. Likewise, the system developed into a bimonetary system based on pesos and dollars (which were effectively interchangeable). The public was free to choose whichever currency they wanted to use, and there was a guarantee that pesos could be converted into dollars. Note that these two features differentiated Argentina from other Latin America economies that were pursuing programs of economic liberalization. (There were, of course, a number of important additional policies; however, their discussion is beyond the scope of this introductory chapter.)

The plan was highly successful and helped restore Argentina's meager credibility in the international markets. In turn, this newly won credibility drove a surge of capital inflows into the country, both direct foreign investments and portfolio capital flows. The plan also allowed Cavallo to restructure the country's foreign debt. Inflation fell from nearly 5,000 percent in 1989 to less than 4 percent in 1994; in the meantime, economic growth returned, reaching levels of some 6 percent—leading a considerable number of analysts to begin talking about an "Argentine miracle." Note that as part of the overall move to open the economy and participate more actively in the global economy, Menem advanced Mercosur; and trade relations with Brazil, in particular, deepened considerably.

The success of Menem's reform agenda was not without problems, however. For example, over time, it became increasingly clear that the currency was overvalued, which eventually led to increasing trade deficits. Likewise, the middle class took a significant hit from the new economic policies. For example, significant job losses resulted from the extensive privatizations. While this may have improved

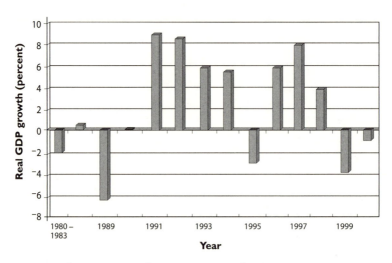

GDP growth in Argentina between 1980 and 1999.

the overall efficiency of the economy, it also resulted in climbing unemployment; from 6.5 percent in 1991, unemployment jumped to more than 12 percent in 1994 and 14 percent in 1997. (Labor did not take its deteriorating situation lying down, as strikes and protests grew in frequency.)

Another problem that hit the lower and middle classes was the increasing cost of living, which was related to the overvaluation of the currency (and was worsened by the rise of the dollar relative to important international currencies). The problem was the lack of a quick means of adjustment. Since the currency could not adjust due to the convertibility law, the brunt of the adjustment came through a combination of deflation and recession, which, for the most part, was cushioned during Menem's years by the easy access to international finance. As you will see, this spigot would eventually be turned off.

For the most part, convertibility worked during the Menem years, mainly because of popular support for the plan. Also, for a good part of the time, growth was coupled with low inflation. Convertibility also survived a number of tough tests. For

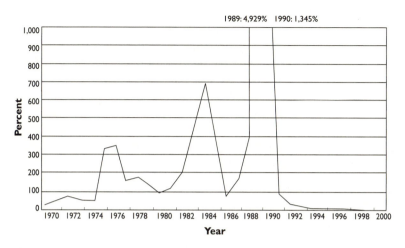

Argentine inflation (in percent) between 1970 and 2000.

example, the so-called Tequila Crisis associated with Mexico's huge devaluation in 1994 led to an attack on Argentina's currency and a run on its banks. Likewise, economy minister Domingo Cavallo's resignation in July 1996 was a significant challenge. Importantly, convertibility survived both crises.

At this point in Menem's term, two key points stand out. First, before Cavallo's resignation, it appeared as though he was having success in bringing government expenditures under control, an important boost for the plan. Likewise, Menem's ability to get the constitution changed so he could run for another term—and his subsequent reelection— seemed to underscore strong public support for the plan. After negative growth in 1995, the economy recovered, posting positive growth rates until 1998; later that year the expansion ended. Likewise, capital inflows were robust from 1993 to 1997 and remained positive overall until 2000. However, the problem of fiscal indiscipline grew. Ironically, as the economy entered recession in 1998, public expenditures actually increased (as they had since Cavallo left office). The fiscal gap had to be covered by borrowing, and this grew increasingly expensive.

To conclude, while the population supported the economic reform agenda, there was growing disenchantment with high unemployment and growing corruption. This would contribute to the victory of Fernando de la Rúa in the 1999 presidential election (and the loss of power by the Peronists).

FERNANDO DE LA RÚA AND THE COLLAPSE OF CONVERTIBILITY

The UCR-FREPASO Alliance was formed in mid-1997 for October congressional elections. Its success during those elections drove the Alliance to challenge the Peronists for the next presidential term. (As you know, Menem made a half-hearted attempt to be able to run for a third term, but highly negative public opinion quickly persuaded him to abandon the effort, although not without substantial damage to the fiscal accounts.) The Alliance candidate was Fernando de la Rúa, and he continued the successful strategy of supporting the existing economic model while criticizing unemployment and corruption. While de la Rúa defeated the Peronist candidate Eduardo Duhalde in 1999, the Alliance fell apart, the president was forced to resign, and convertibility (along with the Argentine economy) collapsed.

De la Rúa ultimately proved incapable of leading Argentina out of its economic crisis. However, the increasingly desperate state of affairs reflected both external shocks and internal policies and politics. On the external side, the most damaging developments had to do with the international financial crisis that hit Asian emerging markets by the end of 1997, worsening throughout 1998 with devaluations and defaults moving from Asia to Russia. For Argentina, the final straw was Brazil's huge devaluation in early 1999.

To understand the huge blow to Argentina's economy that these crises represented, you need to remember two main issues. First, the growing perception that emerging markets as a whole were at risk caused Argentina's capital inflows to dry up, dramatically worsening its financial outlook. Second, currency devaluations in other emerging markets, especially Brazil, contributed to a serious deterioration in Argentina's balance of trade. (In effect, Argentina's exports had just become markedly more expensive while imports from countries such as Brazil were becoming significantly less expensive.)

De la Rúa took power in December 1999; and by January 2000, the economic situation was already looking shaky. (The economy had slipped into recession by the middle of 1998.) For example, the president had to seek medical treatment for a condition that was at first thought to be quite serious; while this turned out not to be the case, several weeks of treatment prevented swift movement on much-needed reforms. Likewise, economic conditions were challenging; recession continued unabated. Unemployment remained stubbornly high (over 15 percent) and exports were weak, a clear result of the Brazilian devaluation (and Argentina's currency overvaluation).

The government pushed ahead with its reform agenda; but early on, it was involved in a corruption scandal, which undermined its credibility. The government faced a fiscal crisis and moved to put austerity measures in place that would further cut spending and increase revenues. In return, the IMF promised to provide the funds so Argentina could make its debt payments in the coming year. Fears of a debt default were growing, and signs of impending economic collapse were increasingly visible—a crisis mentality was taking hold.

One significant political development that seriously impacted the economic crisis was the resignation of the vice-president, Carlos Álvarez, in October 2000 in protest over the government's austerity measures. As head of FREPASO, Álvarez played a key role in attracting votes from the left for the Alliance. To make matters worse, the rest of FREPASO abandoned the Alliance in March 2001, forcing what was now a Radical (rather than Alliance) government to look for allies on the right. The administration's popularity was plummeting.

By 2001, the situation had become a full-blown panic. Bank deposits were falling as people feared a collapse of the banking system and withdrew their deposits; foreign reserves also were plummeting (falling by some $10 billion in 2001). Indicators of country risk (typically measured as the difference—or "spread"—between the yield on Argentine government bonds and the yield on U.S. government bonds) were skyrocketing by the second half of the year.

De la Rúa called in Domingo Cavallo to help avoid catastrophe—in particular, to deal with the convertibility plan. However, Cavallo's announced changes following two quick resignations of economy ministers were interpreted as an indication of indecision and, ultimately, predictive of an end to the regime. At this point, it appeared as though the political leadership in Argentina was unwilling or unable to make the hard decisions needed to exit the crisis successfully.

A second plan—*Plan Cero Déficit* (Zero Deficit Plan)—was announced, promising that each month expenditures would be no greater than what could be covered by revenue; this plan was accompanied by help from the IMF and an agreement by local creditors to reduce interest rates on the government's debts. But by this time, the government was caught in a vicious fiscal trap, a trap that had begun by 1999: Raising taxes and cutting spending during a recession was likely to worsen the recession and, in the process, reduce the government's income (taxes). This would require further tax increases and spending cuts. Argentines continued to buy dollars—and, if possible, to send their money overseas.

In the meantime, Argentina had become increasingly uncompetitive, reflecting the Brazilian devaluation and a soaring dollar (to which the overvalued Argentine peso was pegged). While Brazilian exports were booming, Argentine industry was stagnant and bankruptcies were on the rise. In turn, by 2001, the country's foreign debt had increased to between $130 billion and $140 billion—more and more of the country's resources were used just to pay the interest on the debt.

One major problem was that devaluation was not considered a feasible solution; convertibility was a law, real incomes would be devastated, dollar debts would become crippling, and there was a real danger that hyperinflation could return. A number of attempts were made to avert crisis, including further fiscal adjustment; but the results were disappointing.

Protests increased, putting pressure on de la Rúa to come up with a solution. One increasing form of protest, discussed briefly in the previous chapter, was middle-class housewives taking to the streets, banging pots and pans to highlight their dire straits. As bankruptcies increased, protests escalated, and the economy deteriorated, Cavallo resigned.

One policy in particular enraged the Argentine population, the so-called *corralito*. In early December 2001, the government announced a bank deposit freeze and exchange rate controls in a desperate attempt to stop the run on the banks and to reduce capital flight.

Protests reached a climax that same month in 2001. A huge protest at the *Casa Rosada* (the Argentine White House) sparked a violent struggle with police; the government responded by calling for a state of siege. That pronouncement sparked a spontaneous movement of people to Buenos Aires's central square (the *Plaza de Mayo*), the so-called night of the saucepans in which thirty-five people died. President de la Rúa tendered his resignation that night, December 21, 2001, and used a helicopter to flee the rioting that surrounded him.

For the next two weeks, the environment was characterized by political chaos and constitutional uncertainty; during this short period of time, congress appointed three separate interim presidents. One of the interim presidents, Adolfo Rodríguez Saá, announced the country's intention to default on its external debt, which would lead to the largest sovereign debt default in history.

The final interim president was Eduardo Duhalde, who, ironically, had lost to de la Rúa in the previous presidential election. In January 2002, Duhalde ended convertibility, letting the peso enter into free fall in the open market, although for a short period of time, the government maintained an "official" exchange rate of 1.4 pesos to the dollar. The Duhalde government mandated the so-called pesification of bank accounts, in which accounts denominated in dollars were converted into pesos at the official devalued rate, enraging the country's deposit holders.

Duhalde let the peso float freely, and a huge devaluation followed. In essence, the economic crisis hit bottom in 2002—inflation picked up (due to dependence on imports), the decline in economic growth touched bottom, and unemployment spiked. The peso reached nearly four to the dollar while businesses went bankrupt, real incomes fell sharply, and the overall quality of life diminished. At a minimum, Duhalde got the inevitable devaluation out of the way and helped stabilize the overall situation. Under pressure, Duhalde then called for new presidential elections.

NÉSTOR KIRCHNER

On May 25, 2003, Néstor Kirchner took over as president. One of Kirchner's first personnel decisions was to leave Duhalde's minister of the economy, Roberto Lavagna, in place. (Lavagna was a well-known and well-respected economist who seemed quite capable of managing the ongoing crisis.)

The outlook improved, in part because of the devaluation. While imports were quite expensive, exports were cheap; the government also actively encouraged import substitution. A bit of luck also helped as international prices and demand for Argentina's exports, especially commodities, improved. The return of economic growth since 2003 has been surprisingly strong. (The bottom of the downturn occurred in 2002.) In fact, GDP growth approached 10 percent in 2003–2005 and likely exceeded 8 percent in 2006, albeit with double-digit inflation.

Another factor that eased Argentina's economic pain was aggressive debt restructuring. In short, the country was able to restructure most of its defaulted debt—approximately 70 percent of the holders of the country's defaulted debt accepted a deal that gave them essentially 30 cents on the dollar for their debt. The issue can be seen in several different lights. For example, reducing the debt overhang eases the financial burden facing the country in the near to medium term, although it is certainly no long-term solution to the country's economic problems. Likewise, taking a tough stance with foreigners plays well to a domestic political audience, and Kirchner's approach won him political capital. The president even bragged publicly that investors

Economy Minister Roberto Lavagna (left) signs a letter of intent at the Economy Ministry building in Buenos Aires on March 10, 2004, aimed at restructuring the country's defaulted debt. (Ministerio de Economia/Handout/Reuters/Corbis)

had taken the largest financial "haircut" in history. However, the country may pay a price over time if investors prove less willing to send their money to Argentina (and require a significantly greater reward given the risks of loaning money to a government that seems to brag about breaking contracts). It is too early to tell what the long-term impact of the default will be on the economy.

Looking forward, there are reasons for both optimism and pessimism regarding Argentina's economy. As mentioned previously, the general numbers are positive; while inflation is on the high side, it is nowhere near the numbers seen in the past. At the same time, growth statistics are quite encouraging. As of 2005–2006, the international economy was very supportive of Argentina's economy, with high prices and demand for many of the country's exports. Significantly, while the devaluation caused considerable pain, it is done, which has returned the economy to international competitiveness.

At the same time, there are reasons for caution; and these originate primarily from policies that were pushed by Kirchner. A few examples serve to illustrate. One concern was the president's penchant for nationalist and populist policies; while this type of rhetoric is often used politically, Kirchner backed it up with policies. Shortly after wrapping up the debt restructuring, Kirchner moved to attack largely foreign-owned utilities. These utilities, such as water and electricity companies, were savaged when their dollar fees were converted to devalued pesos and then frozen by emergency law during the height of the crisis. While these contracts were supposed to be renegotiated some four months later, after more than three years, the government has yet to budge (despite significant levels of inflation in the interim). Besides the government having been anything but sympathetic to the plight of these companies, it hinted quite directly that it would take a more active role in business. (There were even hints of renationalizations.)

The problem for the economy is that any new investment in these businesses, whether the owners are Argentines or foreigners, must be based on some degree of confidence that future income will flow from higher rates; but this remains highly unlikely. For now, these companies obviously are not investing, suggesting that the country may face shortages in the future in critical areas such as electricity.

Another issue concerns what appears to be a lax attitude toward inflation—and a growing interest in populist policies in general. One reason for concern, aside from already high levels of inflation (which was over 12 percent in 2005), was the replacement of economy minister Lavagna with Felisa Miceli, who took over in December 2005. One of the central problems is the government's explicit policy of keeping the peso artificially cheap to maintain the benefits of the devaluation. (Technically, the Argentine central bank then has to print pesos to buy dollars, increasing the money supply and fueling inflation.)

In contrast to Brazil, which has used high interest rates to fight inflation and gain credibility, Argentina's interest rates are negative (in other words, well below the rate of inflation). Rather than raise interest rates, the aggressive Kirchner turned to the failed policies of Argentina's past to convince businesses to freeze prices. However, until Argentina adopts prudent monetary policy, prices most likely will continue to rise.

A final concern that is emblematic of Kirchner's penchant for nonmarket means of controlling the economy is illustrated by moves to control prices. For example, Kirchner moved to suspend beef exports from Argentina, with the express goal of keeping beef prices affordable at home. (In other words, more supply with constant demand should lead to better prices for domestic consumers.) While his intentions may have been good, the economics were sloppy at best and reminiscent of the failed economic policies of Argentina's past. In short, as profits decline for those who produce beef in Argentina (due to lower prices), by definition, their incentive to invest also falls. Declining investment, of course, will translate over time into a reduced supply of beef. Assuming the policy stance remains in place, at some point, Argentina will not only lose foreign currency coming from beef exports but also face rising beef prices due to a shortage of beef.

In sum, there are reasons for both optimism and pessimism when looking at the state of the Argentine economy. Current economic performance is undeniably positive, despite relatively high rates of inflation. At the same time, there are growing signs that leaders are adopting failed policies of the past. While these efforts are providing a short-term boost in political capital, they also underscore longer-term risks facing the economy. The hope is that Argentina's leaders have learned the lessons from the country's failed experiments with economic policymaking and are concerned about the basic fundamentals of low inflation, fiscal prudence, and roughly balanced external accounts. If not, when the world's strong commodity cycle inevitably turns, Argentina is likely to quickly return to another stop in the stop-and-go pattern of its modern economic history.

CRISTINA FERNÁNDEZ DE KIRCHNER

Cristina Fernández de Kirchner is the current president of Argentina, succeeding her husband Néstor Kirchner to assume the nation's highest office. It is probably too early to tell whether Fernández will follow her husband's more populist economic policy stance or craft a more centrist position (one unknown, of course, is the level of influence and power which Kirchner will retain). Whichever direction she chooses, the central challenges facing the country and its economy will remain in place. For now the backdrop is a supportive one, in particular as economic growth remains quite strong, although in an environment of relatively elevated inflation. Only time will tell whether Fernández will be tested by the more difficult economic conditions faced by many of her predecessors.

References

Bulmer-Thomas, Victor. *The Economic History of Latin America Since Independence.* Cambridge: Cambridge University Press, 1994.

Cardoso, Eliana, and Ann Helwege. *Latin America's Economy: Diversity, Trends, and Conflicts.* Cambridge, MA: MIT Press, 1995.

Conde, Roberto Cortés. "The Growth of the Argentine Economy, c. 1870–1914," in Leslie Bethell (ed.), *The Cambridge History of Latin America, Vol. V.* Cambridge: Cambridge University Press, 1986: 327–358.

De la Balze, Felipe A. M. *Remaking the Argentine Economy.* New York: Council on Foreign Relations Press, 1995.

Díaz Alejandro, Carlos F. *Essays on the Economic History of the Argentine Republic.* New Haven, CT: Yale University Press, 1970.

Di Tella, Guido, and Rudiger Dornbusch, eds. *The Political Economy of Argentina, 1946–1983.* London: Macmillan, 1989.

Donghi, Tulio Halperín. "Economy and Society in Post-Independence Spanish America," in Leslie Bethell (ed.), *The Cambridge History of Latin America, Vol. III.* Cambridge: Cambridge University Press, 1985: 299–346.

French-Davis, Ricardo, Oscar Muñoz, and José Gabriel Palma. "The Latin American Economies, 1950–1990," in Leslie Bethell (ed.), *The Cambridge History of Latin America, Vol. VI.* Cambridge: Cambridge University Press, 1994: 159–252.

Lewis, Colin M. *Argentina: A Short History.* Oxford: Oneworld Publications, 2002.

Lewis, Paul W. *The Crisis of Argentine Capitalism.* Chapel Hill: University of North Carolina Press, 1990.

Love, Joseph L. "Economic Ideas and Ideologies in Latin America Since 1930," in Leslie Bethell (ed.), *The Cambridge History of Latin America, Vol. VI.* Cambridge: Cambridge University Press, 1994: 393–462.

Paolera, Gerardo della, and Alan M. Taylor, eds. *A New Economic History of Argentina.* Cambridge: Cambridge University Press, 2003.

Rock, David. "Argentina, 1930–1946," in Leslie Bethell (ed.), *The Cambridge History of Latin America, Vol. VIII.* Cambridge: Cambridge University Press, 1984: 3–72.

Rock, David. "Argentina from the First World War to the Revolution of 1930," in Leslie Bethell (ed.), *The Cambridge History of Latin America, Vol. V.* Cambridge: Cambridge University Press, 1986: 419–452.

Scobie, James R. *Argentina: A City and a Nation,* 2nd ed. New York: Oxford University Press. 1971.

Skidmore, Thomas E., and Peter H. Smith. *Modern Latin America,* 5th ed. Oxford: Oxford University Press, 2001.

CHAPTER THREE
Politics and Government

INTRODUCTION

Argentina has been governed as a democracy since its transition from military to civilian rule in 1983 and the presidency of Raúl Alfonsín. The return to democracy was in many ways quite difficult, particularly due to the severe economic crisis taking place at the time (and, for that matter, affecting much of the rest of Latin America as well). However, given the military's humiliating defeat to Great Britain in the Falkland Islands in 1982, coupled with overwhelming public outrage over the excesses of the dirty war, there was not much chance that the country might quickly slip back into authoritarian rule. That the country was gaining traction with civilian democratic rule was underscored by the relatively smooth transition from Alfonsín to Carlos Menem: Occurring in 1989, this was the first time in Argentine history that a civilian president of one party peacefully handed over power to a democratically elected opposition president from another party.

Following Menem's presidency, the new democratic institutional setting was severely challenged by the 2001–2002 financial and political crises, which resulted in the early resignation of President Fernando de la Rúa in December 2001, when he was forced to flee the *Casa Rosada* by helicopter. De la Rúa's resignation of the presidency was followed by an institutional crisis, as four interim presidents were appointed in a matter of days. While the process was not elegant, in the past, the military would have likely stepped into the void, using political and economic chaos—not to mention protests, looting, and violence—as a pretext to assume power and control of the government.

Instead, in January 2002, Eduardo Duhalde was appointed interim president by legislators; the irony, of course, is that Duhalde was the Peronist candidate who lost the election for president to de la Rúa in 1999. As such, the opposition-controlled legislature picked one of its own Peronists to fill the vacant post rather than someone from de la Rúa's Radical Party. Despite the unusual circumstances, Duhalde succeeded in stabilizing the economic and political situation and called for new presidential elections for early 2003—elections that were won by Peronist Néstor Kirchner.

Formally named the *República Argentina,* or Argentine Republic, Argentina follows the Constitution of 1853, which was revised in 1994. The constitution, which strongly resembles the U.S. Constitution, mandates a separation of powers into executive, legislative, and judicial branches of government, both at the national and provincial levels. The president and vice-president are elected directly to four-year terms. They are limited to two consecutive terms, but may be reelected to a third term or more after an interval of at least one term. The president has considerable power in Argentina, including the authority to enact laws by presidential decree under conditions of "urgency and necessity."

The legislature is a bicameral National Congress, the *Congreso de la Nación,* which consists of a Senate with 72 seats and a Chamber of Deputies with 257 seats. Since 2001, senators have been directly elected, with each province and the federal capital represented by three senators (their terms are six years). One-third of the Senate stands for reelection every two years via a system of partial majority. Members of the Chamber of Deputies are directly elected to four-year terms via a system of proportional representation; voters elect half the members of the house every two years. Argentina is divided into twenty-three provinces and the federal capital of Buenos Aires.

As discussed in the preceding chapter, Argentina has experienced considerable economic and political instability,

Argentina's National Congress building in Buenos Aires. (Anthony Cassidy/JAI/Corbis)

particularly since the military coup that took place in 1930. In many ways, this instability reflects a vicious circle: Often economic instability has led to regime changes and abrupt shifts in economic policies; likewise, political instability has often made it impossible to carry out effective economic policies, leading, in turn, to economic collapse and regime changes. In this sense, then, the problem of instability has been both political and economic.

As the previous chapter suggests, one of the biggest questions relating to the study of Argentina today is why the rapid economic growth of the late nineteenth and early twentieth centuries did not consolidate into sustained growth and economic development during the second half of the twentieth century. Remember, at the turn of the century, Argentina was one of the wealthiest countries in the world (and would remain so until as late as the 1940s). As you will see in the following discussion, one of the biggest reasons is political—namely, the failure of the political system to develop as a legitimate mechanism to resolve distributional disputes (i.e., to resolve the inevitable clashes over access to resources and the benefits of development). Unfortunately, in Argentina, the process has often devolved into a zero-sum game, in which one group's gains have represented another group's losses rather than one in which legitimate political institutions have resolved conflicts for the common good.

THE HISTORICAL BACKDROP

As was discussed in the chapter on the Argentine economy, a key point to understand about early colonial Argentina is that its territory existed as a sort of backwater in the greater Spanish Empire. In effect, to understand the politics and government of early Argentina, the territory must be seen as a sort of unexciting appendage, with its small settlements depending on (and answering politically to) the viceroyalty based in Peru. It was only toward the end of the colonial era that Buenos Aires emerged as an important economic and political center.

Remember, the Spanish Crown pursued its objectives in its colonial empire based on the concepts of mercantilism. In essence, mercantilist economic theory held that the wealth of a nation depended primarily on the amount of gold and silver in the national treasury. As a result, governments imposed considerable restrictions on their economies to ensure a surplus of exports over imports; as the benefits of the industrial revolution became apparent, mercantilist thinking was increasingly challenged by the idea of laissez-faire.

The Spanish Crown built its New World mercantilist empire based on the accumulation of riches; given Argentina's lack of mineral wealth and scarcity of Indian labor, the country was quickly written off as an unimportant component of the empire. In this context, the colonial trading system, with all of its mandated rigidities, was solidified, guaranteeing Argentina's backwater status. Given the apparently inhospitable environment in the Río de la Plata region, early settlement took place largely in the Northwest and Andean regions of the territory.

Following this theme, early communities in what would later become Argentina were largely satellites of the viceroyalty based in Peru; these communities were supposed to serve the goals of the Crown and its New World officials, which meant supplying the mining areas with agricultural and other products. To this end, by the 1600s, these settlements were largely dedicated to the production of livestock and agricultural products.

THE EARLY GROWTH OF BUENOS AIRES

Additional attempts at settlement in the eastern part of Argentina were pursued by the Spanish, in good measure as a response to growing Portuguese interests in the region; one of these settlements would eventually become Buenos Aires. However, Buenos Aires developed with a distinct disadvantage. Specifically, the capital of the viceroyalty was based in Lima and the Spanish Crown's mercantile regulations required that all goods from Buenos Aires be exported through the viceregal capital (despite the economic absurdity of overland travel to Peru when Buenos Aires was located on the Atlantic coast).

In effect, this was part of the Crown's attempt to control the colonial economy, in the process, maximizing taxes and preventing the growth of activities that might compete with those taking place in the mother country. One important but unintended consequence of these regulations was the growth of smuggling and other illegal activities. One of the first was illegal trade in silver, which originated in the mines of Peru and flowed to Portuguese merchants based in and around Buenos Aires; this silver was exchanged for manufactured goods, circumventing Spanish controls in the process.

In this manner, Buenos Aires developed independently of the official colonial trading system, at least in part. In this respect, the Spanish faced two related problems. First, there often were not enough inspectors to enforce the official system. Second, even when there were, Spain was, for the most part, unable to supply the goods demanded by the colonial economy—in short, the Crown could not stop illegal trade. The treaty that gave England the role as the sole supplier of slaves for Spanish America (discussed in the preceding chapter) contributed to this trend since it allowed English merchants to operate freely in Buenos Aires. Of course, these merchants were usually prepared to trade in more than just slaves.

THE BOURBON REFORMS (1702–1800)

As discussed in the history chapter, the Wars of Spanish Succession in the early 1700s led to significant political changes in Spain, which ultimately had a dramatic impact on the development of Argentina. The wars ended the line of Habsburg rulers in Spain and led the Bourbons to the throne. Initially, the Bourbon rulers focused on asserting and consolidating authority at home in Spain. However, over time, they began a program to invigorate the colonial bureaucracy, in good part to encourage more rapid economic expansion in the Americas.

There were three basic avenues by which the Bourbons pursued their new agenda. First, bureaucratic reforms were initiated to bring the colonial territories under more effective control. (The Habsburgs had been notoriously ineffective in this regard.) Second, the Crown pushed to expand colonial industries and develop new economic activities that would increase the flow of resources to Spain. And finally, the Spanish government strengthened the military defenses of the colonies and the trading system that connected them. The Río de la Plata region and Buenos Aires specifically became a zone of increased activity.

The most significant component of the Bourbon Reforms for Argentina came in 1776 when South America was divided into two viceroyalties. A new Viceroyalty of the Río de la Plata was created, with Buenos Aires as the capital. Crown administrators ruled the territories of Argentina, Uruguay, Paraguay, and Upper Peru from Buenos Aires. Around the same time, the Bourbons moved to expel the Jesuits, who were a perceived threat to Crown authority. By 1768, the Jesuits were banned from Spanish colonial territories. The second viceroyalty, created earlier, was the Viceroyalty of New Granada, which consisted of Colombia, Venezuela, and Ecuador. Another major catalyst to change was the 1778 policy of *comercio libre,* or free trade, which allowed additional approved ports, such as Buenos Aires, to trade directly with Spain (as well as, in theory, with other ports in the Spanish Americas).

The creation of the new viceroyalty (and the dramatic shift in activity this generated) led to a shift in power in the region that would become Argentina, from the northwest to the southern coast. Buenos Aires became a major point of entry for goods from Europe, as well as a point of exit for goods produced by the late colonial economy. In fact, these reforms laid the groundwork for Buenos Aires to dominate Argentina in the nineteenth and twentieth centuries. Likewise, just as in Britain's colonies in North America, the Spanish Crown's overriding concern with the revenues of the viceroyalty helped plant the seeds of the independence movement.

The reforms created a stream of new royal officers, bureaucrats, clergy, etc., heading to the colony; officers were charged with inspecting the territories and reporting to the Crown. One of their main objectives was to improve tax collection (and as in Britain's North American colonies, this was not popular with the local creole population). Ironically, as long as Argentina had remained a forgotten backwater, the need for royal control had been relatively low and in many ways, locals had been left to their own devices. Things changed with the establishment of the new viceroyalty. Importantly, the long-standing divide in the Spanish Empire between Spaniards and creoles suddenly became more important in the territory.

Creoles were reduced to second-class status politically, and resentments against the Spaniards rose accordingly.

Another important issue concerned the ongoing wars in Europe. In essence, these dynastic struggles disrupted communication and trade between Spain and its colonies. In particular, the English restricted trade in the Atlantic, especially Spanish trade. This made it very difficult for Buenos Aires to receive manufactures. The French Revolution and subsequent Napoleonic Wars further complicated matters. After the turn of the nineteenth century, the shortage of merchant ships to Buenos Aires led to open calls for the end of imperial trading restrictions. The inability of the Spanish to meet the needs of the colony was highly significant in contributing to the collapse of the colonial system and the move to independence. In short, when Napoleon invaded the Iberian Peninsula—and in particular, overthrew the Spanish monarchy—the creoles in Buenos Aires seized the opportunity, assuming political power and leading Argentina to independence.

COLLAPSE OF COLONIAL AUTHORITY AND THE MOVE TO INDEPENDENCE

To reiterate, the establishment of the new viceroyalty based in Buenos Aires reflected the Crown's desire to promote growth and to improve tax collection. In turn, it also reflected strategic issues, such as the encroachment of the Portuguese into the territory (for the most part, on the opposite bank of the Rio de la Plata from Buenos Aires). However, despite the Crown's new interest in the region, the territory already had a long history of independent thinking, reflecting in good part its long-standing status as a backwater in the colonial empire. The region simply did not attract as much official attention as other areas of the empire. In turn, despite increased attempts to assert greater control on the new viceroyalty, the wars in Europe and their impact on trade with the colonies made the enforcement of Spanish controls extremely difficult. In essence, this period lasted from the time of the viceroyalty's establishment (1776) until independence. By this time, Crown regulations had become a burden and local elites began to call for a loosening of ties to Spain.

Colonial officials faced a big problem: The decline of legal trading opportunities rapidly affected their budgets as revenues declined but the need to fund expenditures, such as administration and defense, continued or even grew. At first, officials ignored trade outside the official system; however, over time, they began to sanction such trade, which took place with the British, Brazilians, Americans, and other British colonies in the Americas. *Porteños* (residents of the city of Buenos Aires) were calling to make open trade permanent. (One of the most famous *porteños* was Manuel Belgrano, who believed that unrestricted trade would bring about considerable political and economic progress.) Of course, many were against open trade, most importantly the commercial interests tied to the official trading system. Still, this system was failing miserably.

In 1806, a British force attacked the city of Buenos Aires, causing the Spanish militia and the viceroy to flee. Importantly, local forces recaptured the city two months later and repelled a second British attack in 1807. As discussed in the history chapter, these events had a profound influence on the independence movement. First, they undermined Spanish authority in the region, largely due to the rapid, even cowardly, retreat of the Spanish authorities. Likewise, the locals' success in repelling the British contributed to a growing recognition of their own power. Eventually, local authorities stripped the viceroy of his rank and authority; and the leader of the forces that repelled the British was named interim viceroy in 1807, which was a major move away from colonial rule.

The most important event at this point was the invasion of Spain by Napoleon and his French forces, which forced

Charles IV of Spain to abdicate in March 1808. In general, the collapse of royal authority encouraged creoles to push for more power at the local level and gave such efforts more legitimacy. While there was some effort by local conservatives to revolt, attempting to preserve colonial authority, these loyalists were defeated, strengthening the hand of those pushing for more political liberty and an end to the onerous colonial trade restrictions.

Events moved quickly at this point. A new viceroy was appointed, the Viscount Balthasar de Cisneros, who faced an immediate fiscal crisis—local supporters of open trade suggested that an end to colonial trade restrictions could help. Most importantly, word reached Buenos Aires that all of the major cities in Spain had been conquered by the French; on May 22, 1810, the viceroy authorized a *cabildo abierto,* or open council of leading local citizens. Backed by the local militia, the group stripped the viceroy of his office; and a new council led by local liberals took power. Since the new leaders wanted to maintain Buenos Aires's authority over the entire territory of the viceroyalty, they did not officially declare an end to the colonial system. However, their actions signaled their intentions and colonists in the other regions of the viceroyalty began to challenge the authority of Buenos Aires.

Immediate challenges to the new authority came from four separate regions of the viceroyalty: Upper Peru (which had already risen in rebellion), Ascuncíon, Montevideo, and Córdoba. Local forces were able to put down the rebellion in Córdoba; but efforts against the other regions failed, ultimately leading to the breakup of the original viceroyalty's territory.

In general terms, the territory of what is today Argentina held together, while the other viceregal territories just mentioned were lost. Note, however, that while the Wars of Independence certainly impacted the viceroyalty, not nearly as much property damage occurred as was seen in other areas

José de San Martín

José de San Martín, an Argentine hero and one of the most famous "liberators" of South America, was born on February 25, 1778, in the province of Corrientes. Importantly, as a result of his family's transfer to Spain, he participated in the wars against the French as a member of the Spanish army and participated in fighting against Napoleon's forces in the Battle of Baylen. However, San Martín also began to associate with other South American officers who were sympathetic to the cause of independence. In 1811, he resigned from the military and returned to Buenos Aires, quickly involving himself in the efforts to liberate South America from Spain.

On February 3, 1813, San Martín and his forces fought and won their first combat against the Spanish arriving from Montevideo. In January 1814, San Martín took control of a larger force, which would ultimately play a role in the liberation of Chile and Peru. In 1816, acting as the governor of Cuyo province, San Martín played an important role in calling for the United Provinces to issue a formal declaration of independence from Spain.

In January 1817, San Martín and his men began a trek across the Andes, soon winning the Battle of Chacabuco and entering the city of Santiago de Chile. Suffering a defeat at the hands of the Spanish, the united Argentine-Chilean forces then defeated the Spanish army in the Battle of Maipu; and Chile achieved independence. The next stop was Peru, which was taken by sea; in July 1821, San Martín triumphantly entered Lima, proclaiming independence. On July 26, 1822, San Martín, liberator of the south, met Simón Bolívar, liberator of the north, in Guayaquil, Ecuador. In February 1824, displeased by the civil wars taking place in the United Provinces, San Martín left for France, where he lived until his death on August 17, 1850. While San Martín's sudden departure from Peru and his resignation from command of his army remain the subject of some controversy, he is, without question, one of the most important "liberators" of South America and an Argentine national hero.

of Spanish America. At this point, the military leaders appointed by the junta tried to keep the remaining parts of the territory under the control of Buenos Aires; regional movements against such control were numerous.

The struggle between regional leaders who wanted autonomy within an independent country and the government in Buenos Aires that wanted no dissent as it continued its efforts against loyalist holdouts became the dominant political theme in the first decades following independence. Importantly, it took some seventy years for Argentina to consolidate as a discrete political unit. The principal political divide in the early national period was between the *Unitarios* (centralists) and the *Federales* (autonomists)—in effect, a clear divide between those calling for strong central government and those who wanted more regional autonomy and a loose confederation of the provinces.

UNITARIOS VERSUS *FEDERALES* (1812–1829)

The new country fought for a decade about the direction it would pursue. As just mentioned, the general divide was between the Unitarians, who favored free international trade and the nationalization of the port of Buenos Aires, and the Federalists, who wanted provincial autonomy. (Most Federalists also wanted the port to be nationalized, but for the purpose of distributing customs receipts to the provinces.) A third group, also called the Federalists, was against the nationalization of the port; this group wanted to keep Buenos Aires's monopoly over customs revenues.

The conflict was deep-seated and would continue well into the 1830s and 1840s, ultimately to be decided by one of Latin America's best-known dictators, Juan Manuel de Rosas, who eventually ruled the entire country. To backtrack somewhat, after losing various parts of the viceroyalty, the ruling authorities adopted a more defensive position. A triumvirate took power, and Bernardino Rivadavia emerged as the leading figure of the new order. Rivadavia pushed for greater centralization of power, but political instability remained the order of the day. The triumvirate quickly fell.

A new government was formed, and a second Revolutionary Congress was held at San Miguel de Tucumán, where on July 9, 1816, the country formally declared its independence from Spain. Eventually, the counterrevolutionary forces were defeated, and Buenos Aires asserted its authority over the rest of the territory. The battles between *Unitarios* and *Federales* continued. Rivadavia, the leading figure in the *Unitario* movement, was responsible for a wide range of liberal reforms, including a major effort to improve education. Still, many of Rivadavia's efforts, such as his attempts to promote small landholdings and crop farming, failed.

A constitution was drafted in 1826 (following one written in 1819, which was annulled by the Federalists) declaring the formation of a republic; it also asserted the authority of Buenos Aires. Still, political instability reigned as regional caudillos rejected centralism. Rivadavia resigned in frustration in 1827, and the United Provinces fell to rebel forces in 1829.

This defeat of the *Unitarios* helped set in motion the rise of Juan Manuel de Rosas, the dominant political figure of Argentina's early national period. Rosas was a caudillo, or strongman. In general, caudillos dominated politics in the first half of the nineteenth century, following the elimination of colonial control and the failure of any central authority to be consolidated. (These caudillos were military leaders who led cavalry and militia forces for various factions and their ability to gather armed forces was the foundation of their political power.) As many historians point out, the early national period was represented by fourteen largely autonomous provinces, with caudillos emerging in each province to become the principal element of local order and stability. While Argentina's caudillos helped postpone the political unification of the country, they also may have helped save it from anarchy and disintegration.

THE ROSAS DICTATORSHIP (1829–1852)

As you know from the discussion of Rosas and his economic policies in Chapter Two, the contribution of Juan Manuel de Rosas to Argentine political history is a hotly debated subject. Nineteenth-century liberals and intellectuals who were attempting to pursue modernization efforts portrayed Rosas as a barbarian and a tyrant. However, nationalists have often presented Rosas as a national hero, a man who fought against exploitation of the country by foreign powers and who put down internal threats to national integrity.

In the chaotic years of the caudillos, Rosas emerged as a defender of the provincial interests of Buenos Aires and as a proponent of stable government. Rosas's wealth (derived from his own interests in *saladeros,* slaughterhouses geared to export trade) and political power rose hand in hand. Ironically, Rosas switched sides from the *Unitarios* to defend the interests of the interior caudillos; in 1829, he captured Buenos Aires and declared his allegiance to Federalism. Rosas became governor of Buenos Aires in 1829; and in response to the instability of the 1820s, he put in place an authoritarian regime. (Rosas was notorious for repressing his political enemies.) By 1831, he had largely defeated his opponents. While Rosas briefly retired, he was back in power by 1835 and managed to retain control of the country until 1852, during which time Buenos Aires came to dominate the rest of the provinces.

Rosas's strategy with rival provinces was to promote (even provoke) internal discord; and over time, each fell under his control. However, challenges to Rosas's authority grew both internally and externally. (These challenges included several foreign-led blockades of Buenos Aires.) While Rosas was victorious in a considerable number of these conflicts, his enemies steadily grew in power and ultimately defeated him. While the *Unitarios* gradually disappeared from the political scene, they were replaced by the Generation of 1837 in criticizing the Rosas dictatorship. Many members of this political opposition lived in exile. The leading resistance figure was Justo José de Urquiza, a one-time ally of Rosas who became an outspoken enemy.

In 1851, Urquiza challenged Rosas's reelection. (Rosas often resorted to outright fraud to retain his leadership.) This

---

Domingo Sarmiento

Domingo Sarmiento (1811–1888) was an educator, statesman, and writer (who will be discussed further in the next chapter). He also was the president of Argentina from 1868–1874. Sarmiento's liberal ideas, coupled with his outspoken style, forced him to leave Argentina during the Rosas dictatorship. During his exile in Chile, Sarmiento wrote the famous book *Facundo: Civilization and Barbarism,* a scathing biography of Juan Facundo Quiroga, one of Argentina's caudillos and an ally of Rosas. Sarmiento argued that the forces of civilization must overcome the barbarism of caudillos like Rosas and Facundo.

Sarmiento was one of the most important public figures to focus on the importance of education (in his view, a key ingredient of "civilization"). Sarmiento joined the forces that successfully overthrew Rosas, but then had disagreements with Rosas's successor Urquiza; as a result, he returned to Chile until Urquiza's downfall.

While Sarmiento was abroad in the United States studying the educational system in 1868, he was elected president of Argentina. He returned to Argentina to promote his liberal agenda, including an important push to improve public education and to construct a modern transportation and communication system. Sarmiento left office in 1874, but he continued to lead an active public life and to write until he died in 1888.

challenge ultimately escalated into a military conflict. Notably, the dictator's numerous enemies united behind Urquiza. Rosas was finally defeated at the Battle of Caseros in 1852 and ousted from power.

As mentioned, many leading political and intellectual figures were forced to flee the country during the Rosas dictatorship. One of the most well-known opposition figures (and an Argentine hero) was Domingo Sarmiento, discussed briefly below. Sarmiento characterized Rosas as a tyrant whose iron-fisted rule destroyed civilization, law, and liberty. The political opposition to Rosas generally favored liberal representative democracy. Under the leadership of Justo José de Urquiza, the opposition got its chance, creating a U.S.-style liberal constitution in 1853.

CONFEDERATION AND CONSTITUTION (1852–1862)

The conflict over the status of Buenos Aires continued. In fact, the province and city of Buenos Aires rejected the constitution drafted in 1853. The Argentine Confederation simply carried on without Buenos Aires. Urquiza actively promoted the new country, but his efforts were constrained by the conspicuous absence of Buenos Aires. Without the port, the Confederation was considerably less attractive to foreigners; and the threat of conflict with Buenos Aires did not go away. Urquiza and his forces defeated Buenos Aires in 1859 at Cepeda, and Buenos Aires agreed to join the Confederation. However, conflict continued. Buenos Aires forces would turn the tables in 1861 and defeat the troops of the Confederation at Pavón.

Bartolomé Mitre became governor of Buenos Aires in 1860 and began to push the Confederation to serve the interests of the province and port. Conflict with Urquiza culminated with Urquiza's defeat in 1861 and his resignation of the presidency. Mitre and his followers continued to push for political reforms and managed to make some important changes to the 1853 constitution. One important point is that Mitre set the government to the task of developing the country through the extension, settlement, and exploitation of the southern and western frontiers.

THE ARGENTINE REPUBLIC

After defeating Urquiza in 1861, Bartolomé Mitre became the first president of the Argentine Republic in 1862, leading the recalcitrant province of Buenos Aires to join the central government. This was a very important achievement: Mitre captured control of the entire federation and used his power to attempt to unify the nation. Following Mitre's assumption of the presidency, liberals held political power for another two

Bartolomé Mitre is remembered by Argentines not only as president of the republic, but also for his contributions to historiography, literature, and the press during the mid-nineteenth century. (Library of Congress)

decades, leaving their mark on the nation's political institutions. While the amended constitution gave strong powers to the national government, the status of Buenos Aires remained a contentious issue. However, the military and financial power of the federal government won out over time and the central government's power gradually increased.

One significant factor leading to increased federal power was the War of the Triple Alliance (1865–1870), which pitted Paraguay against Argentina, Brazil, and Uruguay (and is explained in Chapter One). Argentina's government used the war to pursue a number of objectives, including modernizing its army and developing the country's infrastructure; the war also was a convenient excuse to intervene in provinces that continued to resist federal authority.

Mitre stepped down in 1868. Despite his attempts to orchestrate his own succession, he failed. Domingo Sarmiento, a governor of San Juan province, captured the presidency in 1868 (as outlined previously) and moved to stimulate education and immigration. The political supremacy of Buenos Aires suffered another blow some years later when its governor lost the presidential election to Julio Roca in 1880. A violent rebellion took place, ostensibly to block Roca's victory and Buenos Aires's marginalization from power. Roca and the army put down the rebellion; he then moved quickly to federalize the city of Buenos Aires in June 1880. This ended, at least symbolically, the long dominance of Buenos Aires province over the national government. This was a strong symbol of nationhood as national authorities seized control of the city and forced the provincial government to build its own capital in La Plata. As a result, historians often consider 1880 as the beginning of Argentina's modern era.

The symbolism, while significant in the political consolidation of Argentina, should not be taken too far. The provinces did gain a capital, but the victory of national authorities also confirmed that whoever controlled Buenos Aires would ultimately control the rest of the nation. And ironically, even though the customs house was nationalized, a disproportionally large share of collected funds was still spent in the city and province of Buenos Aires. In this sense, the divide between Buenos Aires and the interior of Argentina would continue.

The period of the 1860s through the 1870s represented an era of growing central authority. It also was a period in which the power (and tolerance) of regional caudillos waned.

Conquest of the Desert

Following increasing tensions between native groups and settlers in Argentina, debate raged in the 1870s about how to solve the "Indian problem." Two positions predominated. One called for containment and a gradual integration of indigenous populations into the mainstream. The second, more radical position, propounded by Julio Roca, was based on the uncompromising conquest and subjugation of native groups; this strategy, it was argued, would help accelerate the country's territorial expansion to the south.

From 1879 to 1880, Julio Roca, a professional soldier, politician, and minister of war, led a military expedition to the Río Negro valley. Gone were the days of defensive forts and treaties; the government's superior weapons (Remington rifles) and communications now quickly defeated the native inhabitants. National troops destroyed the Indian settlements and dispersed their inhabitants. Many of the losers in this fight were sent to become servants in Buenos Aires. This Conquest of the Desert opened vast areas of land to exploitation while removing the "Indian menace" that had, until this time, constrained the westward and southward expansion of *estancias,* settlements, and railroads.

With his victory and his new status as a national hero, Roca was swept to victory in the 1880 presidential election. He then called for the country to push even farther south in its efforts to conquer territory; he ordered another campaign to take place in 1881. The last battle was fought on October 18, 1884; the last of the rebel indigenous groups surrendered some two months later. The Indian-fighter-turned-politician became a central figure in the movement to "Europeanize" Argentina.

Between the 1850s and 1880s, the modern state of Argentina emerged. The 1880s were particularly important in this development process. For example, the position of Buenos Aires was finally cemented with its federalization. Other significant developments included the introduction of a new currency and the strengthening of national systems of law and administration. Perhaps most importantly, the emergence of the modern state and political institutions corresponded to a period of peace after so many years of instability, conflict, and violence.

THE GENERATION OF 1880 AND THE ERA OF LIBERAL RULE

The liberal politicians who dominated this era (known as the Generation of 1880 for their emergence that year) were typically elites and members of the landowning class. They controlled the army and the elections, resorting to fraud, if needed, to win. In effect, these elites operated a very effective political machine. Major decisions were made by so-called *acuerdo,* or agreement, which essentially were informal agreements made between members of the executive branch. (Unlike in the United States, at this time, the Argentine legislature was largely unimportant.)

The PAN developed in the 1880s, in essence as a coalition of regional oligarchies. Party politics of this era were more an issue of internal rivalries within the PAN than disputes between contending parties. This alliance among Argentina's elites controlled political life for almost forty years. The PAN played an important role in ending the conflict between nationalists and autonomists, acting as a mechanism to stabilize regional conflicts (mainly by using the growing resources of the state to "grease the wheels" of the political system). The Baring Crisis, described in detail in the preceding chapter, was a threat as well as a wake-up call to oligarchic politics. The crisis underscored the fact that politics had become excessively centralized; the leadership struggled to restore its legitimacy.

Argentina's elite leadership faced increasing challenges, as highlighted by the 1890 crisis and political revolt. Spreading economic prosperity led to a number of groups that were unhappy with the status quo. Among these groups were newly prosperous landowners, old aristocratic families of the interior who had failed to benefit from the export boom, and members of the middle classes who were doing well economically but resented being excluded from the political system. (Over time, the dissident oligarchic component of the party was diluted by the growing numbers of urban middle-class professionals.) Together these groups created the Radical Party in 1890. The early Radical Party, or UCR, alternated its political strategy between insurrection against the system, electoral abstention (as a manner of protest), and collaboration with the oligarchic regime. The party was led by Hipólito Yrigoyen.

Dr. Roque Sáenz Peña, president of Argentina from 1910 to 1914. (Library of Congress)

In the early days, the Radicals were frustrated by their inability to make any electoral headway, due quite often to electoral fraud. However, they continued their efforts to change the system. Eventually, a moderate group within the elite leadership decided the system should be more open to the Radicals. They had their say in 1911 with President Roque Sáenz Peña, who proposed wide-ranging and significant electoral reform. The new bill called for universal male suffrage, a secret ballot, and mandatory voting. In essence, the Sáenz Peña reform can be understood as an effort by the ruling oligarchy to co-opt the groups making up the Radical Party since the real threat was the working class. The measures were designed to promote more participation, bring conflict into the system (and off the streets), and legitimize the state.

The Radical Party quickly took advantage of the new rules, managing to elect its leader Hipólito Yrigoyen president in 1916. Then from 1918 to 1919, crisis hit Argentina (and the rest of the world) with a series of strikes, reflecting anger at declining purchasing power. Yrigoyen responded harshly, but the situation was exacerbated by open conflict between workers and ultra-rightist groups—in essence, class warfare ensued. In the end, hundreds of demonstrators were shot and labor leaders were repressed. Despite continuous efforts to organize workers (by the socialists, communists, and later syndicalists), labor groups were largely subdued by 1930.

Conservative forces grew frustrated over their attempts to co-opt the Radicals, who ignored long-standing traditions such as the *acuerdo*. Reforms by the Radicals led to real changes in the system as the electorate quickly expanded and political parties increased in importance. In short, the conservatives, long used to controlling the political system, were moved farther and farther from power as Radicals controlled the presidency and dominated the legislature. The conservatives grew increasingly dissatisfied with their electoral experiment.

MILITARY COUP

While the 1920s witnessed relative prosperity economically, the political system was characterized by drift. President Yrigoyen and the Radicals faced looming disaster with the onset of the Great Depression. Corruption was widespread; and the government was unable to develop a credible, substantive response to the Depression. Chaos threatened in a number of cities. As conditions deteriorated, the military began to conspire openly with conservatives.

On September 6, 1930, a group of military officers and civilian elites ousted Yrigoyen from power, claiming that his government was illegitimate. This marked the end of the country's first experiment with government by the middle classes. After seizing power, the military and elites formed a provisional regime. Thus, by 1930, the military had concluded that the only solution to the existing political mess was to change the system, which was plagued by corruption, cronyism, abuse of power, and the like. The coup and subsequent provisional regime represented steps in this direction.

However, there was considerable division within the military. One faction, for example, wanted to get rid of open class struggle, remove the Radicals from power, and return to the previous system that had been controlled by conservative oligarchs before the Sáenz Peña reforms. The other faction had a different idea altogether: This group thought that democracy was the problem in Argentina and wanted to establish a semi-fascist corporate state (similar to those existing in Europe at the time). This group wanted to put an end to class-based politics.

In the end, the more moderate faction won out and created a pro-government coalition that was labeled the *concordancia*. Military officers in a number of government posts were removed and replaced with prominent civilians. However, even the more moderate route proved incapable of creating a broad national authority with widespread political legitimacy. The urban working class continued to grow, and its demands on government expanded. Likewise, the Radicals refused to play by the old rules (i.e., those that were in place before they assumed power). They managed to regain control of the congress, and they continued to fight against electoral fraud. However, electoral frauds continued, which, in turn, highlighted the fundamental illegitimacy of the new civilian government. Once again the military was growing impatient with the status quo.

At the time, Europe was embroiled in World War II; and at least in the early 1940s, the Axis powers seemed to have an advantage. Argentina's military (or at least a number of its leaders) believed the country needed strong and disciplined leadership of its own; to them, the main obstacle was weak, self-interested civilian leadership. In terms of the war, Argentina attempted to maintain its neutrality (in contrast with its neighbor Brazil, which joined the U.S.-led military effort and received significant post-war support from the U.S. in return).

Military dissatisfaction with civilian leadership in Argentina continued to climb, and a number of plots to seize control of the government were created. Ultimately, power was seized by the GOU. The group justified its move to take power by declaring that its action was a response to popular demand. While Argentina's democracy was widely seen as one of the strongest and most stable in Latin America, scholars point out that beneath the surface, it was quite fragile; the military coup in 1943 underscored the fragility of democratic institutions in Argentina. This time around the country's military officers wanted to remake the political system completely; they moved in that direction by closing congress in 1943 and decreeing an end to political parties in 1944.

The key political player to emerge at this time was Juan Perón, a military man who had been an active player in the GOU. Working in a series of political roles in the government, Perón courted the large and important working class. Over time, Perón and his wife, Eva, became heroes to the lower classes of Argentina, with Perón winning the presidential election in 1946 with a 54 percent majority of the vote.

PERÓN AND PERONISM

Juan Perón built his popularity and rose to power by attacking the nation's oligarchy and playing on class antagonisms present in Argentine society. With help from his wife, Perón was able to mobilize the previously disenfranchised urban working class. Skillfully, Perón was able to convince the masses that his

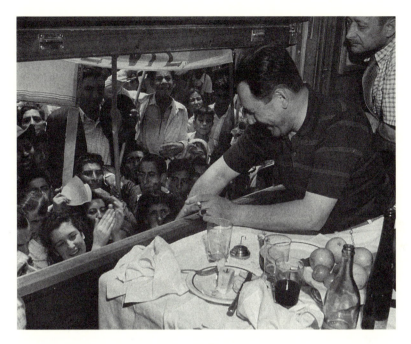

Presidential candidate Juan Perón greets supporters from the dining car of a train on his campaign tour of the country, February 1, 1946. (Thomas D. Mcavoy/Time & Life Pictures/Getty Images)

government was their own. In addition to being a populist, Perón was a nationalist who advocated industrialization led by the government. Importantly, throughout his leadership, Perón relied on the support of the urban working class and on nationalistic economic policies to maintain his power.

Clearly, Perón had opponents, including the rural landed oligarchy, foreign business, and middle- and upper-class political parties. Likewise, the U.S. and British governments were opposed to Perón. (The United States denounced him as pro-fascist.) Finally, factions within the military opposed Perón; and as was discussed previously, he lost the support of the Catholic Church after he legalized divorce.

Remember, Argentina's elite conspired with the military to intervene in 1930 due to concerns that the Radicals could not (or would not) defend the traditional order against rising social conflict. The political elite had invited the middle sectors into the political system after the turn of the twentieth century, but leaders proved unwilling to contemplate a more significant political opening.

Thus, the military intervened in 1930 and installed a conservative regime two years later using wholesale electoral fraud. However, the conservatives alienated a number of key interest groups, including nationalists and the working class. By the 1940s, Argentina's industrial workforce was flourishing, but its efforts to organize were consistently cut short by the government. This would be exploited by Perón after the military coup of 1943.

Political scientists often point out, though, that political change also was driven by the sheer incompetence of the conservative regime; the political landscape proved more complex after the 1930s, given the dramatic changes taking place in the Argentine economy and society. The middle classes had already asserted themselves and could be excluded only with fraud or force; in turn, the working class was increasingly demanding, often provoking repressive responses from the government. But the conservatives continued to assert control despite the fact that they were undermining the credibility of the existing system of government in the process. Over time, the military lost confidence, and ultimately intervened in June 1943.

While Perón did not lead the coup, he participated as a function of his role as a member of the nationalist, pro-Axis wing of the military. For this, he was rewarded with various posts, which he then used to develop his large, dedicated following (which included not only the working classes but also factions of the military).

Perón faced a significant final hurdle on his path to power: In October 1945, a group within the military that opposed Perón convinced the military president to put Perón in jail until after elections were held. This turned out to be a big mistake, as Perón's numerous supporters marched on the presidential palace, remaining there until he was released. (He then addressed the supportive masses in triumph.) Four months later he won the presidency, beating an alliance of Radicals and conservatives.

Once in power, Perón ruled Argentina for a decade. Ironically, although he had used his alliance with labor to secure power, once in power, he prevented further radicalization of the working classes. Perón ruled in an authoritarian fashion, but not dramatically so. Likewise, while he admired European fascist governments, he did not construct a true fascist state; while he did intimidate his opponents, there was little in the way of coherent political ideology or a sophisticated organization like those seen in Europe. Perón's system was corporatist, with interest groups represented through organizations such as labor, business, and agriculture. As discussed, his economic policies targeted rapid industrialization and national independence (even if they did not succeed in achieving those goals).

Despite some early success, Perón's strategy soon ran into serious problems. His response was an orthodox stabilization program of tightened credit, reduced government spending, and wage and price controls. The idea was to get the economy back on track quickly to enable a swift return to his ambitious social agenda. In the meantime, Perón managed to amend the constitution to run for president again; he won the election in 1953 with 67 percent of the vote. Perón's beloved wife, Evita, died in July 1952, becoming an even larger figure in death than she had been in life.

While Perón pushed a less strident nationalist and populist economic stance (he even convinced workers to accept a two-year wage freeze), his political strategy became ever more radical; Peronist rhetoric grew increasingly antagonistic. A Peronist mob attacked the Jockey Club in 1953, a well-known symbol of the country's wealthy elite. In turn, in 1954, Peronist radicals took on the Catholic Church,

Argentines grieve over the wreckage of a Catholic church burned during an uprising in June 1955. (Hank Walker/Time & Life Pictures/ Getty Images)

legalizing divorce and assuming control of parochial schools—another sharp blow to traditional Argentines. After demonstrations at a few important cathedrals, which led to some high-profile vandalism and destruction of Church property, the Vatican responded aggressively by excommunicating Perón and his cabinet.

In hindsight, clearly, Perón made a dramatic blunder. In addition to there being an obvious loss of political control by the leadership (in an already weakened economy), by attacking the Church, Perón gave his enemies in the military an excuse to oust him from power. In September 1955, military conspirators gave Perón an ultimatum—leave the presidency or lead the country to civil war. Perón backed down, leaving Argentina for an extended period of exile, eventually settling in Spain.

MILITARY STEWARDSHIP

There is an interesting historical debate as to why the masses of Perón's faithful did not rally to his support following his ouster, as they had when he was jailed before his first presidential victory. The answer remains unclear, but the political fact is that Perón left Argentina, in large part, without even attempting to mobilize workers. However, although Perón left the country, he did not by any means disappear from the Argentine political scene, nor did the Peronist movement. Rather, Perón remained a dominant political figure for Argentina for nearly two decades, despite his exile. He eventually returned to power, albeit briefly, and died in office in 1974.

The military officers who ousted Perón had other ideas. They were focused on ridding the nation not only of Perón but also of Peronism. Thus, they not only expelled Juan Perón from Argentina but also forced the Peronist rank and file to participate in non-Peronist political parties. Their efforts largely failed over time, as Perón remained an active player in politics, behaving, in essence, as the head of a government in exile from abroad. (He continually sent messages to his followers, promising to return to Argentina if the party remained faithful). In essence, Perón's behavior made it nearly impossible for any government, military or civilian, to govern effectively.

In the decade following Perón's departure, the military held two presidential elections, one in 1958 and another in 1963, in addition to placing its own officers as presidents. The Peronist party was banned from both elections. As a result of this exclusionary process, sitting governments were unpopular with the working class and widely denounced as illegitimate. The first military president was Eduardo Lonardi (1955), a relatively moderate general. He was rapidly deposed and replaced by a hard-liner, Pedro Aramburu (1955–1958), who was prepared to purge the country of Peronism—at this point, the party was even outlawed. The Peronists did not give up easily, however. A pro-Peronist revolt in the military provoked a harsh government response, ending with the execution of some forty leaders. (Aramburu would later pay a heavy price for this action, as he was murdered by revolutionaries in the 1970s, at least in part as retribution for this anti-Peronist move.)

At the time, the anti-Peronist civilian politicians were split: The largest party was still the UCR, or Radicals; but the party was split between the so-called Popular Radicals and the Intransigent Radicals. The first post-Perón presidential election was held in 1958 and was won by the Intransigent Radical Arturo Frondizi. Frondizi's wing of the party also was victorious in congressional elections. It is widely believed that Frondizi cut a deal with the outlawed Peronists. (Given the strong split in his own party, he most likely traded a promise to restore the Peronist party to legality in exchange for votes.) The military was deeply suspicious of Frondizi as a result of his conciliatory stance toward the Peronists.

Frondizi's tenure was a difficult one. Economic conditions were harsh; and despite his plans to accelerate industrialization, Frondizi was forced to implement tough and unpopular stabilization plans in 1949 and 1952. There were some early signs of a turnaround in conditions, but not nearly enough to save the president. Frondizi had lost the support of both labor and nationalists due to his stabilization policies and his supposed sellout to foreign oil companies. Frondizi's declining support was visible in 1960, as the Popular Radical faction gained control of the congress.

The climax in this process came when Frondizi made good on his earlier promise to the Peronists, allowing them to participate in the 1962 gubernatorial elections (most likely based on the belief that his own party would win). This proved to be a costly miscalculation. The Peronists won easily, and the armed forces then moved to oust Frondizi for his blunder. On March 29, 1962, army tanks took to the streets and removed Frondizi from power.

After Frondizi's fall, the president of the Senate, José María Guido, served as acting president for a year and a half. However, real power was held by the military during this period. The military remained sharply divided over how to deal with civilian politicians. Perón did not help the situation, sending repeated messages from exile to his party's faithful. The military called for elections in July 1963, and the presidential contest was won by Radical Arturo Illia.

Illia, like Frondizi before him, would not see the end of his term in office. He was opposed by the Peronists since they were excluded from the elections. The Peronists began to organize a series of strikes and workplace takeovers as part of a "battle plan" aimed at the new government. The Peronists were allowed to participate in congressional elections in 1965 and once again performed well. Juan Perón, encouraged by his party's performance, sent his new wife, Isabel, to consult and negotiate with feuding factions of the Peronist party.

At this point, the economy was facing serious trouble and the military was again frustrated and alarmed by the direction of civilian politics. In June 1966, the military again chose to intervene, ousting Illia from office in large part due to his inability to repress or otherwise control the Peronist masses. This time the armed forces made it quite clear to the country that no elections would be held any time soon; the military was prepared to assume full control of the Argentine government.

BUREAUCRATIC AUTHORITARIANISM I (1966–1973)

The new authoritarian government, headed up by General Juan Carlos Onganía, was modeled in part after the authoritarian government created in Brazil two years earlier. The coup this time represented a sharp break with the past—the sharpest, in fact, since the coup of 1943. The resulting government was also the most repressive. The generals in charge closed the legislature; they did not even bother with rigged elections. As long as Argentines did what they were told, the generals promised the country political order, social discipline, and economic stability. Onganía proclaimed the onset of the "Argentine Revolution."

General Juan Carlos Onganía salutes at a parade to celebrate the 152nd anniversary of Argentina's independence on July 9, 1968. Onganía led the authoritarian government set up after the 1966 military coup that deposed Arturo Illia. (Bettmann/Corbis)

The military removed civilian politicians from positions of authority and created alliances with technocrats and foreign investors; the technocrats were needed to help run the government and the economy, while foreign capital was needed to bolster economic growth. Labor, in turn, was repressed; and real wages were held down (in part to give incentives to investment). The generals believed that economic behavior had to be changed to allow the country to advance. In their view, the nation's problems (an overgrown state, an antagonistic working class, lethargic entrepreneurs, etc.) were largely the result of Perón and his policies. Thus, they aimed to remake the Argentine state and economy, undoing the damage wrought by Perón. The military blamed Perón and the Peronists for the country's economic decline. They also blamed the Radicals who came after the Peronists for doing nothing substantial to fix the nation's pressing problems.

Onganía launched the "Revolution's" economic program, freezing wages for two years in 1967. Initially, the plan brought results, as inflation fell to its lowest level in years while investment picked back up. It even appeared that labor's defiant stance had eased. At the time, a significant group within organized labor wanted to work with the government. Onganía exploited this opportunity, working to divide labor with at least some initial success. However, serious trouble was brewing.

In May 1969, riots broke out in the city of Córdoba (culminating in the so-called *Cordobazo*). Protests, which lasted a week or so, were repressed by the military when local police could not do the job successfully. At one street protest, police opened fire, killing protesters and innocent bystanders. The riots never really threatened the military government, but they did make a mockery of the government's claim to have subdued labor. Likewise, in the days that followed the violence, there was shock at the degree of repression and visible disagreement within the government about how to deal with working class militancy. Some officials called for more repression, while others advocated a more accommodative stance. Ultimately, officers taking the middle ground removed Onganía from power in 1970 and decided reluctantly to hold elections in the not-too-distant future.

To understand this volatile period in Argentine politics, it is important to recognize that a dramatic rise in political violence was taking place. The left was increasingly resorting to kidnappings and assassinations, while the right responded with torture and executions. Argentina's left had been repressed before, but this time they chose to fight back with violence. Revolutionary groups were created, and kidnappings of prominent businessmen for ransom became common. In 1970, leftist terrorists succeeded in kidnapping ex-president Aramburu, who had ordered the Peronist executions in 1956. He was subsequently murdered. Argentine politics had turned violent, and the country was quite literally on the brink of civil war.

While Argentina's military rulers had attempted to replicate Brazil's authoritarian regime, their efforts proved unsuccessful. For one thing, Argentine political parties were far stronger than those in Brazil. Domestic politics also was far more polarized. In turn, Argentina's rulers were unsuccessful in creating a military-civilian alliance that could create sustained economic growth. Importantly, key economic interest groups doubted the ability of the military to change the nature of the economy. In the end, they were correct: only modest adjustments were made to the economy, while its basic structure and the behavior of its main participants changed very little.

After Onganía, a new military leader, Roberto Levinston, took control in 1970; he faced rampant inflation. A military coup removed him and put Alejandro Lanusse in place in 1971. (Lanusse had been the mastermind of Onganía's ouster eight months earlier.) As suggested previously, Lanusse had no grand plans for remaking the economy. However, he did have plans for the political system. Taking a huge gamble,

Lanusse wanted to reach a new national political accord. This hoped-for agreement was to be based on allowing Perón to return from exile. The gamble was that Perón might be the only person capable of reining in the leftist threat. By this time, the situation in Argentina was bad enough that Lanusse was willing to risk it.

PERÓN'S BRIEF RETURN

Elections were scheduled for March 1973, although violence continued unabated. (Guerrillas began targeting high-ranking military officers, as well as striking prisons and military barracks.) Héctor Cámpora served as the stand-in for Perón until Perón's return to Argentina could be arranged. Cámpora received 49 percent of the vote, far higher than the next highest candidate. Again, many in the military, and now the new president, believed that Perón might be the country's only hope in calming the left and restoring peace. Cámpora's stand-in government attempted to gain the cooperation of the country's various interest groups, and it appeared for a time to have put together a workable coalition (in part, a reflection of many Argentines' exhaustion with the status quo).

Still, the leftist guerrillas refused to recognize the new Peronist regime. And unfortunately, Perón, who had once been a dynamic and charismatic leader, had become old and was in poor health (he was seventy-seven at the time). Elections were scheduled for September; Perón succeeded in getting his third wife, Isabel, on the ticket as his vice-presidential running mate. They won the election quite easily with 62 percent of the vote. Once in power, Perón moved swiftly against the revolutionary left. At least initially it looked as if the military's gamble on Perón, as the only person capable of leading a counteroffensive against the left, had been justified.

However, in July 1974, Perón died, leaving his wife as president. Isabel, whom Perón had met when she was a nightclub dancer in Panama, was ill-prepared to assume the presidency,

Isabel Perón, president of Argentina following the death of her husband, gives a television address on February 20, 1975. Her policies were conflicting and ineffective, and she was removed from office by the military in 1976. (Bettmann/Corbis)

given continued political violence, a deteriorating economy, and fierce infighting within the Peronist party (not to mention a mad scramble among Peronists to gain influence over the new president).

Political and economic conditions deteriorated rapidly under Isabel Perón. Her policies were often inconsistent. In one well-known instance, she fought against large wage increases for unions and then reversed herself to reinstate the wage gains after massive strikes. The economy quickly spun out of control, with inflation reaching 335 percent in 1975, forcing Argentina to attempt stabilization. To make matters worse, the left continued its violent attacks, which included some dramatic assassinations; the right responded in kind with violence. At this point, the population, particularly the urban middle class, was terrified by the violence, which came from both the left and the right. Unfortunately, the president was terrified as well; and she was incapable of taking control of the situation.

Many have argued that this time the military appeared ready to let Isabel Perón serve out her term, which ran until 1977, to avoid taking responsibility for the chaos; others have speculated that the military was willing to let things deteriorate to the point where there could be no doubt about the need for their intervention. In any case, by 1976, a well-anticipated coup occurred: Isabel Perón was placed under house arrest, and once again the military put an end to civilian government.

BUREAUCRATIC AUTHORITARIANISM II (1976–1983)

To summarize, complete chaos within the government, an economic meltdown, infighting within the Peronist movement, and all-out urban terrorism brought Argentina to a standstill. The military stepped in to restore order; and by this point, no one was very surprised. Those who were opposed to Peronism hoped that the "old man's" death, the abysmal management of the economy, and the chaos that ensued would undermine support for Peronism and propel dramatic change by the military. However, as with previous military interventions, events did not follow the military's plans.

As the military stepped in to assume political power in 1976, many believed that the previous experiment with bureaucratic authoritarianism had failed due to mistakes made by Onganía rather than more general problems with military rule. In other words, this group thought that a more organized effort by the military to rule the country could succeed. This was their opportunity. This time they were determined to impose a solution that would last. The effort was led by Jorge Videla, who banned all political parties, took control of the labor movement, and unleashed an all-out war against terrorism. Known as both the holy war and the dirty war, the military unleashed a vicious campaign against its enemies, arresting so-called subversives at will.

By this point, the revolutionary effort had become quite organized. Through robberies and kidnapping for ransom, the revolutionaries had built up a huge war chest. (Some estimates put it at about $150 million.) Likewise, their targeted executions and paramilitary strikes represented a threat to the entire country. The revolutionaries aimed for the violent overthrow of the government, to be replaced with a revolutionary Marxist-Leninist regime. Ironically, the revolutionaries were typically from middle-class backgrounds. Another irony is that these middle-class revolutionaries sought to overthrow a socioeconomic order that was among the most modern and progressive in Latin America at the time. For the guerrillas and for the military, this became a fight to the death; the military would win, but at a horrific cost to the country.

Videla unleashed the three military services' intelligence and counterinsurgency units to battle the revolutionary groups terrorizing the country. Subversives were abducted by armed squads; most were never heard from again. These people became the *desaparecidos,* or "the disappeared" of the dirty war. These people were typically tortured and executed, sometimes tossed from planes in groups of 15–20 while still alive. Babies born to mothers in detention were taken and the mothers then executed. However, some survived; and in this fashion, word of the harshness of the repression spread throughout the country. There is no way now to determine how many of the *desaparecidos* were actually revolutionaries and how many were simply sympathetic to leftist causes (or even completely innocent). However, estimates put the number of dead as high as 20,000.

As mentioned, the generals won the war, but at a tremendous price to the country. Argentina became a pariah state internationally, along the lines of Chile and South Africa,

Members of the human rights group Mothers of the Plaza de Mayo march in front of the Government House in Buenos Aires on March 22, 2001, in commemoration of the military coup that unleashed seven years of terror in Argentina. Thousands of people disappeared or were killed during the military regime, a conflict now known as the Argentine dirty war. (Miguel Mendez/AFP/Getty Images)

condemned by world leaders for its flagrant abuses of human rights. It is important to note that the middle classes supported the dirty war, at least at the onset. This is understandable given the complete collapse of order that occurred under Isabel Perón from 1974 to 1976. This was to be the coup to end all coups; the generals stepped in not only to restore order but also to restructure Argentine society.

As discussed in the previous chapter, despite some initial economic successes (not to mention national pride at hosting and winning the World Cup soccer championship in 1978), things began to unravel. By 1981, Argentina was suffering inflation over 100 percent and a serious recession, reflecting the dire economic conditions of the Latin American debt crisis. At this time, the presidency passed from Videla to General Roberto Viola. Dissatisfied colleagues in the military quickly replaced Viola with General Leopoldo Galtieri in 1982, who was at the time the commander-in-chief of the army. The country would soon become involved in the Falklands War with Britain, a disastrous military adventure that would lead to the fall of the military government.

THE FALKLANDS WAR (AND THE END OF MILITARY RULE)

Galtieri surprised the nation—and his military colleagues—by invading the Falkland Islands on April 2, 1982. (In Argentina, the islands are known as the Malvinas.) The remote and desolate islands are claimed by Argentina but have long been controlled by Great Britain. In essence, the Argentines thought that the English had shifted their position and would not defend the islands, which, at the time, had only 1,800 inhabitants (and 600,000 sheep). Likewise, the Argentines miscalculated the response of the United States—they thought the United States would defend the Argentine claim to the islands. A large Argentine force invaded the islands and rapidly defeated the royal marine garrison. However, quickly mobilizing their own forces, the British landed thousands of troops on the islands in late May. (In one instance, the British sunk the Argentine battleship *General Belgrano,* killing more than 360 Argentines.)

The British military quickly routed the Argentine forces, inflicting a humiliating defeat on the nation (although more than 300 British soldiers died). The major question surrounding the Falklands War is straightforward: Why did Galtieri invade these relatively insignificant and remote islands? The answer seems to center on the decline of the military regime. Economic conditions were deteriorating and had reached crisis levels. The regime also was plummeting in popularity, and massive antigovernment demonstrations

Signifying the end of the war, the British flag flies again over Port Howard, West Falkland, for the first time in more than two months, on June 16, 1982. (Bettmann/Corbis)

were mounting. (For example, more people were joining the "Mothers of the Plaza de Mayo" to protest against the military regime and its repressive policies.)

The idea, presumably, was that a quick victory would strengthen the government and build popular support for the regime. (Most likely, the generals also wrongly assumed that the British would not respond militarily.) In the short term, Galtieri was correct, as Argentines demonstrated their patriotism en masse—a quick turnaround from antigovernment protests. However, as the superior British forces rapidly routed the Argentines and the Argentine commander quickly surrendered, the tide shifted—patriotic zeal quickly turned into outrage, protest, and demonstrations. The regime did not survive this critical blunder.

The military responded to defeat by sending Galtieri into retirement and replacing the entire junta. A relatively unknown general, Reynaldo Bignone, took over. In turn, the military announced that open national elections would take place within eighteen months and that the country would return to civilian government by 1984. Significantly, the generals' incompetence, which ranged from economic mismanagement to military defeat, helped restore legitimacy to civilian politics and politicians. Both the Peronist and Radical parties had survived the brutal dictatorship and would return to the forefront of civilian politics. Once again, despite its intentions to do so, the military had failed to dramatically change Argentine politics (and the country's economy).

TRANSITION TO DEMOCRACY

Argentina faced a big challenge as it looked to restore civilian rule: Democratic institutions had to be strengthened, the feeble economy had to be improved, and society had to decide how to go about prosecuting the military and police officers who were responsible for the atrocities of the dirty war. In general terms, the transition to civilian democratic government was quick, a reflection of the defeat in the Falklands and the rapid loss of all legitimacy surrounding military rule. In fact, civilian party leaders even refused to negotiate the terms of transition—they simply called for elections and told military leaders to leave.

Elections took place in October 1983. One interesting development at the time concerned the status of the Peronist party. The Peronists seemed to have become a "permanent majority" in Argentina—it seemed to most that they would lose elections only if they were excluded from power, as the previous military government had done. In 1983, the Peronists assumed that a return to full democracy, with open elections, would bring them back to power. However, this was not to be the case, as the Radical Party's Raúl Alfonsín delivered the Peronists their first defeat ever in free presidential elections. On October 30, 1983, despite polls indicating a likely Peronist victory, Alfonsín won against the Peronist candidate Italo Luder with 52 percent of the vote.

This was an interesting political outcome for Argentina and, many argue, a good one for the country's return to democratic politics. The Peronists lost the presidency but won a slight plurality in the Senate; they also came in second place in the Chamber of Deputies. Thus, free elections took away from the Peronists their claim to be the country's only legitimate political party. Since the 1950s, they had attacked the legitimacy of all governments that were chosen in elections in which they had been excluded. By losing to the opposition in an open election, they could not claim the outcome was illegitimate. However, by running a strong second place, they also retained a strong incentive to play by the rules of the constitution.

One of the toughest questions facing the country at the time concerned the issue of torture and murder during the dirty war. The question was what to do with those people responsible for the thousands that were murdered or disappeared. The new president appointed a commission, which documented almost 9,000 deaths or disappearances. Nine military commanders-in-chief were charged, and five were convicted and given prison sentences. Three of the four who were acquitted were tried by military courts and were sentenced to prison. A thorny issue was how far down the chain of command the prosecution should go. The issue was so complicated that few were satisfied with Alfonsín's approach. Alfonsín limited future trials to the rank of colonel or above; but when members of the military revolted, congress exempted all officers below the rank of general. While society expressed its outrage, Alfonsín pointed out that no other Latin American societies were willing and able to prosecute their own militaries for similar abuses.

Other serious problems confronted Alfonsín's new civilian government. As discussed in the previous chapter, the economy remained a serious problem, in large part due to the poor policies of the military regime. Inflation, huge external debt, and economic recession were the economic legacies of the failed military regime.

While the Radicals managed to win the presidential election, subsequent elections would weaken their hold on power. In 1987, the Radicals lost their majority in the lower house and the Peronists managed to take sixteen of twenty-two governors' races. President Alfonsín did not recover from this defeat. In essence, the end for Alfonsín corresponded to the horrendous state of the economy—deep recession, rampant inflation, and massive foreign debt plagued the administration, which lacked the political power to fix matters. It tried with the Austral Plan (described in the previous chapter), but this proved to be a failure. By mid-1989, the country had succumbed to hyperinflation, with prices rising 100 percent a month.

The economic chaos of the Radical leadership presented an opportunity for the Peronist party. In May 1989, its presidential candidate, Carlos Menem, won the presidential election with 47 percent of the vote (and a majority in the Electoral College). Amazingly, this was the first time an opposition candidate had won a presidential election in Argentina in seventy years. However, the economic crisis deepened, as food riots broke out across the country. While Menem won the election, there was considerable concern for the future. Many doubted whether Menem and the Peronists were prepared to govern a country wracked by foreign debt, recession, and hyperinflation. In the midst of the chaos, Alfonsín announced that he was going to leave office ahead of schedule.

CARLOS MENEM

Carlos Menem led Argentina for ten years, from 1989 to 1999. He was the first Peronist to be elected president since Juan Perón in 1973. Menem was the child of Syrian immigrants. (While he had been raised a Muslim, he converted to Argentina's official religion, Roman Catholicism.) When

Carlos Saúl Menem was elected president of Argentina in May 1989.
(Consulate General of the Argentine Republic)

Menem came to power, the country's high inflation forced him
to abandon the typical Peronist party line, adopting instead
fiscally conservative market-oriented policies. Throughout

his two-term presidency, Menem cultivated his flamboyant image and was quite popular (although he was criticized for handing out pardons to those convicted of dirty war crimes, not to mention the allegations of high-level corruption).

Menem began his first term by asking for help from all sectors of society, adopting a nonconfrontational stance—he also invited both business and opposition politicians into his cabinet. As discussed, Menem's policies put an end to hyperinflation, but also sent the country into recession. In general terms, Menem, contrary to Peronist history and beliefs, took the country in the direction of market-based reforms, including the implementation of a massive privatization program. Perhaps the signature piece of Menem's economic policy package was introduced by his most important economy minister, Domingo Cavallo. This was the so-called convertibility program. Launched in 1991, convertibility helped Argentina restore its credibility within the global economy (and attract large quantities of foreign capital).

As mentioned, one controversial move made by Menem was giving pardons to parties found guilty of abuses in the dirty war. As a result, Menem was sharply criticized by human rights leaders. He also was profoundly embarrassed by officers who admitted publicly to throwing political prisoners out of planes into the sea in the 1970s. However, these criticisms never seriously threatened his presidency.

Menem was able to change the constitution, cutting a deal with Radical leader Raúl Alfonsín, which shortened the presidential term to four years but allowed reelection in return. Menem then won the presidential election in May 1995, soundly defeating the Radical Party candidate. However, public opinion grew increasingly unsupportive of Menem and his political cronies. Several issues stood out. For one, the convertibility plan was not free of costs. The public, in particular, was unhappy about the high rate of unemployment it seemed to cause. Likewise, there was growing evidence of rampant corruption in government.

However, there seemed to be little in the way of a viable political alternative. The Radicals had seen a steady decline in their popularity, in particular due to Alfonsín's disastrous presidency. In turn, a center-left coalition, called FREPASO, was organizationally weak.

However, in mid-1997, the two groups joined to form a coalition (the Alliance, or *Alianza*) for the October congressional elections. Their political stance focused on two main ideas: They supported the basic economic model represented by convertibility, but they attacked the Peronists for high unemployment and widespread corruption. In effect, their stance was to maintain the economic status quo but change the political leadership.

The Alliance coalition made significant progress. The Peronists retained a majority in the Senate, but Alliance gains meant the Peronists would have to cooperate with them in the lower house. At this point, Menem tried to make a third run for the presidency (based on a flimsy interpretation of the constitution and populist spending increases). Highly negative public opinion put a stop to his efforts, but not before significant damage to the country's fiscal stance had been done. (As you know, this fiscal vulnerability would come to haunt the country, as convertibility ultimately collapsed.)

Democratic institutions prevailed, and Menem's own party forced him to give up his quixotic attempt at a third term as president. Eduardo Duhalde was chosen as the next Peronist presidential candidate for the 1999 election, but the battle within the party over reelection had done severe damage to reforms and to the ruling coalition. The Peronist party was deeply divided between the Menem and Duhalde camps; other internal conflicts existed as well. The Alliance mimicked its midterm political strategy, picking Fernando de la Rúa as its candidate for the 1999 presidential elections. Again, the Alliance expressed support for the country's economic model, but it sharply criticized the high unemployment and rampant corruption now synonymous with Carlos

Menem's administration. De la Rúa won the elections, but the economic crisis facing the country was deepening, mainly because of Brazil's steep devaluation of its currency, which further underscored Argentina's lack of competitiveness.

FERNANDO DE LA RÚA

Several points are worth repeating in the discussion of de la Rúa's rise to power. First, it is generally agreed that Menem's drive to obtain a constitutionally prohibited third presidential term hurt Argentina in a number of ways. For example, economic reform momentum was slowed and Menem's turn to populist policies hurt the country's fiscal stance. This led to a second major problem, which was a tremendous split in the Peronist party, with a sort of free-for-all taking place between Menem and the Peronist leaders. (As mentioned, the main split was between Menem and Duhalde.) In essence, Menem's ambitions were seen as blocking the rise to power of other Peronist politicians; and they fought back, against Menem and among themselves.

Unfortunately, this battle contributed to the worsening fiscal stance, increasing the country's vulnerability to the global financial shocks that began in late 1997 and worsened from 1998 to 1999. Finally, the Alliance had come upon an effective strategy: They attacked corruption and unemployment, but promised to leave the basic economic model untouched. For most Argentines, this was enough to tip the balance in favor of de la Rúa.

As you know, what was initially seen as an important positive development in Argentine politics—a coalition between two opposition parties taking the presidency—turned into disaster. In an important way, following the debacle of Alfonsín's presidency, de la Rúa initially represented the recovery of the UCR to political importance. However, like Alfonsín before him, the Radical de la Rúa was forced to leave office prematurely in 2001, having presided over economic and political collapse.

De la Rúa took office in December 1999, and several issues immediately hurt the new administration. The first was the president's need for medical treatment, which delayed quick movement on economic reforms (and certainly did nothing to strengthen his image among the population). The economic situation also was rapidly deteriorating. Then the government was hit hard by a vote-buying scandal, significantly impacting its credibility. Ironically, it was not so much the issue of vote-buying, but the fact that different amounts were paid to different people that led to the crisis.

In the face of deteriorating economic conditions, the weakened president agreed to IMF austerity measures in return for its financial aid. But then as a form of protest against austerity, the Alliance's FREPASO vice-president resigned in October 2000. (Amazingly, the *Alianza* wanted more government spending rather than less, despite the perilous fiscal stance of the government.) The remaining FREPASO members abandoned the Alliance in March 2001, signaling the end of the much-heralded *Alianza*. De la Rúa was forced to look elsewhere—primarily to the right—for help in pushing his policy initiatives. In desperation, de la Rúa brought in Menem's old economy minister in 2001, Domingo Cavallo, to work economic miracles; but this amounted to very little in terms of concrete success. (For many, Cavallo's policies amounted to "too little, too late.")

Protests mounted as Argentines called for the president and his team to put an end to the crisis. One rising group of protesters was middle-class housewives, who took to the streets banging pots and pans to protest the deterioration in their standard of living. Cavallo quickly resigned. The climax to this shortened regime came in December 2001 in the so-called night of the saucepans. A huge march on the *Casa Rosada* took place, leading to violent clashes with the police. The government called for a state of siege, which, in turn, sparked a spontaneous movement of people marching to the center of Buenos Aires; thirty-five people died in the violence and chaos.

Argentine demonstrators gather at the Plaza de Mayo, in front of the Casa Rosada, *to demand the resignation of President Fernando de la* Rúa *on December 20, 2001. (Reuters/Corbis)*

President de la Rúa resigned, fleeing by helicopter the widespread protest, looting, and chaos that surrounded him.

It must be noted that the IMF played a significant role in the economic crisis that led to the downfall of de la Rúa, the impact of which continues to be debated to this day. While some place the majority of the responsibility with the Fund, there is also considerable truth to the argument that Argentina's faulty economic policies, especially the inability to get its fiscal house in order, were the ultimate cause of economic disaster (especially given the rigidities of convertibility).

After years of showcasing Argentina as an example of prudent economic reform, the IMF adopted an increasingly hard line with the country. This contributed to a rapid loss of confidence in Argentina, both domestically and internationally. The bottom line is that the combination of the loss of the IMF's confidence as well as the disintegration of the

Alliance (and serious internal struggles in the Radical Party) doomed de la Rúa to failure. His lack of charisma and often sluggish demeanor exacerbated the problem. In the end, the president was forced to resign, ushering in a period of even deeper economic and political crisis.

POLITICAL CRISIS

The premature resignation of Fernando de la Rúa in December 2001 led to a serious crisis of political succession. Four presidents followed quickly de la Rúa's term in office. First, Ramón Puerta took the role of acting president December 20–22, 2001. Puerta was then followed by Adolfo Rodríguez Saá, who lasted December 23–30, 2001. Eduardo Camaño became acting president December 31, 2001, and January 1, 2002. Finally, Eduardo Duhalde assumed the top position on January 2, 2002, acting as president until Néstor Kirchner won a presidential election and took office on May 25, 2003.

The musical chairs surrounding the office of president reflected severe conflict within the Peronist party; despite the major political and economic crisis facing the country, the Peronists were unable to select and then stand behind a president. Much of the conflict reflected intraparty and interregional conflict. For example, interior factions were fearful of Duhalde, as the head of the dominant faction from Buenos Aires. However, the leaders of regional factions seemed able to agree only on opposing Duhalde—serious conflicts arose among these same regional factions.

As outlined previously, after two weeks of chaos and constitutional uncertainty that started with de la Rúa's resignation, Duhalde emerged in early 2002 as the man to take the job. Of course, the irony here is that he was actually the Peronist candidate who lost the presidential election in 1999 to de la Rúa. The interior power brokers were unable to exclude Buenos Aires's political boss from power, despite their intentions to do so. (They also unsuccessfully tried to limit

Duhalde's authority.) So Duhalde, rejected by the electorate two years earlier, was endorsed by congress. Since the legislature was controlled by the opposition, it chose a president from its own ranks; thus, Duhalde's rise represented a change of ruling parties without the consent of the electorate.

Duhalde faced two fairly daunting tasks once installed in power. First, he had to deal with economic chaos and political unrest within Argentina. In turn, he also needed to restore the IMF's confidence in Argentina and the direction of its policies. Duhalde rejected the economic model that his own party, through Menem, had been advocating for a decade or so; at the same time, he ended convertibility, devalued the peso, and then "pesified" domestic bank accounts at the new devalued rate (both assets and liabilities, of course). For the most part, Duhalde followed IMF advice; but relations remained tense throughout his tenure. However, public support for Duhalde declined over time and public unrest remained significant. In the end, Duhalde was forced by circumstances to call for presidential elections, announced to take place in March 2003.

In the end, Duhalde managed to serve as Argentina's president for more than a year. In that time, he confirmed the country's massive default on its external debt. He also engineered the end of convertibility and the peso's significant devaluation. This led to a spike in inflation and an outpouring of public discontent. However, he did manage to stabilize the chaotic environment; and while under significant public pressure, he called for elections in 2003 and announced that he would not run.

Initially, many saw Duhalde's support for Néstor Kirchner in the presidential elections as an attempt by Duhalde to retain political control. However, Kirchner quickly distanced himself from Duhalde and won the elections, assuming office in May 2003. Initial election results did not give Kirchner a resounding political victory; subsequent developments have given him more power and probably signal the end of a long political career for Eduardo Duhalde.

NÉSTOR KIRCHNER

Néstor Kirchner was active in the Peronist party from a relatively young age; he was even incarcerated by the government during the military regime. Starting as a mayor, he became governor of the state of Santa Cruz, a relatively sparsely populated province in Patagonia. Over time, Kirchner emerged as a sort of center-left Peronist, assuming a somewhat critical stance regarding Carlos Menem's "neoliberal" policies. Kirchner also opposed Menem's decision in 1990 to pardon the leaders of the dirty war. Finally, Kirchner opposed Menem's attempt to run for a third presidential term—in this, he joined Menem's chief intraparty rival Eduardo Duhalde.

While Duhalde was able to partly restore order to Argentina following de la Rúa's resignation, popular sentiment was growing more negative regarding politicians in general. A popular phrase heard at the time was *"que se vayan todos,"* or roughly, "away with them all." It was in this relatively cynical environment that Duhalde announced new presidential elections for 2003.

While Kirchner won the 2003 election, there was considerable debate surrounding the strength of his victory. The first-round vote was held on April 27, 2003, and was won by Carlos Menem. (At only 24 percent, his tally was not enough to win the election outright and was just 2 percent above Kirchner.) However, by this time, although it was constitutionally legal for Menem to attempt to regain the presidency, he had developed a highly negative image with the Argentine public. It was widely noted that Menem would have no chance of winning the run-off election; in fact, polls were predicting a Kirchner landslide. Menem chose to withdraw rather than face defeat, making Kirchner president by default. He was sworn in on May 25, 2003, to a four-year term. As a result of these somewhat unusual circumstances, there was widespread belief that Kirchner entered the presidency with a relatively weak mandate.

Néstor Kirchner was sworn in as Argentina's forty-ninth president in May 2003. (Reuters/Corbis)

Still, Kirchner won the contest through legitimate means and assumed the presidency. As president, Kirchner was partially lucky, especially when it came to the state of the economy. First, while the economy was still suffering from lingering effects of the economic crisis, the cycle actually hit bottom in 2002 and economic recovery was starting to gain traction as Kirchner came to office. Kirchner wisely retained Duhalde's well-respected economy minister, Roberto Lavagna; and together the two tackled the country's debt default (and managed a rescheduling of debt with organizations such as the IMF). As discussed in the previous chapter, the restructuring of the private debt was massive, with investors receiving a "haircut" that left them with a fraction of the face value of their Argentine bonds.

Kirchner managed to use the aggressive stance taken with foreign investors to his political advantage domestically. In general terms, the president adopted an antagonistic stance with international financial institutions such as the IMF as well as with large foreign investors (many of whom made significant investments in the Argentine economy well before the crisis and have been significantly negatively impacted in its aftermath). Likewise, he took an antimarket approach in his policymaking.

As discussed in the preceding chapter, Kirchner played a somewhat risky game, although it appeared to pay off politically. His populist and nationalist approach obviously paid political dividends domestically. This was most evident in the 2005 parliamentary elections, which were widely viewed as a referendum on Kirchner and his political power. (Remember, Menem's withdrawal from the presidential race robbed Kirchner of the ability to receive a huge vote tally and, as a result, a clear mandate.)

In fact, Kirchner lobbied publicly for the country to consider the midterm elections as a plebiscite for his administration. Kirchner's candidates performed quite well in the elections, including the high-profile victory of his wife, Cristina, over the wife of Peronist party boss Duhalde for a Senate seat for the province of Buenos Aires. Kirchner's wife won by a wide margin, signaling not only strong political support for the president but also the waning power of Duhalde and his faction of the Peronists.

However, the risks of Kirchner's nationalist and populist approach were not insignificant. As discussed, a simple example of his approach concerns the price of beef. To hold down the price of beef and, in the process, gain political support from Argentina's beef-consuming voters, the president announced a six-month ban on beef exports in early 2006. Of course, the political motivation for such a ban is to keep beef cheap for domestic consumers, rather than export it to "rich" international buyers. The problem is that the move simultaneously reduces the incentive for domestic cattlemen to produce beef. Assuming that this slowdown in production causes beef supplies to decline over time, the irony is that domestic prices will likely increase. Assuming this is the case, besides domestic consumers losing out, the country will lose the valuable foreign exchange from an important export.

For now, this is only guesswork; and many groups are working to overturn the policy. (By the time this book is published, the policy may well have been reversed.) But it serves as an example of the dangers of nationalist and populist policies. Most recently, the president replaced the respected Lavagna with a lesser-known and less well-respected economy minister. Likewise, in a dramatic way, the country repaid its debt to the IMF in early 2006, projecting an antagonistic attitude toward this important international institution. In general, the two actions are further signals of Argentina's move away from market-oriented policies, as well as of an antagonistic stance toward the world economy. This stance may be acceptable in the current environment, when the global economy is booming and prices for Argentina's commodity exports are strong. However, it may become considerably more costly when the global commodity cycle turns and Argentina faces more difficult global economic conditions.

Fortunately, the country has exited the deep economic and political crisis it faced upon the resignation of Fernando de la Rúa. Historically, his chaotic exit would have been an easy excuse for the military to step in, either to fill the void directly or to orchestrate the political transition to a new civilian government. However, the crisis was "handled" by congress, albeit somewhat clumsily. In turn, Eduardo Duhalde was able to stabilize the chaotic situation and call for new elections, leading to the presidency of Néstor Kirchner. In this sense, democratic institutions worked and conditions in the country improved significantly. That was certainly a much-needed victory for the country as a whole.

CRISTINA FERNÁNDEZ DE KIRCHNER

As mentioned in the previous chapters, Néstor Kirchner has been succeeded by his wife, Cristina Fernández de Kirchner, as the president of Argentina. Fernández is the nation's second woman president, and the first woman president to be elected to the highest office. Remember, Isabel Peron assumed the presidency upon the death of her husband, Juan Domingo Peron. In addition to being the nation's "first lady," Kirchner has had a notable career in national politics as a legislator. Although it is far too early to make any judgments about Cristina Fernández and the direction of her government, her path to the presidency has been rather unusual, to say the least. Unfortunately, the fact that her husband, Néstor Kirchner, chose not to run for a second term, despite high popularity, raises questions about what role he will play in Fernández's government. Cynics of course suggest Kirchner is attempting to establish some sort of "family dynasty," perhaps with the goal of returning to the presidency after sitting out a term. It is even suggested that the two will attempt to alternate in power repeatedly. While this path would be rather unorthodox, assuming it takes place under legitimate elections and with popular support, it is hard to be too pessimistic about the implications. Most important for Argentina and its political system is the continuation of stable, democratic politics—in this sense the individual players are probably less important than the continuity of the institutional framework. Still, interested readers will want to watch closely for clues about the direction of the Fernández administration and role assumed by ex-president Néstor Kirchner.

A NOTE ON ARGENTINA'S FOREIGN POLICY

Argentina's relations with the external world, like its domestic politics, have undergone some fairly dramatic fluctuations.

A concise, straightforward way to categorize these relations is provided by Colin Lewis, who divides Argentine foreign policy into four distinct phases (Lewis, pp. 17–25). The author would add a fifth phase to this framework, corresponding to the contemporary environment.

The first phase, labeled the "American phase," took place roughly from the time of independence to the 1860s. As you know, the period was one of considerable instability for the country and this instability fundamentally affected the country's relations with the world. For portions of this period, Argentina was still forming as a country and national identities in the region had yet to form.

Remember, Argentina was but one country to eventually form out of the territory of the Viceroyalty of the Río de la Plata, which itself was created only late in the eighteenth century. Thus, the key issues in the "American phase" involved securing recognition from countries around the world as well as defining relations with neighboring countries. Importantly, territories were ill-defined at the time, leading to numerous territorial disputes. Likewise, at the same time that national identities were forming, internal civil disorder and provincial rebellions took place. In effect, some of these early struggles led to separate countries being carved out of the original viceroyalty, while others were settled internally as the territory of today's Argentina was finally settled.

A second period of foreign relations grew out of the first tentative phase as national boundaries became concrete. This period is labeled "independent internationalism" by Lewis, and it lasted roughly from the 1870s to the 1920s. The period was characterized by tentative steps into more significant interaction with the global community—in effect, a move beyond specifically Latin American concerns. One critical factor (and probably *the* critical factor) driving this more independent stance toward the world was the country's rapidly growing economy. In effect, the boom Argentina experienced as it became an agricultural exporting powerhouse supported a more independent stance. Remember, as measured by GDP per capita, at the time, Argentina was one of the richest countries in the world, which supported a move beyond regional issues to active engagement in world affairs.

The third phase of external relations, labeled "combative isolationism," lasted from about the 1920s through the 1970s. One important factor in the country's more combative stance with regard to world affairs was a period of difficult relations with the United States. Argentina assumed a stance of "active neutrality" at the onset of the World Wars, a stance that differed dramatically from its neighbor Brazil, which adopted a more pro-U.S. stance. "Combative isolationism" could also be seen in other aspects, which, in general, led Argentina to challenge the dominant internationalism of the time. (For example, Argentina challenged the U.S.-inspired Bretton Woods agreements that followed the Second World War.) Argentina also fostered relations with the Soviet Union and with the nonaligned movement in the 1970s.

The fourth period, the last one labeled by Lewis, is called the phase of "realism." In effect, the period followed the country's combative isolationism and represented a return to a more constructive, collaborative engagement in world affairs, as well as greater integration into the global economy. For example, relations with Chile were normalized. Likewise, the country entered into Mercosur, a trade agreement with Brazil, Uruguay, and Paraguay, which was discussed in detail in the economics chapter. In particular, President Menem went to great lengths to improve Argentina's relations with the United States; and economic cooperation between the two countries increased dramatically. For a time, Argentina became the "darling" of the international business world, seeing dramatic increases in both financial and real foreign investments.

The fifth period, corresponding to the contemporary era, can best be labeled "combative internationalism." Unfortunately, one of the principal drivers of the country's turn to a more combative stance was the financial collapse and massive debt default of the early 2000s. The country remains engaged in world affairs—at a minimum, attempts to close itself off from the global economy seen in the period of "combative isolationism" have not returned. However, the default soured relations with international investors—largely because of the country's aggressive stance vis-à-vis its creditors. This stance also can be seen in Argentina's somewhat cold relations with the IMF. Other aspects of this stance include anti-U.S. rhetoric and closer relations with Venezuela, which has stepped into the fray to lend financial and political support to Argentina's current government. This was seen most recently when President George W. Bush of the United States toured a number of Latin American countries to demonstrate U.S. solidarity with the region and its struggles. On the day Bush visited Argentina's neighbor, Uruguay, Argentina's President Kirchner hosted Venezuelan President Hugo Chavez—anti-U.S. rhetoric was, of course, abundant. This stance of "combative internationalism" is only in its early stage and corresponds to a period of strong economic recovery in Argentina. It remains to be seen whether this phase will cause meaningful problems for the country over time.

The preceding comments are meant to provide a conceptual framework for students interested in pursuing this topic in further detail; however, numerous examples of the main periods can be found in the first three chapters of this book. At a minimum, the conceptual framework should illustrate that Argentina's foreign relations have been cyclical in nature and have often been a function of specific domestic developments, both political and economic. For example, the transition to "independent internationalism" can be viewed quite logically as a result of the country's growing stature in the global economy. Likewise, the recent transition to more "combative internationalism" is without question a result of the country's financial and economic collapse. It remains to be seen whether the country can develop a more constructive stance in foreign relations as its economic recovery solidifies over time. At present, the signs point in several directions.

References

Brown, Jonathan C. *A Brief History of Argentina*. New York: Facts on File, 2003.

Burns, E. Bradford, and Julie A. Charlip. *Latin America: A Concise Interpretive History,* 7th ed. Upper Saddle River, NJ: Prentice Hall, 2002.

Crawley, Eduardo. *A House Divided: Argentina, 1880–1980*. London: Hurst, 1985.

Di Tella, Guido, and Rudiger Dornbusch, eds. *The Political Economy of Argentina, 1946–1983*. London: Macmillan, 1989.

Di Tella, Guido, and D. C. M. Platt, eds. *The Political Economy of Argentina, 1880–1946*. London: Macmillan, 1986.

Erro, Davide G. *Resolving the Argentine Paradox: Politics and Development, 1966–1992*. Boulder, CO: Lynne Rienner Publishers, 1993.

James, Daniel. *Resistance and Integration: Peronism and the Argentine Working Class, 1946–1976*. Cambridge: Cambridge University Press, 1988.

Lewis, Colin M. *Argentina: A Short History*. Oxford: Oneworld Publications, 2002.

Lewis, Paul W. *The Crisis of Argentine Capitalism*. Chapel Hill: University of North Carolina Press, 1990.

O'Donnell, Guillermo, Philippe C. Schmitter, and Laurence Whitehead. *Transitions from Authoritarian Rule: Latin America*. Baltimore: Johns Hopkins University Press, 1986.

Potash, Robert. *The Army and Politics in Argentina,* 3 vols. Palo Alto, CA: Stanford University Press, 1969–1996.

Ramos, Monica Peralta. *The Political Economy of Argentina: Power and Class Since 1930*. Boulder, CO: Westview Press, 1992.

Rock, David. *Argentina, 1516–1982: From Spanish Colonization to the Falklands War*. London: I.B. Tauris, 1986.

Rock, David. *Argentina, 1516–1987: From Spanish Colonization to Alfonsin*. Berkeley: University of California Press, 1987.

Rock, David. *Authoritarian Argentina: The Nationalist Movement, Its History, and Its Impact*. Berkeley: University of California Press, 1993.

Rock, David. *Politics in Argentina, 1890–1930: The Rise and Fall of Radicalism*. Cambridge: Cambridge University Press, 1975.

Scobie, James R. *Argentina: A City and a Nation,* 2nd ed. New York: Oxford University Press, 1971.

Shumway, Nicholas. *The Invention of Argentina*. Berkeley: University of California Press, 1991.

Skidmore, Thomas E., and Peter H. Smith. *Modern Latin America,* 5th ed. Oxford: Oxford University Press, 2001.

Smith, Peter. *Argentina and the Failure of Democracy: Conflicts Among Political Elites, 1904–1955*. Madison: University of Wisconsin Press, 1974.

Torre, Juan Carlos. "Argentina Since 1946," in Leslie Bethell (ed.), *The Cambridge History of Latin America, Vol. VIII*. Cambridge: Cambridge University Press, 1984: 73–194.

Wynia, Gary W. *Argentina in the Post-War Era: Politics and Economic Policy Making in a Divided Society.* Albuquerque: University of New Mexico Press, 1988.

Wynia, Gary W. *The Politics of Latin American Development,* 3rd ed. Cambridge: Cambridge University Press, 1990.

CHAPTER FOUR

Society and Culture

INTRODUCTION

This chapter will focus on the society and culture of
Argentina, a fascinating and complex subject. The preceding
chapters, covering geography and history, economics, and
politics and government, can be seen as providing the background and introduction to this largely contemporary topic.
Over time, those factors helped shape Argentina's culture—
the country's soul, as some might call it—but at the same
time, those factors have been changed by the culture.

For the most part, this chapter will focus on culture as
defined from an anthropological perspective: the collection
of beliefs, customs, traditions, and creative pursuits that
make up and differentiate a given society. In the process, the
chapter will try to identify the factors that make Argentina
unique, searching for something best expressed in Spanish:
Argentinidad.

Argentina is not well-known internationally—just as people in the United States often do not realize that Argentina's
neighbor Brazil speaks Portuguese, a variety of misconcep-
tions about Argentina abound. It is safe to say that Argentina's
international image is puzzling. On the one hand, the country
is viewed as sophisticated—some might even say glamorous.
On the other hand, Argentina is viewed as a third world country, a somewhat odd, underdeveloped country that seems
European in manner. The goal here is to move beyond image
and stereotype.

This chapter will begin by looking at Argentina's people,
focusing in particular on the main groups of people that make

up the contemporary population: the Spanish; Indians; Africans; and, perhaps most importantly, immigrants. Those four groups make up the unique blend of Argentine people today. Remember, from a historical perspective, Argentina is rather unique in the Latin American context. Namely, during most of the colonial era, the territory that now makes up the country of Argentina was largely a backwater in the Spanish Empire. The Spanish searched for mineral wealth and concentrated Indian populations (for labor), but Argentina had neither. As a result, the territory was largely ignored. What settlements were developed were largely concentrated north of the territory and fit into the colonial system centered in Lima, Peru. However, over time, the port of Buenos Aires gained in importance. The Bourbon Reforms discussed in Chapter One represented a reorganization of Spanish America that explicitly took this growing importance into account.

Over time, the part of the country defined by the pampas (a word derived from the Indian language Quechua, signifying

Guaraní men, ca. 1980s. (Ricardo Azoury/Corbis)

"upland meadow" and representing the main physical feature of the central region of the country) became the economic, political, and population center of the country. One of the key issues in the search for *Argentinidad* centers on the tensions existing between the city and province of Buenos Aires and the rest of the country's provinces. This debate is inextricably connected to the issue of immigration, another defining characteristic of Argentine national identity.

Argentina is typically considered the most Europeanized country within Latin America. Immigration has been the most important driving variable, as European immigration to the country has had a greater demographic impact in Argentina than in any other country in Latin America. While the statistics were presented in preceding chapters, remember that between 1857 and 1900, some 3.5 million people arrived in Argentina; and of these immigrants, approximately 46 percent were Italian and 32 percent were Spanish. By 1914, roughly 30 percent of the population in Argentina was foreign-born—at roughly the same time, only about 13 percent of the U.S. population was foreign-born. Again, the process has given the country a distinctly European quality and has contributed to the ongoing discussion about national identity.

Immigration and issues of national identity are also intimately tied to the divide between the city and province of Buenos Aires and the rest of the country. In general terms, some two-thirds of the country's population (and a large part of the country's resources) are concentrated around Buenos Aires and in surrounding areas, while the remaining population (and resources) is scattered throughout the rest of the vast territory. As a result, students of Argentina often speak of "two Argentinas": one that is wealthy and centered around the port, supporting a vibrant, cosmopolitan culture and one that is sparsely populated, underdeveloped, and culturally backward. This chapter will discuss these issues in detail, in the process looking closely at the specific groups of people that make up the population of Argentina.

The first half of this chapter will discuss two more key topics. The first is language. While a number of indigenous languages are still spoken in Argentina, the national language is Spanish. However, the Spanish spoken in Argentina differs considerably from the Spanish spoken in Spain and, indeed, from that spoken in the rest of Latin America (neighbor Brazil speaks Portuguese). One key reason is the country's history of massive immigration, especially the influence of Italian immigrants. The chapter will then turn to religion in contemporary Argentina, an important contributor to the country's unique culture. While the country is, for the most part, Roman Catholic, it is also made up of important Protestant and Jewish populations.

The second half of the chapter is dedicated to a number of specific topics that have been chosen to give insight into Argentina's culture and illuminate the daily lives of the Argentine population. You will take a look at local customs and a few components of social relations. You also will examine in detail factors such as the country's food and drink, religious holidays, sports culture, and the like. You should find that these everyday topics shed some light on the daily realities that people in Argentina experience.

The chapter will then turn to literature and briefly to a number of other arts, including music and film. Argentina has played an important role in Latin America as a cultural innovator. It is the birthplace of the tango; such internationally-famous authors as Jorge Luis Borges and Julio Cortázar; and vibrant film, theater, book, and magazine industries. Finally, you will look briefly at popular culture, women, and education. While this chapter is, at best, a quick introduction to these interrelated subjects, it will point the way for those who are interested in further study. While Argentina has seen its share of political and economic instability, its culture and society are fascinating and quite unique in Latin America and the modern world. This chapter will serve as an interesting window to these topics.

POPULATION IN ARGENTINA: HISTORICAL BACKGROUND

Many analyses of modern Argentine culture pass over the colonial era—often starting somewhere in the early nineteenth century in the post-independence, nation-building era. This oversight reflects factors such as the supposed lack of "high culture" among indigenous peoples and the territory's backwater status in the colonial era. In turn, it also reflects an undercurrent of thinking that equates modernity in Argentina with the waves of immigration that took place in the nineteenth and early twentieth centuries. However, an accurate understanding of Argentina's modern culture and society requires a brief examination of the colonial heritage, if only to understand the basis of nation-building and the cultural continuities that exist today in the national identity.

For most of the colonial era, Argentina was a part of the provinces of the Río de la Plata—a vast region territorially, but really just a minor component of the Viceroyalty of Peru. Offering little of obvious immediate benefit to the Crown, the cities of the interior of this region were largely dedicated to facilitating the flow of minerals to the viceregal capital, Lima, Peru. The Spanish considered the territory as largely vacant and therefore needing to be filled with Christianity and European culture. (The Spaniards became the masters of the land and the existing people, which were for the most part nomadic.) It was no accident that the earliest settlements took place in the country's north, where the most sedentary, agricultural people were located. A look at the three original groups of people making up colonial populations—the Spanish, Indians, and African slaves—serves as a starting point.

Peninsulares *and* Criollos

The earliest Spaniards came to Argentina in large part to control others. They did not come to work the land, toil in mines, or tend livestock; rather, their desire was to dominate others. Unlike the English that settled North America, the Spanish tried to subdue, exploit, and absorb Indian populations. (Many would argue that a resulting disdain for manual labor would last for generations.) As a result of this predisposition, the towns and economic centers of early Argentina centered on Indian agricultural communities, based largely in the valleys and foothills of the Andes. The Spanish *conquistadores,* or conquerors, were not frontiersmen or farmers; they were, for the most part, soldiers, administrators, and masters. Settlement, then, took place in the northwest, in Cuyo and the Mesopotamian provinces, while the pampas, Patagonia, and the Chaco remained Indian territory for most of the colonial period and during much of the nineteenth century, a reflection of the lack of settled agrarian indigenous populations.

Again unlike English settlers, the Spanish, especially early on, did not emigrate as families; and the result was considerable mixing of races. This mix of races was primarily between Spanish men and indigenous women, resulting in the mestizo. However, by the second half of the sixteenth century, enough Spanish women had arrived or had been born in the New World to provide a foundation of "pure" Spanish families. From these families developed the *criollo,* or creole, elite. Creoles were Spanish people born in the New World.

Still, mestizo offspring multiplied, forming a unique social group that aspired to the dominant Spanish culture but was not totally accepted as a part of it. Some mestizos succeeded in integrating into the creole elite; but the majority did not, becoming artisans and laborers in the colonial towns, as well as gauchos, herdsmen, and the like in the countryside.

Indigenous Populations

It is widely believed that the sixteenth-century indigenous population of Argentina did not exceed 300,000. In turn, the populations of the pampas, Patagonia, and the Chaco, representing as much as one-third of the existing Indian population, were largely beyond the effective reach of Spanish exploitation. In general, Argentina's indigenous cultures lived in a more dispersed manner than was seen elsewhere in the Spanish Empire, especially when compared to places such as Mexico and Peru, which were famous for the Aztec and Inca civilizations.

Still, the variety of cultures was noteworthy despite the Spanish tendency to lump diverse groups into similar categories. The Río de la Plata region during the colonial era contained a multitude of tribes. The pampas, or plains, contained the Pampas, Charrúas, Timbúes, and Kaigang. The North held the Matacos, Abipones, Mocobíes, and Tobas. Tribes such as the Puelches, Tehuelches, Araucanians, Selkman, and Yamanas lived in Patagonia. The Huarpes lived in Cuyo, while in the center and Andean Northwest there were Comenchingones and Diaguitas. As discussed earlier in the book, each tribe had its own complex oral histories, traditions, and religions.

The Indian population, as in other parts of Latin America, plummeted early in the colonial period, the victim of violence as well as epidemic diseases. However, by the time of independence in the early nineteenth century, estimates put the total population of Argentina at some 500,000, with as much as 30 percent of that number still indigenous. (Ten percent or so was black and mulatto; the remainder, creole and mestizo.)

African Slaves

Early on in the colonial era, African slaves began to add another layer to the cultural and racial makeup of Argentina. Several factors contributed to the growing African population. Proximity to Portuguese Brazil, the main importer of African slaves in the Americas; the growing trade in contraband in Buenos Aires; and the growing need for coastal labor led to substantial importation of slaves throughout the seventeenth and eighteenth centuries.

By 1680, some 23,000 Africans had been imported legally based on royal licenses; and without question, a good many more had been brought in "under the table." The majority of slaves were shipped inland, but they were concentrated in urban areas. At the time, the prevailing view was that Indians were sullen, while mestizos were crafty and ambitious. African slaves, on the other hand, were characterized as docile and cheerful and were sought to toil as servants and workmen (in trades and small industry). By the early eighteenth century, blacks (made up of slaves and those who had purchased their freedom) consisted of between 10 percent and 30 percent of the population in the growing towns of Argentina. Importantly, blacks tended to blend in with the lower classes made up of mestizos, Indians, and some whites.

Argentine Race and Ethnicity, Continued

For most of the colonial era, the territory of Argentina, like the rest of Spanish America, was governed by a race-based social system that some called the "petit apartheid" of the empire. Thus, colonial society was categorized along ethnic lines in a system in which status, occupation, and dress were determined by race (and that was firmly established in law). The social spectrum was a sort of continuum, with social degrees ranging from peninsula-born whites (called *peninsulares*) to whites born in the Americas (called *criollos*) through a gradation of mixed races—from mestizo (mixed Indian/white) to *pardo* (black/white) to *zambo* (black/Indian) and many more—to liberated blacks. Slaves were at the bottom, existing literally as chattel. In theory, Indians were protected subjects of the Crown; and their lives were governed by a distinct code.

A largely white creole elite developed over time (and eventually pushed for independence due to growing differences with the *peninsulares*). By the early 1800s, the creole-mestizo stock predominated in Argentina, with darker shades of mestizo and Indians pronounced, for the most part, in the countryside and the interior.

One interesting puzzle has been the disappearance of blacks from Argentina. For demographers studying Argentina, this has been a far larger dilemma than the vanishing of the Indian population, which will be examined later. Typical explanations focus on the wars of independence and subsequent civil wars as a cause. Likewise, diseases such as tuberculosis have been identified. However, far more important was a process of gradual absorption into the creole and mestizo populations. In other words, while the disappearance of blacks was often identified with racial theories of inferiority (and thus attributed to disease, overwork, and the like), it is more reasonable to assume that as a group, blacks simply merged with other groups existing on the fringes of Argentine society. In this sense, blacks became a part of indigenous groups, mestizos of mixed blood and poor creoles, to form the Argentine lower classes. On this point, it is interesting to note that *negro* in Argentine Spanish does not refer specifically to being black or of African descent, but has come to mean "nonwhite." As such, it has been applied to a host of groups, including Italians, Arabs, and Jews and even to Spaniards from southern Spain.

The mestizo population of Argentina also has witnessed a process of absorption, impacted most importantly by the waves of European immigration that took place from the 1880s to the early part of the twentieth century. Likewise, a huge process of internal migration from the provinces and countryside to the coastal cities took place in the 1940s and 1950s, again contributing to this process of absorption (leading to the term *cabecitas negras,* or "black heads," a reference to the mestizo ethnicity of migrants). Mestizo populations can still be seen in rural areas such as the Andean regions. But this distinction has become much less significant in contemporary society, which is a blend of creoles, mestizos, and immigrants.

Again, while native Argentines lived throughout the territory at the time of discovery, they had largely disappeared by

An immigrant family at their homestead, ca. 1920. Argentina's robust agricultural economy attracted a large immigrant influx. (Library of Congress)

the beginning of the twentieth century, killed by soldiers and settlers as well as by epidemic diseases. Today some indigenous peoples continue to survive in relatively isolated parts of the country, and many of them continue to follow their native customs. In turn, a few native practices and customs have been incorporated into the mainstream Argentine culture; but the list is not a long one. For example, a handful of native words or words derived from indigenous languages exist today in Argentine Spanish. In turn, there are a number of well-known folksingers with indigenous backgrounds. And finally, the *bombo,* which is a base drum carried by musicians, has been adopted from indigenous culture.

Argentina has nothing like an ideology of mestizo culture, as is seen in modern-day Mexico. Argentina's sociocultural consciousness has had very little identification with the Indian over the course of its history. As a result, aside from isolated groups at the fringe of Argentine society, the role of indigenous culture in the country's modern identity is mostly historical. In essence, the conquest of indigenous peoples was an integral part of the "conquest of the desert" and, therefore, an essential component of national identity. In turn, since they were virtually exterminated, indigenous groups no longer play a meaningful role in national debate, as they do in countries such as Peru, Mexico, and Brazil.

The concept of the frontier is a key component of Argentine history and national identity. First, the modern country's political boundaries were established and the conquest of its vast internal territories soon followed. For the most part, indigenous peoples were considered "savages," while the lower classes were deemed barbaric. Overcoming those obstacles was seen as one of the key components of modernization. A more sympathetic viewpoint regarding local culture and the gaucho would eventually emerge, but only after the Indians were nearly exterminated and the gaucho lifestyle was on the wane.

Interestingly, over time, there has been an undercurrent of belief that racial conflict does not exist in Argentina— particularly evident during the period of civil unrest in the United States in the 1960s. U.S.-style democracy was even seen as an important cause of unrest, while defenders of Argentine authoritarianism suggested their own system kept society focused on a long-standing national identity that did not emphasize racial and/or ethnic conflict. Events have, of course, proven this to be wishful thinking, at best. In reality, Argentina has experienced periods of intense racial and ethnic conflict, including not only the "conquest of the desert" discussed previously but also the Tragic Week in 1919 that targeted Jews. (See Chapter One for details.) Argentine writer David Viñas has pointed out that Argentina's indigenous peoples can be seen as the country's first *desaparecidos,* or disappeared. In this sense, the author underscores the fact that much of the disappearance of Indians, like the disappeared of the dirty war, can be attributed to state policy—hardly a display of racial harmony.

WAVES OF EUROPEAN IMMIGRATION

Argentina's ethnic mix has been fueled by the tremendous waves of immigration, emanating primarily from Europe. Despite the Spanish, slave, and indigenous roots, probably no other nation in Latin America has closer ties to Europe; and that topic of European immigration will be discussed next.

Note that by the 1860s, the non-Spanish European population was no greater than approximately 100,000; these people were concentrated, for the most part, in and around Buenos Aires and were made up primarily of Basques, Irish, English, French, and Italians. In less than 100 years, 4.5 million Europeans would emigrate to Argentina; in the decades before World War I, these immigrants (55 percent Italian and 26 percent Spanish) would largely overwhelm the existing creole-mestizo stock. By 1914, foreigners outnumbered native Argentines by a ratio of 2:1 in most of the country's big cities and an amazing 4:1 in Buenos Aires. Another wave of immigration after the wars included new groups such as Poles, Syrians, and Slavic people; but Southern Europeans continued to predominate. Even as late as 1960, foreign-born people in Argentina still numbered in the millions.

Again, as late as the 1820s, the creole-mestizo stock predominated in Argentina, with mestizo and Indian elements pronounced in the countryside; blacks and mulattoes were still in evidence in the towns. But by and large, the process of mixing was slowly absorbing both black and mestizo elements. Then in the late nineteenth century, the country underwent a wholesale transformation. First, population as a whole increased dramatically, driven by massive immigration. Black and Indian populations largely disappeared, while mestizos were, for the most part, absorbed. Population was increasingly concentrated in the coastal region, focused largely in Buenos Aires and surrounding areas. Cities and the population were Europeanized, while the balance of population shifted from the countryside to more urban centers.

The philosophical underpinnings of this great transformation have already been covered briefly, but it is worth examining in more detail. Remember, while the *criollos* of Argentina had developed an identity based in good measure on interests that were opposed to those of the Spanish, the immediate catalyst for independence in the early nineteenth century was the loss of authority on the part of colonial authorities due to Napoleon's invasion of the Iberian Peninsula (and his brother's assumption of the Spanish throne). While independence eventually was achieved, there was by no means a broad consensus among the creole population about the country's direction, due mainly to the existence of subgroups among the creole elite. There was a split between Buenos Aires and the outlying provinces, as well as between a number of subgroups, such as the army, merchants, and landowners. Strife (even civil war) filled the vacuum after independence until president Juan Manuel Rosas imposed authoritarian discipline on the country with the nation's longest period of dictatorship. Rosas imposed a sort of authoritarian populism that relied on a strong alliance with the popular classes as well as protection of large landowners.

Rosas's mid-nineteenth-century iron-fisted rule was contested by a liberal opposition, led by such figures as Domingo Faustino Sarmiento and Juan B. Alberdi. These liberals wanted to turn what they considered a marginally important former colony into a modern secular society that was based on a capitalist economy similar to those seen in the United States and Europe. The liberals believed that for their agenda to succeed, local customs would have to be radically changed. In large part, it was assumed that this change would result from two key processes: wholesale public education of the popular classes and massive immigration from Europe. A good number of these liberals were concerned about the nation's racial identity, subscribing to racist theories propounding the need for "whitening." Thus, while education was important, immigration was essential. In the words of Juan Alberdi, "to govern is to populate." Resulting immigration policies would profoundly and permanently alter the ethnic and racial profile of the country.

While Rosas relied on his popularity with the lower classes, liberals in general were not so inclined. They viewed the popular sectors as obstacles to be overcome in building a modern Argentina, largely assuming that this could be built from the top down. The antagonism between the two viewpoints constitutes an important theme and a significant hurdle in Argentine history that has played a large role in culture and society.

Another critical issue that is inextricably tied to immigration is the role of Buenos Aires in the formation of Argentine society. While some immigrant groups settled outside the city (examples include Germans who settled on the border with Chile and Jewish farmers who settled in the Mesopotamia region), the vast majority of immigrants chose to settle in Buenos Aires. One major reason for this was policy-related: Unlike the United States, land in Argentina was not given to farming families or homesteaders, but rather was distributed in large tracts. As discussed, this led to a lack of a meaningful peasantry in Argentina. Immigrants, for the most part, settled in ethnic enclaves; but over time, they experienced a pattern of upward mobility in which they blended into the general population.

Argentina's *fin de siecle*—a term coined in France meaning literally "end of the century" but also referring to decadence—was a time of triumph. The country's dreams were indeed coming true. It was during this period that the myth of Argentina as a modern nation built from scratch was born, as the country emerged from its long period of civil strife, dictatorship, and economic hardship to rapid progress. Argentina was ruled by the so-called oligarchy that pushed prosperity via public education, massive immigration, and urbanization. The highlight of the era came in 1910, with the centennial celebrations of independence from Spain. The country showed off its affluence with a newly remodeled Buenos Aires, whose broad avenues, public buildings, and private mansions truly looked like the "Paris of South America."

As for the immigrants, the single largest group were the Italians, although the Spanish were not too far behind. People

In the late-nineteenth century, Argentina's growing prosperity became most obvious in the capital, Buenos Aires. People acknowledged its cosmopolitan culture by calling the city the "Paris of South America." (North Wind Picture Archives)

of Italian descent now make up a major part of the population of the capital, as well as other urban and surrounding areas. (A quick look in the phone book in Buenos Aires will dispel any doubts about this.) Today Italian is no longer widely spoken, but various Italian dialects have made great contributions to Argentine Spanish, especially to *porteño,* the local Spanish of Buenos Aires. As will be discussed in more detail, *tango* is another great store of this immigrant Italian culture. One also can see Italian influence in Argentina's food, which in addition to beef, is dominated by Italian cooking. Finally, a quick look at the names of presidents and other government officials over time helps illustrate the process of upward mobility and assimilation of Italian-Argentines.

Another important group of immigrants are Jews. Interestingly, Mediterranean and Sephardic Jews have been in Latin America since the time of the conquest. However, German and Eastern European (the latter often called Russian) Jews became an important component of the wave of immigration in the later 1800s that included other Europeans such as the Italians and Spanish. Over a period of time, the Jewish migration became so significant that Argentina became the largest center of Jewish population and culture in Latin America— and one of the biggest in the world.

Unfortunately, Argentina has experienced considerable anti-Semitism; in addition to the "Tragic Week," bombings against Jewish sites occurred in 1992 and 1994, one at the Israeli embassy and the other at an important Jewish center in Buenos Aires. Scores of deaths occurred, but the perpetrators have yet to be brought to justice. In response to these crimes, however, the Argentine population expressed support for its significant Jewish population in public demonstrations. The Jewish presence in Argentina remains quite strong and can be seen in academic and intellectual pursuits, in business, and in entertainment, among other areas.

Immigrants also have come from other areas of the world. For example, the country has received refugees from the

Spanish Civil War as well as immigrants from the Arab world. There is an Asian presence, with people from countries such as Japan, Vietnam, and Korea. Many observers point out that a number of Koreans have moved into areas typically considered "Jewish" in Buenos Aires, as the city's Jews move uptown or to the suburbs. Two more points deserve mention: Argentina has been an important destination for people coming from other Latin American countries, both as political exiles and economic opportunists. Finally, the most recent economic crises have caused a considerable number of Argentines to leave the country, heading primarily for Europe and the United States in search of a better life. Unfortunately for Argentina, these people are often from the middle class and are highly educated. The hope is that the unfolding economic recovery can slow or stop this process.

To conclude this section, it is important to underscore the dramatic nature of the change that took place in Argentina in the late 1800s and early 1900s and to understand the tremendous role that immigration played in this wholesale cultural and social change. As one important student of Argentina notes, the old Argentina did not die, but relative to the new Argentina, it simply stood still. As a result, over time, two worlds appeared, as their differences truly split the nation, between *porteño* and provincial, between free trade and the desire for protection, between rejection of the church's temporal power and a conservative acceptance of the church's authority over all aspects of life, and between a search for new cultural values abroad and a reaffirmation of creole or native values.

Therefore, modern Argentine society and culture, a product of this great transformation and the people who created it, is a complex mix of various influences—from Indian, conquistador, and slave to mestizo, gaucho, creole, and immigrant. The process has created a number of themes, even myths, that permeate the culture. Likewise, the search for Argentine identity seems to have become something of a national pastime.

One of the deepest divides may have been best introduced by Domingo Sarmiento; although by the time he took up the debate about "civilization versus barbarism" in his book *Facundo,* it was already an established theme. Sarmiento was one of the most outspoken proponents of the view that Argentina had to shed its traditionalist past (and all of the "archaic" values that went with it) to achieve modernity. A strong undercurrent in Argentine culture, this view stressed educated, secular, urban, cosmopolitan, and democratic values. The country embraced this view enthusiastically, and it helped drive policies pushing education and immigration. It was also linked to centralist or *porteño* views.

However, an alternative view that developed over time was expressed in one of the masterpieces of Argentine literature, *Martín Fierro* by José Hernandez. The epic, written in 1872, which centered on the gaucho's struggle and defeat by civilization, underscored and dignified an alternative set of values. These values included the role of the masses, intuitive and practical knowledge, the creole and the Spaniard, the church, the countryside, and the caudillo. In general, these alternative views were stressed in provincial or autonomist positions.

In sum, there is a strong sense that Argentina has been a country "built from scratch," formed by immigration and liberal policies. As you have seen, this is only partly true; while immigration and liberal policies have played an enormous role in creating modern Argentina, to ignore what existed before immigration—the Spanish-mestizo origins of the population—is to miss the essence of Argentina. Likewise, there is the ever-present tension of the divide between Buenos Aires and its surrounding areas and the rest of the country. In large part, this is simply a component of the "modern" versus "traditional" debate, perhaps simply more temporal and less intellectual. At a minimum, this debate has often been heated and has provided the context for numerous major national political events.

RELIGION

Argentina is, without question, a Catholic country—roughly 90 percent of Argentines are Roman Catholic. As will be discussed next, the Catholic Church has a long history in the country and was brought to Argentina by the original explorers, conquerors, and settlers. Of course, indigenous populations already had their own religious practices. While these cultures have largely disappeared over time, a number of communities still practice traditional beliefs—sometimes blended with Catholicism.

However, just as the population is a complex mix of a variety of people, religion in contemporary society is more than simply the dominant Catholicism. For example, more than 1 million Argentines follow some form of Protestantism. Likewise, as was already discussed, a significant minority—perhaps as many as 500,000 people—consider themselves Jewish, the result of the significant wave of Jewish immigration from Europe. Finally, there are even a few hundred thousand followers of Islam, a point that was underscored when ex-president Menem converted from Islam to Catholicism, in large part to facilitate his political career. This section will look briefly at the most common religions that exist in Argentina today.

Roman Catholicism

In the 1500s, the Spanish first introduced Christianity to the territories now making up Argentina—and converting "heathens" to Catholicism was a central goal of the Spanish Empire. One of the most important groups to arrive in the region were the Jesuits, who arrived in 1585 and had a significant impact on the colony until they were expelled in 1767 (when the kings of Spain and Portugal moved to expel the Jesuits from the New World). The Jesuits traveled the world, believing it their duty to teach about Christianity and convert nonbelievers to the faith. They built missions where both converts and the Jesuit priests lived. The importance of the prosperous Jesuits and their missions in the north of Argentina can be seen to this day in the name of one of its provinces: Misiones.

The Jesuits were the most influential religious order in the provinces of the Río de la Plata and helped define the cultural profile of colonial life. Their dominance of life in the colony often led them into conflict with Spaniards and creoles, as well as with the Crown. Until the end of the eighteenth century, the Jesuits dominated all institutions of higher learning, educating a good many of the colonial elite, especially at the University of Córdoba and the School of San Ignacio.

Although the Jesuits were eventually expelled, religion—especially Catholicism—continued to play a central role in Argentines' lives. Of course, much of the tension between the modern and the traditional, between the urban and the provincial, between the secular and the religious, etc., underscores the debates that took place later, as liberals tried to separate church and state and secularize the country. They were partially successful; but the church, specifically the Catholic Church, has remained one of the most powerful and enduring institutions in the country. (In fact, many argue that president Juan Perón's loss of support from the Catholic Church was his "last straw," helping bring down his powerful regime in 1955.) In fact, Catholic nationalism, arising in the late nineteenth century as a sort of backlash against liberalism, argued that the union of the church and the state was the only viable way to preserve the country's Hispano-Catholic cultural heritage. Again, this gulf between competing notions of Argentina and its true cultural identity remains a wide one.

Interestingly, while the country is overwhelmingly Catholic today, it is more secular than religious—and in this sense, differs greatly from many other countries in the region. One Argentine joke even has it that the country's true religion is Freudianism, a reference to the widespread popularity of psychoanalysis in the country. The country's secular nature also can be seen in the lack of widespread popular Catholicism that is seen in countries such as Brazil and Mexico (the latter having developed around the Virgin of Guadalupe, an integral part of Mexico's national identity).

However, Argentina does have some degree of popular Catholicism and many would argue that its popularity grows as one moves away from Buenos Aires. It also has its own home-grown version of the miraculous appearance of the Virgin Mary. According to this legend in which the Virgin appeared in 1630, a man was transporting two statues of the Virgin Mary from Brazil to Peru; and while crossing a river near present-day Luján, his cart became stuck in the mud. The cart was finally freed when one of the statues was removed to lighten the load. This was taken to be a sign that the Virgin wanted to stay put, and a shrine was erected in her honor to hold the statue on this spot. This statue of the Virgin Mary became known as the Virgin of Luján, and is now mounted above

Thousands gather at the Basilica of Luján during Pope John Paul II's visit to the Argentine city on June 11, 1982. (AP Photo/Mark Foley)

the altar of an immense basilica. Twice a year thousands of faithful make a pilgrimage to the basilica, and images of the Virgin of Luján can be seen throughout the country.

Another popular celebration takes place in September in and around the northern city of Salta during the Fiesta del Milagro. This event celebrates the statue of Christ that stands in a local cathedral. It is believed that in 1592, a ship carrying the statue sank off the coast and that the statue floated miraculously to shore, where it was discovered and taken to Salta. For the most part, the statue was forgotten until a priest dreamed about the statue during a series of earthquakes. This dream was taken to be a message from God, and the priest asked the people to find this statue and carry it through the streets. According to legend, the earthquakes then stopped; and to honor the miracle, the residents of Salta reenact this event each year, parading through the streets with the statue.

La Difunta Correa

La Difunta Correa (Spanish for "The Deceased Correa") is a mythical figure popular in Argentine folk religion whose popularity has spread beyond the country's borders to neighboring countries such as Chile and Uruguay. According to legend, the woman's sick husband was abandoned by his companions during a period of civil war in the 1840s. The woman took her baby and went to find her sick husband; when her supplies ran out, she died; and her body was found a few days later. Amazingly, the child remained alive, nursing "miraculously" from her dead mother's breast. As news of these events spread, *La Difunta Correa* grew to become an unofficial popular saint. A sanctuary was created near her grave and has, over time, grown into a small town with a number of different chapels. One of the main chapels contains a life-sized statue of *La Difunta* lying with her child at her breast. The site remains widely visited to this day, at times attracting enormous crowds of the faithful.

Judaism

Historically, Jews have constituted an important component of the Argentine population. While Jews make up only about 1 percent of the population, the Jewish population in Argentina is the largest in Latin America (Brazil is second) and the fifth largest in the world. Estimates of the Jewish population vary considerably, from as low as 200,000 to as high as 500,000. An estimate of between 250,000 and 300,000 is reasonable.

The largest groups of Jewish migrants began to arrive in Argentina in the late nineteenth century, coming from Eastern Europe, Russia, and the Mediterranean. These areas were marked by various political upheavals and often experienced pogroms against Jewish populations. This resulted in a significant migration of these populations westward, and many arrived in the Río de la Plata region. This corresponded to the period of colonization in Argentina, although similar, but perhaps less dramatic, events were taking place in other areas of the New World, such as the United States and Brazil.

Life was by no means easy for the Jewish immigrants— although undoubtedly it was better than it had been in the homelands. Many early immigrants dedicated themselves to agriculture; but over time, many Jews found that they could do better in Buenos Aires than on the farm. As a result, the early agricultural colonies dwindled in size and some even disappeared. One major issue for Jewish immigrants was education, which was scarce and often of poor quality in rural settings while of higher quality and more available in urban areas.

For the most part, the children of Jewish immigrants were able to merge into mainstream Argentine culture, although not without causing some conflict between the generations. (Intermarriage with non-Jews was and continues to be a point of contention among the Argentine Jewish population.) As mentioned previously, Jews can be found in nearly every facet of Argentine cultural and economic life. The Jewish presence in Argentina is quite visible, with numerous synagogues, institutions, and related schools. Unfortunately, anti-Semitism also has been a part of Argentine reality. On this front, the bombings described earlier are the worst examples.

The majority of Argentina's Jews are quite secular—in fact, it has been argued that many of the country's Jewish immigrants were not that religious to begin with. As a result, assimilation led many to lose their active connection to religious practice. Thus, many maintain Judaism as much as an ethnic and cultural identity as a religion. Still, it is difficult not to observe Jews practicing their religion in parts of Buenos Aires, among other select areas. Literature has proven to be an important vehicle for preserving and transmitting Jewish cultural values and traditions.

Protestantism

It is widely, and incorrectly, believed that Protestantism is a relatively new phenomenon in Argentina—due at least in part to the rapid spread in recent years of various "Protestant sects," especially Pentecostalism, throughout much of Latin America. On this score, the growth of this type of Protestantism has been less significant in Argentina than in other Latin American countries. The arrival of Protestantism in Argentina dates back to the nineteenth century, corresponding to the arrival of early immigrant groups who brought with them their religions. Among the first were Scottish Presbyterians who settled near Buenos Aires in 1825. Other groups importing various Protestant denominations came from England, France, Italy, Germany, and Holland. These early groups did not attempt to proselytize, or convert people to their beliefs. Rather, they conserved their religions, which, as minority groups, aided in supporting their cultural identity.

There have been few large studies of Protestantism in Argentina; and much of what exists tends to have a bias, projecting Protestantism as a sort of "transplant" religion and Catholicism as the true religion of the land (ironic, of course, since Catholicism was transplanted to the region at an earlier date). Within South America, Protestantism has been most successful in Brazil; and here the most rapid growth has been among evangelical, and often Pentecostal, groups. As suggested, Protestantism has at times been seen as a threat to Catholicism and to the Hispanic tradition in general. Some suggest this is a continuation of the struggle that started in Europe hundreds of years ago, now playing out in Catholic Latin America whose Catholic traditions differ from Protestant cultures of the Northern Hemisphere.

One factor associated with the modern growth of Protestantism in Argentina has been the trend of migration from rural areas to urban centers—from the countryside to the cities (especially Buenos Aires). It has been suggested that Protestantism, which is structured as a community in which all participate, is at times more attractive than Catholicism, which is structured as a hierarchical institution. Furthermore, as traditional structures break down as societies modernize (rural-urban migration can be seen as one facet of this process), the switch from traditional Catholicism to Protestantism may be supported. Whatever the reasons, evangelical and Pentecostal groups are now more common. For example, the trend of movie theaters and storefronts being converted into church meeting places is widespread. Some estimates suggest that as much as one-third of regular Sunday church attendance in Buenos Aires is made up of Protestants. Among the most successful in recent years have been the Seventh-Day Adventists, the Baptists, and the Plymouth Brethren. Argentina also has been home to the so-called Billy Graham of Latin America, Luis Palau, who has built a highly successful evangelical movement.

In 1960, Protestants made up only 1.6 percent of Argentine society. By 1985, this figure grew to nearly 5 percent; and many project that by 2010, the figure could be as much as

10–15 percent of society. While the growth is considerable, the figures are still low compared with other Latin American countries. Some have argued that this is a reflection of migration patterns in Argentina—notably that migration to urban centers took place earlier in Argentina than in other countries. Another variable that is often highlighted is the ethnic nature of religion in Argentina. Whether Catholic, Protestant, or Jewish, religion is often closely tied to ethnicity in Argentina, perhaps acting as a barrier to more rapid growth of Protestant denominations.

Note that the Church of Jesus Christ of Latter-day Saints, whose members are typically called Mormons, is the most prominent Christian, non-Catholic church in Argentina. (Mormons do not consider themselves Protestant.) The growth of the Mormon faith in Argentina, as elsewhere in the world, has reflected its highly organized missionary program as well as the church's remarkable wealth. Spanish is the second most spoken language of the Mormons, followed by Portuguese, underscoring the success its missionaries have had in Latin America. Mormons have encountered some difficulties in Argentina, having been targets of both the left and the right. For example, some Argentines have accused Mormons of being spies for the CIA, while others have accused the Mormons of being compliant with Argentina's repressive military regimes. Others have considered Mormons, along with Jews and Jehovah's Witnesses, as representing a subversive threat to the nation.

ARGENTINE SPANISH

Spanish, the official language of Argentina, was brought to the country by explorers and settlers of Spain in the 1500s. At this point, nearly all Argentines speak Spanish as their first language. However, native languages such as Quechua, Guaraní, and Mapuche continue to be used in parts of the country. For the most part, European immigrants have been assimilated, and later generations speak Argentine Spanish.

Interestingly, the Spanish spoken in Argentina is quite distinct from that of Spain, as well as the Spanish of other Spanish-speaking Latin American countries. Many observers suggest that Argentine Spanish sounds a bit like Italian, a reflection of the millions of Italian immigrants who arrived in the country, adding words and pronunciations here and there as they learned the local language.

Argentines have maintained an old-fashioned piece of Spanish grammar that ended in Spain centuries ago. In Spain, people say *tú* for *you,* while in Argentina, they use *vos* in a somewhat more formal manner. Another peculiar characteristic of Argentine Spanish is the use of the word *che* (pronounced chay) in popular speech. The word is used to grab the attention of the listener—perhaps similar to *man* or *buddy* in English.

Many in Buenos Aires use words and expressions from *lunfardo,* a slang or dialect spoken only in Buenos Aires. It is said that the language developed about a century ago, perhaps first among gangsters who did not want people to understand them. Over time, the dialect gained in popularity throughout the city. Often it can be detected in the words of tango songs. The dialect is witnessing something of a revival as it regains popularity—there is even a *Lunfardo* Academy in Buenos Aires dedicated to the study of the dialect.

SOCIAL CUSTOMS IN ARGENTINA

Thus far, the chapter has discussed the various people (and historical processes) that have come together to create the modern Argentine population, underscoring in the process the main themes contributing to the national social and cultural identity. Discussion then moved on to religion in modern Argentina, identifying the country's dominant Roman Catholicism as well as significant minority religions such as Protestantism and Judaism. Finally, the chapter briefly examined the national language, Spanish. As noted, Argentina's "brand" of Spanish is unique, again reflecting the country's distinct historical tradition.

This section of the chapter on Argentine society and culture will examine a number of social customs, focusing specifically on aspects of the national identity and the Argentine personality. Discussion will then turn to a related but more specific topic of some of the unique components of the country's food and drink. The second half of the chapter will address a number of individual topics: the arts, education, and women in modern Argentina.

THE NATIONAL IDENTITY

One popular current of thinking suggests that the recent years of "neoliberal" policy have contributed to an erosion of national culture—that truly Argentine characteristics, customs, and rituals are dying out and being replaced by more global, and often American, practices. This is probably true to some degree throughout the world, a process facilitated by nearly instantaneous communication that results from cell phones, cable television, and the Internet. However, one simple visit to Argentina would illustrate the uniqueness of Argentine society and culture—underscoring various aspects of the distinct national identity, or *Argentinidad.*

In attempting to identify some of these national characteristics, this section will first turn to a few aspects of the Argentine personality. In assessing this personality, regional differences can be underscored and similarities that exist across the country can be identified. As has been discussed at length, perhaps the biggest differences that exist in terms of personality or character are those between the *porteños,* who make up roughly 40 percent of Argentina's population, and those residing in the interior, scattered among the provinces making up the rest of the Argentine territory. To a certain extent, these differing characteristics are stereotypes; but they are nonetheless instructive, since they are widely accepted by Argentines themselves.

In general terms, *porteños* are characterized—most often by those from the interior—as aggressive, high-strung, and often pretentious. Like the stereotypical American in Europe, they are also seen as loud—at times to the point of obnoxiousness. By contrast, provincials see themselves as humble, down-to-earth, and filled with common sense. *Porteños,* however, see provincials as unworldly, to the point of being ignorant and often even superstitious. (In the worst form, *porteños* even see provincials as ugly—a thinly veiled negative stereotype associated with provincial ethnicity.) *Porteños,* by contrast, see themselves as attractive, sophisticated, and cultured. Such self-awareness, often bordering on obsession, is underscored by the fact that Buenos Aires has one of the largest numbers in the world of people who have undergone plastic surgery.

Turning to national characteristics—those seen as pervasive both in the city and the countryside—many students of Argentina identify an attitude of melancholy as existing among Argentines. This sadness—many suggest even a sort of soul-searching—is unique in Latin America, which is typically seen as more upbeat. Neighbors in Brazil, for example, are considered fun-loving and-happy-go-lucky. Despite their somewhat melancholy outlook, Argentines are generally warm people, a trait immediately apparent to outsiders in the extensive physical contact that takes place

U.S. President Bill Clinton embraces Carlos Menem during the Argentine leader's visit to the White House in 1999. Argentine greetings are more intimate and physical than is customary in the United States. (Mike Holmes/Getty Images)

in greeting and saying good-bye—kissing and hugging are typical and expected. The normal level of physical contact between men can, at times, make those from more reserved cultures uncomfortable. In general, Argentine families are very important and are likely to be close-knit. Interestingly, compared to the United States, Argentine children are likely to live with their parents for a longer period of time, often well into adulthood.

Both outsiders and Argentines are likely to consider the average Argentine to be highly opinionated. In the Latin American context, Argentines are among the most politically well-informed and active. Reflecting the highly literate population and the pervasive influence of the press (when not suppressed by authoritarian government), the population is also well-informed on national and international events. Passions about politics run deep in Argentina.

In relative terms, Argentines dress more formally and stylishly when compared to the rest of South America and North America; grooming is meticulous. Argentines, especially in Buenos Aires, are quite conscious of the quality of clothing. It is often pointed out that Buenos Aires is one of the few cosmopolitan cities in the world where one still sees a pervasive use of fur coats, which are literally paraded by the elite in the high-class neighborhoods and shopping districts of the city. (The latter are often compared to Beverly Hills and Palm Beach in their opulence.) Outsiders are also struck by the attention Argentines pay to shoes—perhaps a legacy of their Italian origins and their cattle/leather history.

As discussed, the overwhelming majority of Argentines are Roman Catholic; but whether Catholic or Jewish or other, Argentina is a more secular society than is most of the rest of Latin America. Despite this fact, until fairly recently, it was mandated that the president of the country be Catholic. Divorce was not legalized until 1987, and abortion remains a hotly debated issue. While secular attitudes are pervasive, it can be argued that religiosity increases as one moves away from the metropolis of Buenos Aires; in fact, popular Catholicism also grows in importance, as does the role of religion in daily life.

As mentioned briefly, Argentina's secularism corresponds to a national obsession with Freud and psychoanalysis. As the joke goes, Argentines do not need religion since they have Freud. (Ironically, the heavy focus on Freudian psychology continues in Argentina despite the fact that the field has moved on in the rest of the world.) The importance of psychoanalysis is highlighted by the fact that there are roughly three times as many psychiatrists and psychologists per capita in Buenos Aires than in the state of New York; while this ratio might decline if one were to do the comparison with Manhattan alone, the point still stands. In the end, it is safe to say that a majority of middle-class Argentines in Buenos Aires (as well as in other large cities) have undergone psychoanalysis.

Many suggest that this near obsession with psychoanalysis, coupled with the melancholy mentioned previously, can be attributed to the existence of a national identity crisis. Ironically, this national identity crisis is often identified as an actual characteristic of Argentine national identity. In other words, the search, conflict, and debate over national identity has become an integral part of that identity. Put somewhat simplistically—and stereotypically—Argentines are not certain whether they are Latin Americans or Europeans; in fact, a common joke is that Argentines are Spaniards who speak like Italians, dress like the French, and think they are British. The country's immigrant history can clearly be heard in its spoken Spanish, not to mention its dialects, such as *lunfardo,* which can be identified in urban speech. On a more serious note, many analysts stress the fact that not only are so many Argentines of foreign origin but that for a good part of modern history, many Argentines have retained dual citizenship—both factors contributing to a confusion about national identity.

Another possible factor has been identified more recently: that the country's economic decline in recent years has contributed to the identity crisis. After displaying such promise at the turn of the twentieth century—highlighted by the triumphant centennial celebrations in 1910 and the concomitant beautification projects of Buenos Aires—the slide back into the third world has had important ramifications in self- and national analysis in Argentina. Still, whatever the reasons, Freudianism is highly popular in Argentina, which is the case regardless of class. In fact, the Peronists established state-run psychiatric clinics for the use of the working classes. However, the last military dictatorship deemed Freudianism as subversive and books were removed from libraries and university departments were closed. As one can imagine, the end of military rule saw a rapid return of psychoanalysis and its popularity.

Unfortunately, any discussion of national personality characteristics must at least mention authoritarianism. As you know from the discussion in the history chapter, Argentina has had its share of authoritarian rule. Even during apparently democratic periods, authoritarian and exclusionary tactics have, at times, been close to the surface. Most analysts point to the period inaugurated by the coup of 1930 as the beginning of authoritarian government since this was the first military government in more than 100 years of nationhood. However, disenfranchisement (class, regional, and gender) and electoral fraud were pervasive before 1930; so it is difficult to argue that liberal, representative democracy was a way of life then.

Many experts point out that authoritarianism in Argentina can be seen not only in the power the military (and other authoritarian governments) exercised in national affairs over 200 years of history but also in the degree of public support for authority and authoritarian tactics. Significantly, this can be extended from the concrete wielding of power by authoritarian government to a more symbolic sense; namely, to the wide-ranging and well-understood concept of privilege. Undoubtedly, the existence of privilege has been illuminated in periods of questioning or protest—whether protests of torture and brutality, complaints about Church complicity with military rule, regional dissatisfaction with Buenos Aires–imposed policy, or women's questioning of Argentina's patriarchal society.

One final component of national character must be included: Argentina's gaucho heritage. This text has covered extensively the divide between city and countryside, between the urban and rural, etc. It has also discussed the country's history—in particular, the disappearance of the gaucho from the countryside as Argentina slowly modernized its rural economy. Still, the countryside and the gaucho represent extremely important themes in the national identity—so much so that this chapter will return to them yet again when exploring the country's literature and art. For now, the discussion will add just a few more specifics about the gaucho and gaucho culture and what remains today.

Gauchos dressed in knee-length boots, striped cummerbunds, and berets lean against a wire fence at a rodeo in Pampas, Argentina, in 1991. (Barnabas Bosshart/Corbis)

Interestingly, to this day, a debate continues in Argentina about gauchos and their role in the country's history and culture. On the one hand, there is the argument that for the most part, the Argentine gaucho, like the American cowboy, disappeared in the late nineteenth century. In effect, as the rural economy was modernized and gauchos were stripped of their independent lifestyle, they were forced to become hired hands on the nation's large ranches.

Others argue that the gaucho lives on, with the gaucho culture surviving today in the people who remain tied to the cattle economy and horsemanship in general. Thus, the gaucho spirit lives on, in their view, despite the radical changes that have taken place in the Argentine countryside. There is probably some degree of truth in both arguments. Even if the true gaucho has disappeared from the countryside, his legacy lives on in the culture and in the day-to-day lives of Argentines, especially those who participate in the rural economy.

Remember, traditional gauchos, for the most part, were mestizo, of mixed Indian and Spanish blood. They survived on cattle and horses that had escaped from the earliest Spanish explorers and settlers and then multiplied on the pampas. The gauchos caught and tamed wild horses and then used them to pursue the wild cattle, which initially were used for hides (since there was no effective way to utilize the meat, other than for immediate consumption). These gauchos sold the hides, exchanging them for items such as tobacco, rum, and *mate;* their possessions were few in number—typically just a horse, a saddle, a poncho, and a knife. Gauchos prided themselves on their knives, not to mention their knife-fighting abilities; and over time, the gaucho knife—called a *facón*—became elaborately decorated and a symbol of craftsmanship.

The gaucho's reputation was tied, more than anything, to his horsemanship; and like the American cowboy, the gaucho and his horse were inseparable. Most of the gaucho's work was accomplished on horseback. Initially, gauchos hunted with *boleadores,* which consisted of three leather-wrapped stones or metal balls, which were attached to the ends of connected ropes. Gauchos threw the *boleadores* to trip cattle. Eventually, and not unlike the lasso and rodeo, the *boleadores* became part of organized contests. One of the most famous organized events is called a *sortija.* In this competition, the rider approaches a ring as fast as possible, using a lance to catch a ring that is dangling from a crossbar. Another competition is called a *marona,* in which a gaucho drops from the corral gate as a group of wild horses is driven beneath him; the gaucho must land on a horse's back, control the horse, and return it to the gate.

Traditional gaucho clothing is elaborate and obviously a source of pride—the main components of which are still seen today. Thus, while the traditional gaucho disappeared by the end of the nineteenth century, the culture remains in such traditions as the competitions and gaucho dress. Another obvious legacy of the gaucho is the country's love affair with red meat, which will be discussed next. A final vestige of gaucho culture is a festival called *La Rural,* which is held in Buenos Aires in July. While *La Rural* is best understood as a sort of state fair, it is held largely for Argentina's cattle-raising elite. *La Rural* is composed of livestock competitions, horsemanship competitions, artwork, and a wide array of Argentina's traditional foods.

FOOD AND DRINK

There is no doubt that upon arriving in Argentina, visitors are struck by the fact that the country's food and drink represent a unique culture. While in part a blend of national influences, like so much of Argentina, this blend has become something unique in its own right. This section will discuss a few of the highlights to give a sense of this uniqueness—yet another facet of *Argentinidad.*

One of the most salient characteristics of the country's cuisine is the love (and significant consumption) of red meat. Of course, this is a direct result of Argentina's history of the gaucho and of cattle raising. Most national dishes are based on beef; and for much of the country, beef is eaten at least once a day, often twice. Remember, much of the economic transformation of Argentina that took place in the late nineteenth and early twentieth centuries was based on beef—specifically on the development of new techniques to store, chill, and ship meat. Because of these developments, huge amounts of Argentine beef began to cross the Atlantic to Europe. Railroads were constructed to speed the cattle's trip to port. The economy boomed as a result of these developments.

Today one of the most enduring characteristics of the beef culture is the *parrillada,* or grill—a sort of afternoon barbecue cookout. The *parrillada* is a tradition on Saturday afternoons, typically attended by large extended families. Argentines are proud of the quality of their beef and the role it plays in national traditions. As an indication of the popularity of beef in Argentina (and Argentines' impressive capacity to consume beef), per capita consumption is some 220 pounds per year, compared to roughly 88 pounds in the United States.

Another ubiquitous national food is the *empanada,* which generally can be found in the Southern Cone region, with some variations existing between countries. The *empanada* is a small pastrylike food, the bread portion stuffed with items such as beef, ham and cheese, hard-boiled eggs, and vegetables. *Empanadas* are baked or fried and can be spicy or bland. They are found nearly everywhere in Argentina and are typically quite inexpensive.

There is no doubt that the Italian heritage is strong in Argentina, which can be seen quite clearly in the national cuisine. Italian food is probably the most popular "ethnic" food found in Argentina, with traditional Italian dishes seen on the menus in nearly all "Argentine" restaurants. One popular national dish is *ñoquis* (gnocci), a potato dumpling typically eaten with red or white sauce and sometimes with meatballs. *Ñoquis* can be found throughout the country and are often one of the least expensive items on restaurant menus. (Often *ñoquis* are considered a "poor man's food.") One interesting national tradition is to eat *ñoquis* on the 29th of each month. The idea is that by the end of the month, this poor man's dish is the only thing that a person can afford. In a unique twist, a peso is often left under each person's place, a sign indicating that *ñoquis* are eaten by choice rather than necessity. (The coin also is considered good luck.) Note that Argentina has a flourishing wine industry, producing many internationally recognized wines. It is no surprise that the country's fine wines are considered perfect accompaniments to both beef and Italian food.

One of the most characteristic drinks in Argentina, indeed a quintessential component of *Argentinidad,* is the nation's love affair with *mate. Mate* (pronounced mah-tay) is an herb that is made into a kind of tea (and has roughly the same amount of caffeine as coffee). The consumption of *mate* can be seen easily throughout the country, provided the visitor looks for it. Importantly, for the most part, *mate* consumption crosses both socioeconomic and ethnic distinctions in modern Argentina. *Mate* is a traditional drink that is typically associated with the gaucho, one of the country's best-known cultural symbols (and typically associated with characteristics such as strength, bravery, and independence of spirit, not unlike the cowboy or pioneer in the United States).

Four essential components are involved in the consumption of *mate.* First, a metal straw called a *bombilla,* which has a strainer on the end to prevent consumption of the leaves, is put in a hollow gourd. Likewise, there must be the *mate* leaves and hot water. In the typical ritual of *mate* consumption, the host pours hot water to fill roughly two-thirds of the gourd, adding a small amount of mate leaves and cold water and then letting the mix brew for a few minutes. The *mate* is sucked in through the *bombilla* until the brew is gone. The process is then repeated, with the gourd passed to the next person in a clockwise manner until everyone has been served. For the most part, everyone uses the same *bombilla.* Gourds range from simple hollowed-out squashes to ornate vessels crafted out of metal; both gourds and *bombillas* have become the objects of artwork in Argentina as well as in countries such as Brazil and Uruguay.

One of the most striking and unique features of the Argentine culture, intimately related to the country's tradition of food and drink, is its "café culture." In a sense, Argentines' love of cafés and the café life are important aspects of Buenos Aires's reputation as the Paris of South America. Thus, in contrast to the gaucho culture of rural Argentina, café culture is very much an urban phenomenon, intimately tied to the sophistication and cosmopolitan image of Buenos Aires.

The popularity of cafés has been tied to the nation's love of sweets, good coffee, conversation, and current events. Social life, business, and politics revolve around the numerous cafés of the capital, which are called *confiterias* (or confectionaries). Cafés can be seen throughout the city on street corners everywhere. While many cafés are fairly humble, a number are quite elegant, often retaining their turn-of-the-century charm and atmosphere. Others, by contrast, are quite modern, even utilitarian, and do a brisk midday business for lunch and coffee breaks. Originally, cafés were for men; only later did "*salons de familias*" develop to include women.

Interestingly, *porteños* display a strong loyalty for their cafés. As a result, cafés often develop a reputation based on the pursuits of their most loyal patrons. For example, cafés become known for the literary, artistic, or political pursuits of their customers. In fact, the *taller literario,* or literary workshop, has developed specifically to take place in cafés of the capital. One legacy of the strong presence of the British in Argentina (and Buenos Aires specifically) is the fact that teatime is still observed in many tea houses of the capital. Like a number of the cafés, many tea houses have retained their elegant turn- of-the-century charm. (Jorge Luis Borges, Argentina's most famous author, was a regular of the Richmond, a tearoom where one can still order tea and scones at five o'clock daily.)

ARGENTINE ARTS, LITERATURE, AND CINEMA

This section of the chapter will try to accomplish two things. First, it will take a detailed look at the arts in Argentina, focusing on art, music, literature, and film. Second, it will turn to a number of specific topics concerning modern Argentina's society and culture, including education, women, and sports. Each of these serves as a snapshot designed to give you additional perspective on the country. Argentina has had a very rich history in the arts—in many ways one of the deepest and most developed in Latin America. The country's high degree of education and literacy has no doubt played an important role in this process.

Over time, a number of themes have been established, including the struggle for nationhood (and the related dichotomy between city and countryside), the issues of immigration and urbanization, and the nation's so-called identity crisis. Likewise, authoritarian and military rule has proven an enduring theme, especially following the coup in 1976 and the repressive regime that implemented the country's dirty war. At the time, freedom of expression was severely curtailed and many artists were forced to flee the country (some in fear of their lives). As these same artists began to return following the restoration of civilian rule, the country's cultural environment received a fresh impulse of creativity. Fortunately, this environment remains vibrant today.

Art

While Argentina has been recognized internationally for its cultural achievements, visual art specifically has not been the focus of this attention (compared to literature and music, for example). This reflects the fact that Argentina has not been a major contributor to the body of Latin American visual art the way countries such as Mexico and Colombia have with artists such as Frida Kahlo, Diego Rivera, and Fernando Botero (or Brazil, for that matter, starting with the famous colonial sculptor Aleijadinho). This fact is somewhat difficult to explain, although some analysts suggest that the tremendous importance of literature in the country somehow overshadowed the importance of the visual arts. Whatever the reasons, there is an important artistic community today, not to mention an interesting history of artwork.

One key event in Argentina's art world occurred in 1895, when President José Uriburu signed a decree laying the groundwork for the *Museo Nacional de Bellas Artes* (National Museum of Fine Arts, known also as the MNBA). This important national institution was inaugurated in December 1896 and now for more than 100 years has housed the work of the country's artists, not to mention traveling international exhibits.

Art movements in Argentina have been closely associated with similar movements in other artistic fields. Perhaps the closest link has been between art and literature, although most of the main movements in visual art have been influenced by a range of fields. As will be discussed in more detail in the section on literature, two major artistic movements that emerged in the twentieth century were the Florida group and the Boedo group. For the most part, the Florida group was made up of upper-class elites and was concerned with aesthetics. The Boedo group, by contrast, was more bohemian—typically of working-class origins and more interested in social concerns. Each group included artists and authors and was particularly influential in the 1920s and 1930s.

Like the MNBA, the *Instituto di Tella,* established in 1958, had a significant impact on the art world in Argentina, corresponding to a boom in artistic activity following the downfall of Juan Domingo Perón in 1958. The *Instituto* was created by two brothers, Torcuato and Guido Di Tella, the sons of a wealthy industrialist who became an important philanthropist and patron of the arts. The institute was devoted to the promotion of the fine arts, thus focusing on theater and music. While the institute eventually went bankrupt, it was replaced by the *Centro de Arte y Comunicaciones* (Center for Art and Communications, or CAYC). The paragraphs that follow will briefly discuss a few of Argentina's most well-known artists.

Florencio Molina Campos. Florencio Molina Campos (1891–1959), well known both in Argentina and abroad, made an impact on the art world with his drawings of rural life and gauchos. Molina Campos has a reputation as one of the

An example of the work of Florencio Molina Campos. His drawings of Argentina's gauchos in their rural settings helped define the national image, leading Molina Campos to become one of the country's foremost artists in the process. (F. Molina Campos Ediciones (www.molinacampos.net) and Fundación Molina Campos (www.molinacampos.org))

country's best-known and most respected artists. Interest-ingly, his work with a well-known Argentine footwear company—specifically, the calendars he helped the company create—led his artwork into the homes of millions of Argen-tines of all social classes.

Like many of the country's well-known literary figures who utilized the theme of the gaucho, Campos's work helped transform the gaucho from something of a rogue figure into a more positive symbol, in the process contributing to the gau-cho's role as an integral component of national identity. The artist focused on the positive characteristics of the gaucho—highlighting the honor, courage, and hard work of this national icon—but he did not go so far as to exaggerate the heroic nature of the gaucho, which others have had a ten-dency to do.

In addition to his focus on the gaucho, Campos dealt with other aspects of rural life, including numerous paintings of the gaucho's companion, the horse. His paintings also depicted the landscapes of the pampas and a variety of rural scenery. In fact, many believe that no other artist in Argentina has had a more important impact on Argentina's national con-sciousness.

Xul Solar. Xul Solar, otherwise known as Oscar Alejandro Agustín Shulz Solari (1887–1963), was prominent during the first half of the twentieth century. The artist was associated with the Florida group, sometimes referred to as the *martin-fierristas* (for purposes here, a term more or less interchange-able with the Florida group). Again, the group embraced avant-garde aesthetics; often irreverent, they generally opposed what they believed were the homogenizing effects of modern culture. The group was associated with the journal *Martín Fierro,* and Solar was an important illustrator of its pages. Throughout his life, Solar was a close friend of the writer Jorge Luis Borges.

In general, Solar focused on the fast-paced urban setting of Buenos Aires. (Some argue that they can see the violent thrust of modernity in his paintings.) He is also well known for his attachment to subjects such as astrology, philosophy, world religions, and the occult. He is best known for his paintings from the 1920s and 1930s, a time of important social change—even upheaval—in Argentina. Some critics argue that his work can be interpreted as a sort of response to the debate over national culture and the issue of nationality during this tumultuous period of history.

Other well-known artists include Raquel Forner (1902–1988), Antonio Berni (1905–1981), and Luis Bendit. Berni focused on issues of social justice and was a leading figure in what came to be known as *nuevo realismo,* or *neo-realismo.* Bendit is an eclectic contemporary artist, working in painting, habitats and installations, and sculpture. Mirta Kupferminc is another well-known contemporary artist, gaining notoriety with her attention to Argentina's history of violence as well as to a number of Jewish themes. She designed a monument to the victims of the 1994 bombing of the Jewish Mutual Aid Society in Buenos Aires, located in the Plaza Lavalle in the city's downtown center. Famous photographers include Benito Panunzi, who worked in the nineteenth century and was famous for works on gaucho and indigenous groups, and Alejandro Whitcomb, who also documented nineteenth-century life.

As mentioned earlier, Argentina's experience with military rule, especially the brutal dictatorship of the *Processo,* has had a profound influence on the country's arts. Besides many artists having to leave Argentina, many focused their works on the brutality of the dictatorship and its implications to society. One interesting, albeit tragic, form of artwork associated with the dirty war was the "silhouettes," which were outlines of human bodies painted in public spaces such as streets and plazas, quite often accompanied by the name of a "disappeared" person. As a result of their locations, the paintings could not go unnoticed. These figures have become permanent in the Plaza de Mayo.

Music

Modern Argentina has a wide range of musical genres, from folk music to Spanish and Latin American music to classical and modern rock music. Folk music, which has a long history in Argentina, often represents a blend of indigenous forms of music with Spanish music. Singers in Argentina have entertained crowds for hundreds of years, both in cities and the countryside. Perhaps the most traditional figure in Argentine music was the *payador,* the folksinger of the pampas who was a key figure of the gaucho's rural landscape.

Musical instruments include both European and traditional Argentine instruments, often legacies from the indigenous heritage. The former include instruments such as the guitar, flute, and violin. The latter include the *quena,* or flute; the *charango,* a type of stringed instrument made from an armadillo's shell; the *siku,* or pan flute; and *bombos,* or drums. Folk music continues to be strong in Argentina today; famous folk musicians, many known around the world, include Mercedes Sosa and Atahualpa Yupanqui.

One of the country's most famous instruments—many would even call it the Argentine national instrument—is the *bandoneón.* The instrument is similar to a small accordion, but with buttons instead of keys for playing notes. The instrument is a key component of the tango, probably the best-known and most popular art form originating in Argentina. The tango, which will be discussed in detail below, is both a type of music and a dance form. It is so popular that many Argentines refer to the popular tango song "My Beloved Buenos Aires" as the nation's unofficial, or second, national anthem.

The tango emerged roughly between 1865 and 1895. More precisely, during this time, a number of musical traditions blended into something that would eventually become the tango. In its early stages, the tango was largely a music and dance of the urban poor—typically second-class citizens and the masses living in working-class neighborhoods. Over time, the dance caught on, moving from the lower classes to the upper classes, eventually catching on around the world.

During the 1870s, one of the most popular dances in Argentina was called the *milonga,* often referred to as "the poor man's *habanera."* The *habanera,* in turn, was a dance that originated in Cuba, but spread to places such as Spain and Argentina. The *milonga* originated as a type of song, in effect derived from the songs of the *payadores* of the pampas. As this song arrived in the city, it evolved steps of its own. Experts typically see the *milonga* as an embryonic form of the tango.

The origins of the word *tango* remain, in part, a mystery, although it most likely came from African languages or from Portuguese. The word existed (and still exists) in a number of African languages and can be found as a place name in certain African countries such as Angola and Mali. In turn, it may have been used in a form of pidgin language used by people in the slave trade—in essence, adopted by both slaves and masters. Whichever origin is correct, it seems fairly likely that the word *tango* arrived in the Western Hemisphere with the slave ships and slaves.

Interestingly, in many parts of Spanish America, the word *tango* evolved over time to mean a place where slaves and free blacks gathered to dance; in Argentina, the word then came to refer to black dances in general. Thus, the term *tango* had been used for quite some time and was common among inhabitants of nineteenth-century Buenos Aires, making its application to a new dance form relatively easy.

In its early form, the tango was simply a new way of dancing the *milonga,* with distinctive features borrowed from African-Argentine traditions. The novelty of the new form was that dancers had partners; not surprisingly, members of Argentina's more privileged classes saw this new dance form as rather lascivious, deeming the Africanized *milonga-tango* as unacceptable. This disdain was due even more so to the dance's lower-class, often delinquent origins.

Again, the origins of the tango were the fringes of Argentine society—poor barrios and questionable circumstances; often the tango was danced in brothels and in establishments that were little more than disguised brothels. Tangos were danced in *academias* (dance academies) and *peringundines,* which were a type of café where waitresses could be hired as dancers (and presumably as prostitutes). Many have pointed out that in this respect—the intimate link between the tango and the brothel—the tango can be compared to jazz that originated in New Orleans. Over time, the tango traveled to high-class bordellos and eventually into higher-class circles of society. Still, its lower-class origins cannot be denied; Leopoldo Lugones, a writer whose work will be discussed in the next section, called the tango "the reptile from the brothel."

While many have considered the dance and music to be a sort of celebration of creole culture in Argentina—even a form of protest against the waves of immigrants—the tango was embraced by Italian immigrants, who began to add accordions and mandolins. Over time, the tango became more refined: As has often been stated, improvisation declined at this point, while composition was born. Professional musicians and dancers began to appear—in fact, true tango stars began to emerge.

However, the elite of Buenos Aires continued to look down on, and even detest, the tango, in large part due to its lower-class, seedy origins. However, a tango craze swept Europe from about 1913–1914. While representing a sort of gentler form of tango, the dance swept European capitals such as London and Paris. Ironically, this overseas success immediately gave the tango credibility and respectability at home; as a result, the tango began to enter its so-called golden age. The most famous tango singer in the history of Argentina was Carlos Gardel, whose music is still famous around the world. (His death, not unlike that of Eva Perón, led to a national outpouring of emotion and mourning.) Another national great was Astor Piazolla, who combined traditional tango with jazz and other types of music.

A couple dances the tango. The dance originated in Argentina but exhibits many different cultural influences. (Corel)

The tango is, without a doubt, the best-known music and dance tradition in Argentina. Still, the country has a rich and varied tradition of folk music and folk dancing. One popular type of folk dance is called the *zamba,* in which dancers perform while holding handkerchiefs. Still, tango, which survives and even thrives to this day, must be added to the short list of truly great contributions that the Americas made to world music.

Literature

As mentioned, Argentina has an amazingly rich history of literature—indeed, one of the most important in Latin America. Argentina's Jorge Luis Borges, who will be discussed in depth below, has been called the most important Latin American writer of the twentieth century. One central theme that permeates Argentine literature is the so-called identity crisis. While the search for national identity, or *Argentinidad,* emerged as the new nation sought to define itself, the ongoing economic and political disruptions that followed also contributed to the search. As a result, many students of Argentina point out that the country's literature can be viewed as almost a social record of Argentina's attempts to come to grips with itself—both its existing culture and the events that shaped it. Given the country's extensive literary tradition, this chapter will cover literature more extensively than the other arts. The chapter will look at the country's best-known authors, in the process developing a general overview of Argentine literature.

Unlike many other countries in Spanish America, Argentina does not have a significant body of colonial literature. While countries such as Mexico and Peru developed bodies of literature from the onset of colonial times, often chronicling discovery and conquest, the peripheral nature of Argentina's territory in the empire impeded any significant literary tradition. A notable exception in the late eighteenth century was a piece entitled *El Lazarillo de Ciegos*

Caminantes, or *The Guide for Blind Wayfarers,* by Alonso Carrío, often referred to as *Concolorcorvo.* The piece describes travel from Buenos Aires to Lima, giving important details about colonial life, such as the cost of living, local customs, availability of supplies, and the like. Often the piece is categorized as Peruvian literature.

The backwater status of Argentine literature began to change as the territory changed—notably with the creation of the new viceroyalty based in Buenos Aires in 1776. However, Argentine literature did not materialize into a meaningful body of literature until the nineteenth century. At the time, writing reflected the historical circumstances of the new republic; for the most part, this work was done by politicians and statesmen—writing, in a sense, was a public forum in which political ideas could be presented and debated. The first generation of writers appeared in the late nineteenth century with the so-called Generation of 1880. This was a group of elites, typically well-known liberal leaders and public intellectuals. Its goal was to transform the nation into a European-style country. Its rejection of Hispanic traditions helped pave the way for subsequent debates about the essence of national identity.

The literary genre of modernism emerged from about 1880–1910 and is considered to be the first truly Latin American literary movement. (Those before were more appropriately offshoots of typically European movements.) Argentina was at the forefront of modernism in Latin America. Shortly after this period, between 1930 and 1950, social realism developed, in large part as a response to the perceived exaggerated artistry of modernism. This school was focused on social justice and was highly influenced by international developments such as socialism and communism. The Peronist era generated a good deal of writing in Argentina, both supporting and condemning the movement. In fact, it has been argued that only the later dictatorship of the *Processo* and the dirty war generated more writing in

Argentina. More recent literature has been influenced by trends such as globalization and neoliberalism, as well as the economic crises experienced by Argentina.

Esteban Echeverría.   Esteban Echeverría (1805–1851) was a leading Argentine statesman and a founding figure in the nation's emerging body of literature. His work was made up largely of political essays. Like most early writers, the author was a member of the elite class. He is known for two texts in particular: *La cautiva* (*The Captive*) and *El matadero* (*The Slaughterhouse*). In a sense, *La cautiva* foreshadows Domingo Faustino Sarmiento's concerns with civilization versus barbarism (discussed next), dealing with a white woman who is held captive by Indians. A "hero" is sent to her rescue; but he fails to overcome the primitive, brutal environment of the interior. Many consider *The Slaughterhouse* to be the first short story written in Latin America. (It was probably written in 1839 or 1840.) It describes the nation's circumstances under the dictator Rosas, highlighting the struggle between the barbarism of the interior and nascent civilization; the work contains a number of fairly graphic scenes of violence.

The author's work is critical of the period of Rosas-induced barbarism, setting the stage for the civilization-barbarism dichotomy to become a major theme in the country's literary history. As Echeverría dealt with the variety of tensions existing at the time—political, ethnic, etc.—he helped establish the concepts that many Argentine writers would tackle. Importantly, *The Slaughterhouse* is a strong critique of Argentina under Rosas. It also falls in line with much of the thinking of the time in identifying the constraints to progress existing in the supposedly barbaric populations and customs.

Domingo Faustino Sarmiento.   Domingo Faustino Sarmiento (1811–1888) is considered one of Argentina's founding fathers, an educator, a diplomat, a statesman, and eventually a president of the republic. Sarmiento and his work have been instrumental in laying the foundation for

Domingo Sarmiento, an influential essayist, journalist, and educator, served as president of Argentina from 1868 to 1874. During his tenure, Sarmiento made many contributions to the consolidation of the national government. (Library of Congress)

critical elements of the national character. As you know, Sarmiento, like Echeverría, was an outspoken critic of the Rosas regime, which lasted from 1835 to 1852; as a result, Sarmiento spent a good portion of this time in exile in Chile. He was an admirer of the United States, which he thought should be seen as a model for Argentina. Of course, Sarmiento's thinking has been criticized over the years, not least of which was due to his adherence to racist views of the time.

It was in Chile that Sarmiento wrote his most well-known work *Civilización i Barbarie, Vida de Juan Facundo Quiroga, Aspecto Físico, Costumbres y Hábitos de la Republica Argentina* (1845). His piece was translated into English as *Life in the Argentine Republic in the Days of Tyrants, or Civilization and Barbarism.* Known popularly as *Facundo,* the book stands as a diagnosis for the country's ills under Rosas as well as a prescription for its cure. The piece was controversial at the time of its writing, but it has become one of the most important texts in the country's history—not to mention a source of inspiration for other authors interested in national identity. One great example of this inspiration to dig down deep for the essence of *Argentinidad* can be seen in the writings of Ezequial Martínez Estrada (1895–1964), whose classics include *Radiografía de la Pampa* (*X-Ray of the Pampa,* 1933) and *La Cabeza de Golíat* (*Goliath's Head,* 1940).

Facundo is a biography of the caudillo Facundo Quiroga (1790–1835); but at the same time, it is a passionate argument against Rosas and the local political traditions he represented. In essence, Sarmiento points to the battle between civilization and barbarism as the explanation for Argentina's history of civil unrest. For Sarmiento, civilization can be equated with European culture, city life, and republican values. Barbarism, on the other hand, is synonymous with colonial and indigenous customs such as the laws of the caudillos and the practices of the gauchos. In this sense, the Rosas tyranny can be seen as a temporary victory of barbarism over the forces of civilization. The way to turn the clock forward was to bring civilization to the retrograde countryside via modernization, massive European immigration, and education of the gaucho population.

José Hernández. Perhaps the best-known opposing viewpoint was written by José Hernández (1834–1886), whom many consider to have written the definitive work of Argentine literature, the epic poem *El Gaucho Martín Fierro* (1872), which was followed by a sequel, *La Vuelta de Martín Fierro* (1879). Hernández spent much of his life, as a result of his health, on a cattle ranch managed by his father for Rosas. There the author was around gauchos and learned their ways. Like many authors of his era, he became a political figure, fighting for the Federalists against the Unitarians. Falling into disfavor with the presidency of Sarmiento, he lived for a period in exile in Uruguay.

Hernández's classic works fit into a genre of gaucho literature popular at the time in which authors used gauchos to comment about (and often satirize) contemporary political events. Hernández went a step further by creating a realistic depiction of the gauchos and their way of life. Many would say this was ironic in that his writings corresponded to the waning of the gaucho lifestyle. *Martín Fierro* rapidly became a best seller and remains one of the best-known literary works in Spanish America. It is an Argentine classic and one of the most impressive attempts to capture the national identity. While it is a romantic work, many also consider it the most successful attempt at capturing the national soul.

The first work tells of Martín Fierro and his struggles with a nation caught up in a process of rapid modernization, a society with seemingly little room for the hero and his kind of people. Fierro ultimately rejects the trappings of European civilization, choosing instead to live with the Indians; he is joined by an army sergeant who was sent to retrieve him. Together the two (and their choice to turn their backs on Buenos Aires–based society) represent a rejection of official policy and highlight the government's failure to integrate the various components of Argentine society.

This first volume is typically called the *Ida,* or departure, of the gaucho Martín Fierro. The second volume is called the *Vuelta,* or return; and to a certain degree, it underscores a change in perspective on the part of the author. The piece represents reconciliation on the part of Fierro, who becomes less rebellious and more philosophical. Fierro seems to come to terms with (and at least to partially accept) the unavoidable progress of society. In the process, the author demonstrates the decline of the gaucho and his lifestyle and transforms him into a national hero and a symbol of Argentine nationality.

Hernández's works have become Argentine classics and have been praised by some of the country's most famous authors, including Jorge Luis Borges and Leopoldo Lugones; in fact, Lugones delivered a series of lectures in 1913 on *Martín Fierro* that were later published in book form, called *El Payador.* In the nation's search for *Argentinidad,* Hernández made a tremendous contribution. However, in sharp contrast to Sarmiento's focus on Argentina's perceived backwardness and its local causes, Hernandez tried to hone in on truly Argentine characteristics using the figure of the gaucho, in the process glorifying these local characteristics.

Leopoldo Lugones.   By the turn of the century, Buenos Aires was the center of the modernist movement in Spanish South America. (Mexico City was the center in the North.) As mentioned, modernism became a truly Spanish American literary movement, in good part as a reaction to what was essentially an imported romanticism. By many accounts, Leopoldo Lugones was Argentina's greatest modernist writer, not to mention one of the top modernists in Latin America. The author gained fame in 1897 with a collection of poems called *Las Montañas del Oro* (*The Golden Mountains*), while his second book of poetry, *Los Crepúsculos del Jardín* (*Garden Twilights*), is considered one of the most important examples of Spanish American modernism. Lugones was also a writer of prose, producing the well-known *La Guerra Gaucha* (*The Gaucho War*). While Lugones is recognized as a top-notch writer, he is also known for his interest in the supernatural and mystical (not uncommon interests in turn-of-the-century Buenos Aires).

As mentioned above, Lugones published *El Payador,* a series of lectures he gave in tribute to Hernández's poem *Martín Fierro.* In the process, Lugones was participating in a nationalist response to the nation's tremendous social diversity, marked at the time by the reality that more than half of the Argentine population was of immigrant origins. For many people at the time, this social diversity was alarming— especially to the country's traditional elite. In this sense, then, Lugones was, at least in part, criticizing the nation's heterogeneity by lauding a return to the traditions of *Martín Fierro.* For Lugones, the essence of Argentina and its people lay not in the hordes of immigrants, but in the vigor of the gaucho and creole traditions.

The Florida Group and the Boedo Group.   While most of this section of the chapter is dedicated to specific Argentine authors, you will now take a look at two specific schools of literature—really, of the arts in general: the Florida group and the Boedo group. Both developed at a time of intense literary activity as well as artistic innovation in Buenos Aires. An avant-garde developed that purported to create new ways of thinking about and creating literature. Both groups pursued those same goals, although what they created differed considerably.

One group organized around a new literary journal called *Martín Fierro* and concentrated on new themes as well as new modes of literary expression. The group, which adopted an aesthetic approach to literature, included authors such as Oliverio Girondo (1891–1967), Jorge Luis Borges (1899–1986), Ricardo Güiraldes (1886–1927), and Macedonio Fernández (1874–1952). The group was associated with an upscale section of Buenos Aires, as well as with elite society and high-class culture. The group was called the Florida group, although given its close association with the literary journal, its members also were often called *martínfierristas*—the vanguard of the Buenos Aires avant-garde movement.

The other main group, the Boedo group, represented, in a sense, an opposite pole in the avant-garde movement. Its members took their name from a working-class Buenos Aires neighborhood from which some of the members came (which, in turn, was named after an important figure in Argentina's independence movement, Mariano Boedo). At a minimum, the group related more to working-class values and less to the high-society milieu of the Florida group; most came from immigrant backgrounds and experienced a very different social reality than the country's elite. The group also aimed to change literary style, but their most distinguishing feature may have been to use literature as a means to promote social change. Among the more prominent members of the Boedo group were Leónidas Barletta (1902–1975), Roberto Mariani (1892–1946), Alvaro Yunque (1889–1982), and Elías Castelnuovo (1893–1982).

In general terms, the Boedo group's literature was less refined than that of the Florida group. However, for the Boedo group, the point was in the message, which focused primarily on the lives of workers and the lower classes in general and whose working conditions were often described in detail.

Ricardo Güiraldes. Ricardo Güiraldes (1886–1927) was a member of the Argentine elite, a wealthy man who traveled the world. The author's second novel was published in 1926, and it very quickly became a classic of Argentine literature. The novel, *Don Segundo Sombra,* follows a young protagonist as he becomes an adult. Similar to *Martín Fierro,* the novel is a celebration of local culture, with numerous descriptions of ranch life, the traditions and values of the gauchos and people of the countryside, and detailed descriptions of Argentine nature.

Many experts point out that the novel reveals a good bit about Argentina in the 1920s; and like Lugones's thinly veiled disdain for Argentine heterogeneity, many see the novel as a prescription for Argentina based on elite values coming from the creole and rural past. This identity is seen as being threatened by the masses of immigrants, in effect "contaminating" the country's social identity. Most consider *Don Segundo* a fairly blatant defense of conservatism and the country's elite oligarchy, not to mention a fairly xenophobic attack on immigrants. Still, the novel was pathbreaking in its use of rural speech patterns and is considered an Argentine classic. Once again, it fits into the pattern of works attempting to isolate what is truly Argentine.

Roberto Arlt. Roberto Arlt (1900–1942) also came to prominence in the Argentina of the 1920s; he was the son of German immigrants, and his primary language was German. Arlt had very little in the way of formal education; among many jobs, he worked as a secretary to Güiraldes, who influenced Arlt considerably. Interestingly, Arlt was associated with both literary groups described previously, but he was not aligned with either. Likewise, despite his association with the wealthy Güiraldes, Arlt's life and work were separate and unique.

Arlt's first novel was called *El Juguete Rabioso* (*The Rabid Toy,* 1926). The novel describes the misery, poverty, and suffering of the poor of Buenos Aires of the time. Likewise, it instills the sense of alienation of the times, in the process incorporating speech patterns of the streets (especially *lunfardo,* described earlier). While Güiraldes's *Don Segundo* has a relatively happy ending, Arlt seems to return to *Martín Fierro's Ida* by underscoring the failure of Argentina to successfully integrate the multitude of newcomers, who suffer a life of difficulty on the margins of society. Arlt produced novels as well as short stories and plays; while his influence is considerable, many think he is underappreciated among Argentine authors.

Victoria Ocampo. Victoria Ocampo (1890–1979) was highly influential in Argentina's literary world, rather unusual for the times since she was a woman. Ocampo was born into one of Argentina's most wealthy and influential families; and over time, she became one of the most prominent women authors. She founded, edited, and financed the literary and intellectual journal *Sur,* which was published continuously from 1931 to 1970, and as such, was one of the longest-running journals in Argentina. Her journal was responsible for launching a number of the country's well-known authors. Ocampo was an outspoken opponent of Perón and Peronism; through her works, she also was an early spokesperson for feminism. At times, critics argued that her works represented the tastes and even political leanings of the oligarchy.

Interestingly, many analysts have pointed out that Ocampo, as a woman, was, in essence, the exact opposite of Eva Perón. Besides coming from a wealthy landowning family, Ocampo was well educated, multilingual, and well traveled—rather different from Evita's humble origins. Likewise, for the time, she was even considered sexually liberated. While both Ocampo and Evita were concerned with women's issues, their perspectives were opposite: Perón worked to improve labor conditions for women workers, encouraged women to become involved politically, and advanced the notion of an ideal woman as a loyal companion to her man. Conversely, Ocampo advanced the goal of women's freedom, demanding a "room of one's own" for the modern, educated Argentine woman, whom Ocampo believed was severely constrained by the country's rigid social structure. Ironically, Ocampo opposed Peronist legislation advancing women's suffrage; while her reasons were not entirely clear, her opposition may simply have reflected the legislation's Peronist origins.

Jorge Luis Borges. Without a doubt, Jorge Luis Borges (1899–1986) is the most influential and famous author in Argentine history. In fact, many would argue that Borges is the most influential figure in Latin American literature. Borges initiated a movement called ultraist, which was avant-garde and opposed to the perceived excesses of modernism. (His was an attempt to strip language down to its essentials, moving beyond forms associated with "isms.") Borges was highly recognized by the 1930s and 1940s and had become a literary icon by the 1960s. It is interesting to note that despite his successful and prolific career, not to mention the widespread recognition of his literary genius, Borges did not receive a Nobel Prize in literature; a considerable number of Argentines consider this an injustice.

Borges was at his best as a short story writer, although he wrote poetry and essays as well. Borges's stories were complex, filled with metaphor, and characterized by multiple levels of reality. Many point out that a unique characteristic of these stories was that they were open to diverse interpretations. Importantly, many also pointed out that Borges was successful in taking Argentine themes and symbols and turning them into universal concepts.

Borges did not avoid the debate on *Argentinidad,* although he addressed the issue from his own unique perspective. At the time Borges broached the subject, Perón was glorifying

An award-winning poet, essayist, short story writer, and editor, Jorge Luis Borges is best known for his early works of short fiction written in the 1930s and 1940s. (Library of Congress)

aspects of local culture; Borges took issue with the Peronist stand. In Borges's view, Argentine culture was not a single culture; in fact, it was a complex mixture of a variety of cultures. Borges used this logic to suggest that gauchos could be used to touch on universal issues—they need not be limited to purely local, often nationalist concepts of tradition and culture. Borges was unique in that he could portray his country's distinctive culture, but at the same time apply it to the world as a whole.

Due to his aversion to Peronism, Borges presented something of a conundrum for a number of socially committed Argentines. Borges went as far as arguing that civilization had to be defended against the primitive forces of the "dictator." The fact that this attack was, at times, expressed in elitist terms was problematic for many Argentines, who saw Peronism as a benefit for neglected sectors of society. By the 1960s and 1970s, many thought Borges was a reactionary, as he had no qualms in opposing the Cuban revolution at a time when nearly all Latin American intellectuals supported it.

Julio Cortázar. Julio Cortázar (1914–1984) is the second leading figure of Argentine literature, no small feat given the international stature of Borges and the depth of the country's literary tradition. Like Borges, Cortázar's failure to win a Nobel Prize has been a disappointment to many Argentines. Cortázar wrote a number of novels, as well as short stories, essays, and poetry (as well as a few works of prose that defy classification). The author was a master with short stories and was particularly gifted in the realm of the fantastic. He was also a somewhat controversial public figure and maintained a high profile in domestic and international affairs. Like Borges, Cortázar was disgusted by Peronism; and he left the country for good in 1951, living the rest of his life in Paris. He did maintain close contact with other Argentine writers.

Cortázar, despite being somewhat overshadowed by Borges, rose to international fame as one of the so-called boom authors of Latin America, a group that included Gabriel García Marquez of Colombia, Mario Vargas Llosa of Peru, Carlos Fuentes of Mexico, and José Donoso of Chile. Cortázar's best-known novel *Rayuela* (*Hopscotch,* 1963) is considered a major work in Latin America's new narrative; and many consider it second only to García Marquez's novel *One Hundred Years of Solitude.* The novel requires the active involvement of the reader, who must piece together the various episodes of the novel, which bounce back and forth between Buenos Aires and Paris. The novel contains no real plot—the main character seems on a slow search for the meaning of life. Many of Cortázar's short stories enter the realm of the fantastic, and the author was significantly influenced by Edgar Allen Poe.

As suggested, Cortázar was no stranger to politics, taking aim in particular at the excesses of Peronism; his feeling of asphyxiation ultimately caused him to leave the country. Also as suggested, he was somewhat overshadowed by both Borges and *Sur,* Ocampo's literary magazine. It was only relatively late in his life that Cortázar's genius was discovered. Interestingly, Cortázar, unlike Borges, also became increasingly radical later in his life, supporting leftist causes such as the Sandinistas in

Nicaragua. Cortázar believed that reading could be a revolutionary activity—while many read to escape, at least some readers change due to their reading.

Manuel Puig.   The post-boom era of Latin American literature witnessed the rise of Manuel Puig (1932–1990). Although Puig wrote at about the same time as the boom authors, he did not receive much recognition until the boom had faded. Puig was unique in one key aspect: He was very interested in cinema as an art form, which came through in his literary work. His first novel was *La Traición de Rita Hayworth* (*Betrayed by Rita Hayworth,* 1968), which was a hit and a critically acclaimed novel. In addition to his fascination with cinema, Puig successfully integrated popular culture (tango, telenovelas, etc.) into his work—many would argue that the author was able to blur the line between "serious art" and mass culture.

Puig's best-known work was his 1976 novel *El Beso de la Mujer Araña* (*The Kiss of the Spider Woman*), which was made into a highly successful movie. The book deals with official repression—not just political repression, but aspects of social and sexual repression as well. One of the main characters of the book is a homosexual who is detained for contributing to the "corruption of minors."

To conclude this section on Argentina's strong literary tradition, it must be mentioned that only a small number of the country's authors were discussed, although for the most part, these men and women have been the most famous and influential. (One additional author worth exploring is Ernesto Sábato, who wrote *El Túnel,* or *The Tunnel,* among other works). Unfortunately, space considerations also prevent an exploration of the country's contemporary authors—despite the fact that a few of them might well become Argentina's next Borges or Cortázar. If you are interested in further exploration, a few contemporary names to consider include Alejandra Pizarnik, Marta Lynch, Enrique Medina, Luisa Valenzuela, and Ricardo Piglia.

Cinema

Argentina is one of the most important filmmaking countries in Latin America—along with Brazil and Mexico. Given solid channels for domestic and international distribution, the country has made major contributions to the region's film industry. Many point out, however, that political instability (most notably the country's various episodes of authoritarian rule) have taken a toll on output. In turn, the last decade or so of relative openness, corresponding to so-called neoliberal economic policies, also impacted the domestic film industry. Most importantly, the widespread importation of Hollywood films has affected demand for domestically produced films. Despite this fact, there is still notable domestic demand for locally produced films—perhaps more so now that such films also can be seen on television.

While a detailed discussion of the history of Argentine film is beyond the scope of this introductory chapter, note that Argentina had a so-called golden age of film from the 1930s to the 1950s, which included a wide variety of genres. Perhaps the most famous Argentine filmmaker was Leopoldo Torre Nilsson, who emerged in the 1940s. His film, *La Casa del Ángel* (The house of the angel 1957) is one of the most internationally viewed Argentine films.

The menu of Argentine films available for English-speaking audiences is fairly limited, but a few high-quality films can be found easily. One of the most well-known of these is *La Historia Oficial* (The official story). The film won the Oscar in 1986 for the best foreign film; it was directed by Luis Puenzo and based on a script by Aída Bortnik. Importantly, the film is a leader in the process of redemocratization, in which Argentines take a closer look at what happened during the dark days of the military regime; it is significant that some of the film's actors were persecuted during this period.

The film focuses on a family preparing to celebrate the birthday of their adopted daughter. The mother becomes increasingly interested in exploring the origins of her daughter, mainly because it is somewhat unusual in Argentina to find a candidate from the same social class. As the mother's interest heightens, the father/husband becomes increasingly violent; his likely corrupt business interests also are taking a turn for the worse with the implosion of the military regime. The mother eventually discovers that the child was taken from a young woman who was arrested for alleged terrorism—as occurred during the dirty war, the woman was executed after giving birth and the child taken and put up for adoption. Often such children were given to officials and their political supporters. The film ends with confrontation between the likely biological grandmother, the adoptive mother and the adoptive father, and then between the parents. The film leaves open the fate of the girl—entirely fitting since this often is the case in real life, in which cases are pending for years.

Another important Argentine film is María Luisa Bemberg's *Camila* (1984). After *The Official Story, Camila* is considered to be the second most well-known film from Argentina. Likewise, Bemberg has emerged as an important feminist director, despite her death in 1994.

The film is based on the true story of Camila O'Gorman, who in 1848 was executed along with her lover, a priest named Ladislao Gutiérrez. Camila, twenty years old, was pregnant and the daughter of an important backer of the dictator Rosas. She seduced the priest and then convinced him to flee with her to continue their love affair out of the reach of Rosas and his men. However, the lovers were found, captured, and returned to Buenos Aires, where they were executed together, despite the fact that this violated the law (and Catholic custom) due to Camila's pregnancy. Camila entered national legend after her execution as a symbol of the forces of barbarism, which many argue can be applied today to more modern Argentine experiments in authoritarianism, militarism, and neofascism.

The film is a historical narrative; it provides an effective re-creation of life in Buenos Aires at the time. While there is no suggestion that the film should signify other periods in the country's history, many have come to see it that way nonetheless. Many have suggested that the film underscores the Catholic Church's complicity with the country's episodes of tyranny, as it does in the film when the Church agrees to Camila's execution despite her pregnancy.

To conclude, filmmaking is an important art in contemporary Argentina; mentioning these two important films available with English subtitles barely scratches the surface. Those readers who are fluent in Spanish might want to explore films by Jorge Polaco and Eliso Subiela, two important contemporary Argentine filmmakers.

Print Media and Broadcasting

Like the discussion of film, the examination of print media and broadcasting will be brief, an attempt simply to introduce this interesting contemporary subject. Like other countries around the world, print media and broadcasting represent important components of modern Argentine life.

As is apparent from the longer discussion of Argentine literature, Argentina is a highly literate society and interest in contemporary affairs is significant. As a result, the so-called print media have played an important role in Argentine life. As noted, "café society" is highly developed in the country, providing another impetus for the purchase and consumption of newspapers and magazines. Argentina's first newspaper is thought to have begun in Buenos Aires in 1810 with the launching of *La Gazeta de Buenos Ayres*. It was founded by Mariano Moreno, who argued that newspapers could provide an important vehicle to transmit the ideals embodied in independence, freedom, and equality.

In the few short years following the first paper, several papers were founded. Early on, papers tended to be tied primarily to politics, often tied to a particular interest. In fact, until 1867, journalists were often regarded as politicians, when *La Capital* was founded in the city of Rosario, covering daily news and a number of general interest topics. By the late 1800s, papers developed that were devoted to humor; *Caras y Caretas* became an important magazine, focusing on humor, art, literature, and current events. Published in the so-called *belle époque,* it was here that Argentines first began to talk of Buenos Aires as the Paris of South America.

As suggested, the country's emphasis on education—and its resulting high level of literacy—was a great support for the print media. It is estimated that by 1926, Argentines consumed some 66 percent of the newspapers circulated in South America. Newspapers played an important role in the country's affairs, with editors, journalists, and the like often directly involved in these events. Many observers suggest that the newspaper *La Critica* helped topple the regime of Hipólito Yrigoyen in 1930.

By the 1930s, magazines began to focus on the country's emerging radio, film, and theater stars. Likewise, the literary and intellectual journal *Sur* began publication under the direction of Victoria Ocampo. While the 1940s saw the publication of one of the country's most important newspapers, *Clarín,* it also saw the rise of Perón, who began to suspend publication of papers critical of the regime; by the time Perón was toppled, the Peronist government controlled a significant portion of the media. Unfortunately, this corresponded to a large increase in newspaper self-censorship as publications attempted to avoid crossing the official line. Not surprisingly, the quality of analysis dropped precipitously. Most experts contend that Perón's departure did little to improve the environment; censorship continued and publications were often shut down due to their content.

In 1962, the magazine *Primera Plana* was launched as a sort of Argentine *Time* magazine, acquiring a good deal of influence in the country over time. One addition to the magazine

Argentine artist Joaquín (Quino) Lavado's comic strip Mafalda *features the commentary of an eight-year-old girl. This strip translates to: 1. Look, that's the world. You see? 2. You know why this world is lovely? 3. 'Cause it's only a model. The real one's a disaster! (© 2008, Joaquín S. Lavado (Quino)/Caminito S.a.s.)*

was a cartoon created by Joaquín Lavado, nicknamed Quino, called *Mafalda.* The cartoon centered on a precocious eight-year-old of the same name who vocalized the views of many Argentines on politics and society. The cartoon was highly popular and commercially successful, often disseminated around the world. Ironically, the cartoon was criticized by both the left and the right, a telling episode about the country's struggle for tolerance and free exchange of ideas. Lavado stopped producing the cartoon in 1973.

The 1970s were a time of severe political instability, with guerrilla activity, the return of Perón, his death, the chaos of Isabel Perón, and ultimately a military government. During these tumultuous years, one important journalist emerged: Jacobo Timerman. He was affiliated with *Primera Plana* and another journal called *Confirmado.* Later, in 1971, Timerman founded *La Opinión,* a newspaper many considered to be his finest. The paper was modeled after France's journal *Le Monde*, covering a limited number of important items in significant detail.

The country's political turmoil took its toll on the media, with kidnappings and murders of many journalists. A climate of fear was pervasive, and censorship increased—prison was a real threat to journalists crossing the line, and many journalists fled the country altogether. (Tomás Eloy Martínez, one of Argentina's best-known and well-respected journalists, was one.)

As you know from the history chapter, a coup occurred on March 24, 1974, in which the generals launched the Process of National Reorganization, often called the *Processo*. The dictatorship proved quite difficult for the press, with newspapers and magazines informed of the new order and what would be expected of them. While every article was to have been reviewed by the military for approval (with imprisonment a real threat), self-censorship quickly ensued.

Initially, the arrival of the generals was a relief to a good portion of the population, a reflection of the violence and sense of anarchy that preceded them. However, few expected what followed—as freedoms were taken away and state-directed violence and repression mounted. One of the first journalists to defy the military was Rodolfo Walsh, who published an open letter to the junta; he was eventually tortured and murdered. Jacobo Timerman was imprisoned and tortured; while his citizenship was revoked, he was somehow spared execution, although the circumstances surrounding his "luck" were not clear. Timerman was forced to leave the country.

Information surrounding the 1982 Falklands War was tightly controlled. Papers and magazines were not allowed to suggest that Argentina was losing badly; in fact, they could not even report the eventual defeat. However, more than any single fact, the rapid and humiliating defeat contributed to the downfall of the regime. Unfortunately, the country's print media was effectively in tatters by this point. Still, the press made a rapid comeback with a number of new publications founded after the 1983 return to civilian democratic rule (for example, *Página/12*). The country's print media is now thriving despite the economic crises; at this point, many of the country's important newspapers and magazines can be found on the Internet (while Argentines also can access the international media).

Argentine radio was born on August 27, 1920, with a concert of Richard Wagner's *Parsifal;* rapid growth quickly ensued. By the 1930s, a number of programs had begun, with the cliff-hanger gaining importance. *Radio El Mundo* started in 1935, ushering in what many call the golden age of radio in the country. Radio played a very important role following the deaths of Eva Perón and Carlos Gardel. (No tango songs were played for an entire week following Gardel's death, a way of mourning the country's loss.) Following Evita's death in 1952, radios played solemn music and occasional readings from Eva Perón's autobiography. Radio, like the print media, experienced censorship during Perón's reign.

One of the most popular radio programs in the country's history was *Los Pérez García*—a show about a family to which most Argentines could relate. Quiz shows and soap operas became popular in the 1940s. Even through the 1950s, radio continued to be the most popular medium; television was introduced in 1951, although only one channel was available to begin with. Only in the 1960s did television begin to threaten radio's dominance. During the 1960s, the state controlled a television channel, although several private channels were launched. By this time, many popular radio programs were turned into television shows.

The 1966 World Cup soccer tournament was the last match to which the majority of Argentines would listen by radio—by the next tournament, the games were broadcast live by television. The 1960s are typically considered the golden age of television in Argentina; the country received many of its programs from the United States, but it also produced a considerable number of its own. Both radio and television suffered after the 1974 military coup. Strangely, even Carlos Gardel was deemed unacceptable for a time. (It was later discovered that this was due to the fact that a navy captain's wife did not like his music.) Television seemed limited to innocuous subjects such as soccer and tourism shows.

As with the print media, the ability to cover the Falklands War was severely curtailed in radio and TV. In fact, the media helped generate a sense of euphoria surrounding the conflict, however misguided this turned out to be. The media were forced to portray heroic accounts of battles, portraying Argentines as the brave victors. (Opinions unfavorable to the military were forbidden.) The result was unfortunate for the media because when the truth was finally known, there was a generalized loss of confidence in the media's credibility. TV viewing audiences dropped at the time.

Fortunately, the return to democracy saw a revival in the media with a considerable amount of new and creative programming. By the turn of the twentieth century, the average Argentine household had several radios and a majority of the population had televisions. Cable television also had arrived in the country, dramatically increasing the quantity of programming—domestic and international—available to the population.

SELECTED THEMES OF MODERN ARGENTINE LIFE

This section will look briefly at a number of diverse aspects of Argentine daily life. Perhaps less academic than issues such as economic development and political institutions, these issues are important and can serve as interesting snapshots of the daily lives of Argentines. This section will examine poor barrios, sports, important holidays, women, and education.

Poverty and Slums

Poverty, and the poor living conditions that come with it, has been common in the historical development of Argentina. However, Argentina has been a leader in Latin America in a number of social indicators, including education levels

Slum neighborhood of Buenos Aires in June 2000. (Michael Brennan/Corbis)

and per capita income. Likewise, inequalities of income and wealth distribution have been far less pronounced than in neighboring countries such as Brazil. Still, poverty and inequality are important issues, worsened considerably by the most recent economic crisis.

Conditions of poverty in rural areas have been a key driver of migration to the city, despite difficult conditions in urban slums. (Indeed, this is the case for Latin America as a whole, where rural-urban migration and urbanization have accompanied the general process of industrialization.)

For these rural poor, slums were a necessary evil to be endured until they could move on to better areas. One of the most visible aspects of poverty in all of Latin America is the *villa miseria,* or misery village (also called *villas de emergencia,* emergency village). Note that the most common word for these villages of poverty is *favela,* which comes from Brazil, whose infamous shanty towns ring its major cities.

From the 1930s and 1940s, the increasing industrialization of Argentina has been accompanied by a dramatic growth in urban populations and, not surprisingly, by the numbers of poor living in urban areas. As many observers of Argentina point out, slums have been symbols of both hope and fear—hope for a better life in the city, but also fear of continuing poverty. Over time, slums in Argentina have been used as symbols in political life. For example, slums have been seen as evidence of the failure of Peronist policies in the 1950s and as breeding grounds for revolutionary activity in the 1970s. The military dictators, in turn, identified the nation's multitude of urban slums as obstacles to growth and development.

Unfortunately for many, the economic crises that Argentina has endured in the last couple of decades have impeded the move to better living conditions. In fact, for many, Argentine slums have become permanent locations of misery. One of the oldest and largest slums in Buenos Aires is called, ironically, *Villa Paradíso* (Paradise Village). Residents endure not only conditions of poverty but also a lack of security and prevalent violent crime.

Sports

There is no question that soccer is the national sport of Argentina, as it is for most of Latin America. (Baseball may come in a close second in some countries of the Caribbean basin.) Like the consumption of *mate,* the love of soccer in Argentina crosses traditional categories of class, wealth, and status. In essence, nearly everyone in Argentina watches soccer. Fans of winning teams in Buenos Aires often gather to celebrate their victory at the Obelisk, the city's most prominent monument. Sunday afternoons see men gathering throughout the country to play soccer, while children do the same. While this might be stretching the point, some observers have noted that Argentines get an extra sense of pleasure from watching a game in which the rules are followed and in which infractions are penalized. According to these commentators, this represents a welcome change from the realities of daily life.

Soccer was introduced to Argentina in the 1860s by British sailors who played the game to pass the time when their ships were docked. By 1891, the British community had organized the first official game; and by the turn of the century, the game had caught on and a domestic league was set up. Argentina's first World Cup was played in Uruguay in 1930—the country came in second to the host country. The game became the national sport in 1931.

Currently, the country's two most popular teams are the River Plate and Boca Juniors; most Argentines favor one team or the other. Perhaps the most popular player in Argentina is Diego Maradona (who at times has been called the greatest player ever, although conventionally this honor is given to Pelé from Brazil).

While soccer is tremendously popular in Argentina, its top players often head to Europe to play during their peak years. This is a simple reflection of the huge pay packages they receive in wealthier countries. Argentina has won the World Cup twice—in 1978 and in 1986—and is typically seen as a top contender in this popular global competition.

Argentina has another game that is less popular than soccer but was developed locally rather than imported. The game, called *pato* (duck), developed in the countryside; many characterize the game as a sort of cross between basketball and polo. (Polo also is relatively popular in Argentina, largely among the wealthy elite.) One can find references to *pato* that date as far back as the seventeenth century. Originally played with a live duck in a basket, teams competed to get the duck back to their settlement. Somewhat dangerous (especially for the duck), the game was banned in 1822. It was then resurrected in 1937 in a tribute to local tradition, although the game now utilizes a ball as opposed to a live duck.

Holidays

Given the nation's Roman Catholic heritage, it is no surprise that many of Argentina's most important holidays are both religious and Catholic holidays. However, there are a number of national holidays, typically celebrating important historical events, as well as a number of smaller regional holidays and festivals. Carnival is an important celebration, a pre-Lenten celebration seen in many Roman Catholic countries. (Well-known Carnival celebrations include the elaborate festivities in neighboring Brazil, as well as Mardi Gras in New Orleans.) Celebrated in February or March, the period is typically one of fasting and sacrifice leading up to Easter. The Carnival celebration is known for its abundant food, music, and costumed parades.

Christmas is another major nationwide holiday. Despite the fact that it takes place in Argentina's summer and the country's location in the Southern Hemisphere, Argentines put up Christmas trees, send greeting cards, and wait for Santa Claus, known in Argentina as Papá Noel. As in many Catholic countries, Christmas in Argentina lasts for two weeks, beginning with Christmas Eve. The Day of the Kings takes place on January 6, honoring the New Testament story of the three kings (or wise men) who visit the infant Jesus. In Argentina, children leave their best shoes outside the front door (or on their windowsills) before going to bed, along with cookies for the kings and water for the camels. The kings visit and leave small gifts in the waiting shoes.

As for nonreligious holidays, May 25 marks the celebration of the Anniversary of the Revolution in Argentina, the day in 1810 when Argentines began their battle for freedom from Spanish rule. July 9, in turn, marks the anniversary of the country's full independence from Spain in 1816. Both anniversaries are national holidays, replete with parades, political speeches, and a day off from work. As mentioned, more regional festivals are celebrated throughout the country, often reflecting the various immigrant communities that have contributed to the country's makeup. One example is the *eistedfodds,* a traditional festival of Welsh music, dancing, singing, and storytelling. The tradition reflects the Welsh and British settlers that immigrated to Argentina about a century ago.

Finally, it is interesting to note what many observers have identified as Argentina's odd obsession with death. Notably, Argentines honor many of their heroes not on the day of their birth, but on the day of their death. Flag Day, for example, celebrates the day of Manuel Belgrano's death; Belgrano designed the Argentine flag and is a national hero. Many suggest that Buenos Aires's Recoleta cemetery highlights this obsession, as the country's wealthy and famous dead are housed in elaborate, often ornate family mausoleums, each with a unique architectural style. Famous dead in the Recoleta include Eva Perón and Carlos Gardel.

Women in Argentina

Without question, Argentina has been characterized as a patriarchal society, a country in which not only wealth and status but also sex determine power. Interestingly, two of the films discussed in this chapter, *Camila* and *The Official Story,* present unique angles on Argentine culture by shedding light on this particular aspect of society. *Camila* is persecuted during the male-dominated terror of the Rosas regime, which, among other things, built its legitimacy on themes such as the return to authentic Hispanic/Argentine values and the defense of the family and moral principles. The dictators' hired guns enforced this vision of society, including the execution of the young, pregnant Camila. One interesting angle in the film is the father's attempts to force his rebellious daughter to conform to existing rules—attempts that obviously fail. Many feminists would argue that the film provides an interesting window into the origins of "patriarchal authoritarianism" in the early days of the nation.

The Official Story provides a more modern angle on the struggle of women in Argentina through the realistic story taking place at the end of the last and most brutal military regime. While the most obvious aspect of the film is its depiction of the dictatorship's brutality and inhumanity, the film provides another window on the struggles of women in Argentina. The husband's response to his wife's questioning about the origins of their adopted daughter not only is harsh but also ends in open physical abuse. Again, while the film provides a unique view of these difficult times in the country, it also underscores the difficulties that the women of Argentina faced.

Probably the best-known Argentine woman to address feminist issues specifically was Victoria Ocampo, discussed in this chapter's section on literature. Ocampo, a member of the Argentine elite, demanded better treatment of the country's educated and ambitious women, who she believed were overly constrained by the country's Victorian mores and rigid family customs. Importantly, Ocampo argued that the twentieth century was not merely the century of recognizing the rights of the worker, but also the century of the emancipation of women—she believed women needed to be treated equally and should be treated as people, not objects.

Eva Perón, more well-known and loved than Ocampo, represents an entirely different angle on Argentine women and their struggles. Eva Perón worked to improve the labor conditions that female workers encountered and encouraged women to become active in politics through voting and party work. However, Perón, unlike Ocampo, also advanced an image of the ideal Argentine woman as a sort of loyal companion, one who would stand by her man. While Ocampo may have been more consistent in her attempts to advance feminist thinking, Evita ultimately became a larger-than-life figure, to the extent that many refer to the cult of Eva Perón and call her Santa Evita. In this sense, Eva Perón not only became the essence of Argentine womanhood but also acquired status

Argentine literary figure Victoria Ocampo, ca. 1943. (Bettmann/ Corbis)

as a religious-political icon that continues to be an essential part of Argentine identity.

To conclude, by the 1970s, groups of educated, typically middle-class women who were identified as feminists began to be seen and recognized in the public eye. Early efforts in the 1970s focused on issues that would unite women with a common identity (more contemporary feminists seem to recognize their own diversity), but at least they now receive considerable attention from state and party organizations. Among contemporary topics being examined by feminists are the meaning of being a woman and the role of the state in sexual politics.

Education

Argentina has one of the most highly educated populations in Latin America, a function of what is arguably one of the region's best education systems. By many estimates, over 95 percent of the population is literate, well above the region's average and nearly equivalent to universal literacy. As you will see, Argentina has long held public education in high esteem; and before the creation of public education, religious education through the Catholic Church was quite important. Thus, while the country faces a number of problems that many developing countries encounter (resource constraints reflecting government budget difficulties, for example), it has still made great strides in creating and maintaining a highly educated population.

Historically, the Catholic Church was in charge of education in Argentina, as was the case for most of Argentina's Latin American neighbors. The University of Córdoba, the oldest university in the country, was founded in 1613. During the colonial era, Córdoba far surpassed other areas of the country as the center of higher education. The church maintained control over education until 1816. Many point out that the country had no effective national educational plan until the second half of the nineteenth century. Still, the country's largest university, the University of Buenos Aires, was founded in 1821 as part of a greater national project launched by Bernardo Rivadavia. One of the first important national educational laws to be enacted came in 1884 during the administration of Julio Roca, Law 1420 of Common Education. This law established compulsory, free, secular education. Reflecting ongoing church-state tensions, the law, which removed the church from the public schools and increased government control in the school system, was initially resisted by local clergy and the Vatican.

Probably the single most important historical figure in Argentine education was national hero and president Domingo Faustino Sarmiento. It is often pointed out that Sarmiento left the country with a "triple legacy" of education that was lay, free, and mandatory (at least through primary school). Remember, Sarmiento lived in exile in Chile during the reign of the dictator Rosas and wrote one of the country's most famous books. Commonly called *Facundo,* the book was a thinly veiled critique of the barbarism he believed held sway in his country. Sarmiento argued that this barbarism was a holdover from the early Spanish influence in his country and was particularly prevalent in rural areas. For Sarmiento, the answer to the country's problems was "civilization"—to him, an enlightened European, non-Mediterranean tradition for the country. Sarmiento pushed for immigration and universal education (and the advancement of science in general) to foster the country's modernization. In the process, he advocated the building of schools and libraries; Teacher's Day on September 11 in Argentina commemorates Sarmiento's death.

Interestingly, Sarmiento's focus on the battle between civilization and barbarism can be seen as a battle between imported and domestic culture, a battle that has raged throughout the country's modern history. As was discussed, Sarmiento argued for the value of imported culture and the importance of more "civilized" urban areas such as Buenos Aires. Alternatively, tracts such as José Hernandez's *Martin Fierro* lauded the country's unique, more indigenous culture, extolling the virtues of the gaucho and Argentina's rural traditions. Ironically, the fact that this battle has taken place in a literary context, playing out in some of the country's best-known literary works, underscores the importance that education and culture have assumed over time.

The first system of national schools was put in place during the 1870s and was quickly followed by the legislation of the 1880s, which established mandatory, free, secular education. The provision of basic education was greatly aided by massive immigration, since immigrants were, for the most part, literate. The educational system played an extremely important role in establishing and cementing a national identity. As in the United States, public education in Argentina emphasized the key events in the nation's history and its national heroes.

In practical terms, education in Argentina is divided into three periods. The first is typically made up of grades one through nine and is called Basic General Education. (Kindergarten is optional.) This is the mandatory period, and it is followed by an optional secondary education lasting two to three additional years. Called polymodal, this second level allows students to choose an orientation. While not obligatory, this level is required for a person to enter university. (Note that there are some variations on the exact lengths of primary and secondary educations.) The third stage of education is the college level. In December 2006, Argentina's congress approved a new national education law making secondary education obligatory and increasing the length of mandatory schooling to thirteen years; the law is likely to be implemented gradually. Argentina has an abundance of free public universities throughout the country. It also has a considerable number of private institutions, both religious and secular; however, many of these schools are expensive and limited to more affluent students.

Clearly, this section can only begin to cover the topic of education in Argentina. More than anything, the content is meant to introduce a few key themes. For example, by Latin American standards, Argentina has one of the region's best systems of education and one of the most educated and literate of societies. This is hard to miss when visiting the country and its major cities. However, another theme is the fact that the educational system, as in most other countries of the world, suffers from budgetary problems; but in Argentina, this has been exacerbated by periods of political and economic instability. The years of military dictatorship were particularly hard on the country's universities as military leaders resorted to censorship and propaganda (as did Juan Domingo Perón). Fortunately, the transition to democracy has put an end to many of these problems. Likewise, some complain that the country's educational system favors the coast and urban areas; in this sense, interior provinces are seen to suffer. Finally, like many countries in Latin America, the public schools have suffered problems related to demonstrations and strikes; while important, these probably pale in comparison to the damage done to schools and learning by dictatorship. In the end, it is difficult to be overly critical of Argentina's educational system, especially considering its successes in light of historical events. In short, despite economic and political instability characterized by frequent regime change, hyperinflation, and economic collapse, the country continues to have one of the best-educated populations in Latin America. This must be recognized as quite an achievement.

References

Andrews, George Reid. *The Afro-Argentines of Buenos Aires, 1800–1900.* Madison: University of Wisconsin Press, 1980.

Baily, Samuel L. *Immigrants in the Lands of Promise.* Ithaca, NY: Cornell University Press, 1999.

Bayón, Damián. "Latin American Art Since c.1920," in Leslie Bethell (ed.), *The Cambridge History of Latin America, Vol. X.* Cambridge: Cambridge University Press, 1995: 393–454.

Carlson, Marifran. *Femenismo! The Woman's Movement in Argentina from its Beginnings to Eva Perón.* Chicago: Academy, 1988.

Collier, Simon. *The Life, Music, and Times of Carlos Gardel.* Pittsburgh: University of Pittsburgh Press, 1986.

Cubitt, Tessa. *Latin American Society.* Essex, England: Longman Group UK Limited, 1988.

Elliot, David. *Art from Argentina.* Oxford: Museum of Modern Art, 1994.

Fisher, Jo. *Mothers of the Disappeared.* London: Zed, 1989.

Foster, David William. *Contemporary Argentine Cinema.* Columbia: University of Missouri Press, 1992.

Foster, David William, Melissa Fitch Lockhart, and Darrell B. Lockhart. *Culture and Customs of Argentina.* Westport, CT.: Greenwood Press, 1998.

King, John. "Latin American Cinema," in Leslie Bethell (ed.), *The Cambridge History of Latin America, Vol. X.* Cambridge: Cambridge University Press, 1995: 455–518.

King, John, ed. *On Modern Latin American Fiction.* New York: The Noonday Press, 1987.

Lafaye, Jacques. "Literature and Intellectual Life in Colonial Spanish America," in Leslie Bethell (ed.), *The Cambridge History of Latin America, Vol. II.* Cambridge: Cambridge University Press, 1984: 663–704.

Lynch, John. "The Literature, Music and Art of Latin America, 1870–1930," in Leslie Bethell (ed.), *The Cambridge History of Latin America, Vol. IV.* Cambridge: Cambridge University Press, 1986: 443–526.

Martin, Gerald. "Latin American Narrative Since c.1920," in Leslie Bethell (ed.), *The Cambridge History of Latin America, Vol. X.* Cambridge: Cambridge University Press, 1995: 129–222.

Morse, Richard M. "The Multiverse of Latin American Identity, c. 1920–c.1970," in Leslie Bethell (ed.), *The Cambridge History of Latin America, Vol. X.* Cambridge: Cambridge University Press, 1995: 1–128.

Nouzeilles, Gabriela, and Graciela Montaldo, eds. *The Argentina Reader: History, Culture and Politics.* Durham, NC: Duke University Press, 2002.

Sawers, Larry. *The Other Argentina: The Interior and National Development.* Boulder, CO: Westview Press, 1996.

Scobie, James R. *Argentina: A City and a Nation,* 2nd ed. New York: Oxford University Press, 1971.

Shumway, Nicholas. *The Invention of Argentina.* Berkeley: University of California Press, 1991.

Skidmore, Thomas E., and Peter H. Smith. *Modern Latin America,* 5th ed. Oxford: Oxford University Press, 2001.

Taylor, Diana. *Disappearing Acts: Spectacles of Gender and Nationalism in Argentina's "Dirty War."* Durham, NC: Duke University Press, 1997.

PART TWO
REFERENCE SECTION

Key Events in Argentine History

1492	Christopher Columbus reaches the New World, arriving at the islands of the Caribbean. Estimates suggest that at the time, some 900,000 indigenous people inhabited the territory of today's Argentina.
1493	The Incas integrate the people of Northwest Argentina into their extensive empire; the indigenous groups of the plains remain independent.
1516	Under the command of Juan Díaz de Solís, an expedition of Spanish explorers arrives at the Rio de la Plata estuary. The expedition claims the territory in the name of the Spanish Crown. Díaz de Solís is killed and supposedly cannibalized by hostile indigenous groups. (Some argue that Díaz de Solís was the victim of a mutiny, with the story of murder and cannibalization concocted by the crew.)
1520	Ferdinão de Magalhães, otherwise known as Ferdinand Magellan, searches for the elusive "southwest passage" to the Far East around the southern tip of the Americas. He succeeds in sailing through the straits now bearing his name and making the first circumnavigation of the world. Magellan continues the exploration of Argentina's southern coasts. Magellan comes into contact

with the indigenous peoples in southern Argentina, immortalizing their physical attributes with the term *Patagonia,* which probably refers specifically to their feet and engenders the myth of gianthood (which while untrue, highlighted the contrast with the physically smaller Spanish, Portuguese, and Italian explorers).

1527–1529   Another Spanish expedition, this one under the command of Sebastian Cabot, explores the Paraná River, establishing in the process the first Spanish settlement, which is named Sancti Spiritus. This short-lived settlement is established near modern-day Rosario.

1536   Fearful of Portuguese expansion into the region, the Spanish Crown sponsors the establishment of a new settlement on the shores of the Rio de la Plata, with the expedition led by Pedro de Mendoza. The town is named *Nuestra Señora de Santa María del Buen Aire.* The expedition comes under violent attack by indigenous peoples; Santa María del Buen Aire is abandoned, its inhabitants leaving in 1541 what is now called Buenos Aires for Asunción in present-day Paraguay.

1543–1565   Additional expeditions establish settlements in Argentina's northwest and in Cuyo. Mendoza is founded in 1561; San Juan, in 1562.

1573   The town of Córdoba is founded by Jerónimo Luis de Cabrera; Juan de Garay establishes the town of Santa Fe.

1579	Franciscans build missions in the Río de la Plata region.
1580	Juan de Garay, aided by supplies from both Santa Fe and Asunción, rebuilds the settlement of Buenos Aires, populated largely by Spanish-speaking mestizos from Paraguay. The permanent colony is reestablished as part of the Viceroyalty of Peru.
1595	The sale of African slaves in Argentina begins in the market of Buenos Aires. (Slaves were first imported into Buenos Aires in the late 1580s.)
1605	The first shipment of salted beef is sent from Buenos Aires.
1610	The first Jesuit mission is established at San Ignacio Guazú. A number of Jesuit missions are founded in the Upper Paraná region for the indigenous Guaraní peoples.
1622	The University of Córdoba is founded by the Jesuits and plays a central role in educating the elite population of colonial Argentina. The Catholic Church controls education in colonial Argentina and maintains a strong influence over society in general.
1713	The first Bourbon monarch assumes the throne of Spain. British merchants gain control of the slave trade in Spanish American ports.
1750	The Treaty of Madrid is signed, with *Colônia do Sacramento* reverting from Portugal to Spain; Spain then returns Colonia to Portugal under the Peace of Paris in 1764. This territory remains

contentious until the independent
country of Uruguay is formed in 1828.

1767   The Jesuits are ordered to leave the
            Spanish American colonies by an order
            of the Spanish Crown.

1776   The Crown reorganizes its colonial
            empire, establishing the Viceroyalty of
            the Río de la Plata, naming Buenos
            Aires the capital of the new viceroyalty.
            (Its territories include today's
            Argentina, Uruguay, Paraguay, and
            much of Bolivia). The move, part of a
            larger set of reforms undertaken by the
            Spanish Crown, paves the way for the
            emergence and dominance of Buenos
            Aires in the nineteenth century.

1788   In a move to partially liberalize the rigid
            mercantilist trade system of the colony,
            the Crown establishes "free trade"
            between the colonies and thirteen
            Spanish ports.

1795   The first *saladero* is established in
            Argentine territory.

1806   Santiago Liniers leads a counterattack
            that pushes British invaders from the
            city of Buenos Aires. The British unsuc-
            cessfully attempt to control the territory
            as part of the larger struggle of the
            Napoleonic Wars.

1807   The local (creole) militia of Buenos
            Aires defeats a second British force
            invading the area, while Spanish troops
            offer little resistance (and Spanish mer-
            chants actually trade with the enemy).

1810   News of Napoleon's invasion of Spain
            leads to a power vacuum in Buenos

Aires, culminating in the May
Revolution. On May 25, the *cabildo
abierto,* with the creation of the
Primera Junta, assumes political
authority over the Viceroyalty of the
Río de la Plata; however, its hold
over outlying areas is tenuous and
ultimately fails. The slave trade is
outlawed.

1811   Military defeats at Paraguarí, Tacuarí,
and Huaquí separate Paraguay and
Upper Peru (Bolivia) from Buenos Aires.
(The final loss of Bolivia comes in
1815.) The First Triumvirate replaces
the existing junta.

1813   The Law of the Free Womb is passed,
which is designed to phase out slavery.

1816   The Congress of Tucumán, an assembly
of provincial delegates, formally
declares independence from Spain on
July 9, establishing the United
Provinces of the River Plate. A royalist
invasion from Peru is defeated by José
de San Martín.

1817   General José de San Martín leads the
Army of the Andes into Chilean territo-
ry, beginning the final portion of the
Wars of Independence.

1818   José de San Martín defeats Spanish
forces at the Battle of Maipú.

1820   In the so-called Terrible Year Twenty,
the armies of independence splinter
into rival regional forces; ensuing political disputes destroy the unity of the
revolutionary government in Buenos
Aires. Caudillos rule the provinces.

1821	Authorities establish the University of Buenos Aires.
1824	The Battle of Ayacucho successfully ends the struggle for independence in Peru, ending, for the most part, Spanish colonial ambitions in South America.
1825	Great Britain recognizes the United Provinces of the Río de la Plata. War breaks out with the Brazilian Empire.
1825–1828	The war with Brazil over the so-called *Banda Oriental,* or the eastern bank of the Río de la Plata, ends with the creation of the independent country of Uruguay.
1829	Federalist armies challenge the authority of *Unitario* rule. Growing military conflict splits the United Provinces of the Río de la Plata. Juan Manuel de Rosas becomes the governor of the province of Buenos Aires, asserting its independence.
1831–1834	Voyage of the *HMS Beagle,* led by Charles Darwin and Robert FitzRoy, visits Río de la Plata, Patagonia, and Tierra del Fuego.
1833	British armed forces invade and capture the Falkland Islands, called the Malvinas by Argentines.
1835	Juan Manuel de Rosas is appointed governor of the province of Buenos Aires for a second time, with dictatorial powers.
1844	An immigrant rancher from Britain, Ricardo Newton, imports barbed wire to use on his properties. The rapid spread of barbed wire later underpins the modernization of cattle and sheep ranches.

1845–1848	British and French forces mount a naval blockade of Buenos Aires.
1851	Rosas is made the Supreme Chief of the Argentine Confederation.
1852	Rosas's army is defeated at the Battle of Caseros; the defeat signifies the end of the Rosas dictatorship. Rosas is replaced by Justo José de Urquiza. The San Nicolás Agreement is signed by all provinces but Buenos Aires on May 31.
1853	The constitution of Argentina is drafted and agreed to by an assembly in Santa Fe, creating the Republic of Argentina and its modern system of government.
1854	Justo José de Urquiza becomes the first (modern) president of Argentina; his presidency is still opposed by Buenos Aires.
1856	The provincial government of Santa Fe sponsors the country's first agricultural colony, called La Esperanza.
1859	On October 23, Argentine Confederation forces win the Battle of Cepeda against Unitarian forces led by Bartolomé Mitre; the leaders of the defeated armies of Buenos Aires agree to join the Confederation.
1861	On September 17, the Battle of Pavón once again blocks Buenos Aires's efforts to remain independent. An earthquake kills some 8,000 to 10,000 Argentines in Mendoza.
1862	A new constitution is adopted, and Bartolomé Mitre is elected the first president of the new Argentine Republic.
1865–1870	War of the Triple Alliance, also called the Paraguayan War in neighboring

	Brazil, pits Argentina, Brazil, and Uruguay against Paraguay. Brazil does much of the fighting for the Triple Alliance; Paraguay is decimated in its misguided attempt to prosecute the war.
1872	*Martín Fierro,* written by José Hernandez and celebrating the country's gaucho tradition, is published.
1877	The first shipment of frozen beef is shipped from Argentina to Europe, inaugurating a period of tremendous growth in such exports.
1878	Merchants ship Argentine wheat from the port of Rosario to Great Britain.
1878–1879	Minister of War Julio Roca launches the Conquest of the Wilderness (or Conquest of the Desert) under President Nicolás Avellaneda. The brutal conquest destroys Native American communities in the pampas and in northern Patagonia. Final surrender takes place by 1884. The conquest opens Patagonia for settlement.
1880	Julio Roca, hero of the Conquest of the Desert, becomes president of Argentina. The city of Buenos Aires is transformed into the federal capital of the Argentine Republic.
1890	The Unión Cívica Radical, or Radical Civic Union (UCR), typically called the Radical Party, is founded. The Baring Crisis creates a financial panic and leads to recession in Argentina. Political dissatisfaction leads to the so-called Revolution of 1890 and the resignation of President Miguel Juárez Celman in 1893.

1895	Argentina establishes mandatory military service. During this year, a monument to *La Difunta Correa* is built.
1912	The Sáenz Peña Law, approved by the national government, mandates universal male suffrage and secret ballots in elections. The law signifies the end of the Generation of 1880.
1916	Hipólito Yrigoyen and the Radical Party (UCR) defeat their conservative rivals in national elections. Power is transferred peacefully to the Radicals.
1919	In the days between January 7 and January 13, Buenos Aires and other urban areas are jolted by fighting between striking workers and the army. The violent repression of these worker protests and the killing of hundreds in Jewish neighborhoods of Buenos Aires is later named the *Semana Trágica* (or Tragic Week).
1924	The Unión Cívica Radical splits into two factions, one pro-Yrigoyen and one anti-Yrigoyen.
1928	Hipólito Yrigoyen is elected president for a second time.
1930	José F. Uriburu and military units under his control stage a successful coup d'état against the Yrigoyen government. The coup sets in motion events leading to the so-called Infamous Decade.
1932	Agustín P. Justo becomes president amid widespread fraud and violence; the Radicals are prevented from participating in the election. The *concordancia* begins its reign over the *Decada Infame*

	(or Infamous Decade), which lasts from 1932 to 1943.
1933	The Roca-Runciman Pact, also known as the Treaty of London, grants Great Britain special economic privileges in exchange for trade regulations favoring Argentine interests.
	The government puts in place the so-called *Plan de Acción Económica* (or Plan of Economic Action) designed by Economy Minister Federico Pinedo and Agricultural Minister Luis Duhau. Among other things, controls on foreign exchange and minimum prices for agricultural exports help Argentina adjust to the impact of the Great Depression.
1936	The great Argentine tango singer Carlos Gardel dies, ushering in a period of national mourning.
1943	Army officers, declaring loyalty to the country's national interests, topple the provisional government of Ramón Castillo and put in place a military dictatorship. This "National Revolution" is led by nationalist military officers that include Colonel Juan Domingo Perón.
1945	Argentina enters World War II on the side of the Allies after a period of "nonintervention."
1946	Juan Domingo Perón is elected president of Argentina.
1946–1949	The Peronist government nationalizes key industries and services.
1947	After a campaign led by Eva Perón (known popularly as Evita), the government grants women the right to vote.

1952	Following a constitutional reform taking place in 1949, Juan Perón wins reelection and assumes his second term in office as president. His wife, Eva Perón, dies of cancer.
1954	Catholic Action leads widespread opposition to Perón as church-state relations deteriorate.
1955	Argentina's military forces Juan Perón from power in a coup deemed the Liberating Revolution. Perón lives in exile for the next eighteen years.
1955–1958	General Pedro Aramburu rules the country as the provisional president, implementing a policy of de-Peronization.
1958	Following rising popular discontent and strife among military factions, the country sees a return to civilian rule. Arturo Frondizi is elected president, but the Peronists are prevented from participating in the elections.
1962	Frondizi promises to allow the Peronists to participate in upcoming elections. To block this possibility, the armed forces remove Frondizi from power and assume control of the government in March.
1963	Given that the Peronists are excluded from participating in popular elections, Arturo Illia is elected president.
1966	The Argentine military, reacting to rising political and economic turmoil, removes Arturo Illia from the presidency. General Juan Carlos Onganía is named president in June and moves quickly to repress political parties.

1969	In an occurrence dubbed the *Cordobazo,* protesters and rioters overwhelm military and police forces in the city of Córdoba, briefly taking charge of the city on May 29 and 30 before being violently repressed.
1970	A guerrilla unit loyal to the Montoneros kidnaps and murders Pedro Aramburu. Rampant political violence coupled with rising economic instability leads to Onganía's removal from office in June. Onganía is replaced by Alejandro Lanusse.
1972	Lanusse, acting as provisional president, begins a process of returning the country to civilian rule. Lanusse approves the pardoning of Juan Perón and allows the ex-president to return (briefly) to the country.
1973	The Peronist party unites behind candidate Héctor Cámpora and wins the May 25 presidential elections. Cámpora then resigns, triggering new elections; on September 23, Juan Perón wins an unprecedented third term as president.

The Ezeiza massacre takes place during Perón's return from exile, when members of the Argentine Anticommunist Alliance (dubbed the Triple A) open fire on the crowd awaiting the leader's return. |
| 1974 | Juan Perón dies on July 1. His wife and the country's vice-president, María Estela Martínez de Perón, or Isabel, assumes the presidency. |
| 1975–1983 | *La Guerra Sucia* (or the dirty war) leads to the death and disappearance of |

	tens of thousands of Argentines, not to mention a substantial number of foreign nationals. The war, considered by many observers to be tantamount to a campaign of state terror, is waged against real and suspected enemies of the state.
1976	The military forces Isabel Perón from power. Jorge Rafael Videla, the commander-in-chief of the armed forces, becomes the nation's president and launches the so-called Process of National Reorganization. A euphemism for the dirty war, the *Processo* resorts to torture, disappearance, and extrajudicial killing to neutralize political and armed opposition, killing as many as 30,000 Argentines.
1977	In Buenos Aires's main square, the Mothers of the Plaza de Mayo, or *Las Madres,* begin their silent protests against the dictatorship. The "Mothers" become an important voice of opposition to military rule and repression.
1978	Argentina hosts and wins the World Cup soccer tournament.
1981	Viola succeeds Videla as provisional president.
1982	Leopoldo Galtieri assumes the presidency. Galtieri orders the invasion of the Falkland Islands, presumably to build popular support for the military government. The British quickly defeat the Argentines, humiliating the Argentine military in the process. As a result, Galtieri is forced to resign amid widespread criticism of military

incompetence. He is replaced by
General Reynaldo Bignone, who begins
negotiations with civilian leaders to end
military rule and return to democratic
government.

1983   Raúl Alfonsín of the Radical Party (UCR)
wins the presidential elections. Inflation
reaches 343 percent, while the foreign
debt approaches $45 billion.

1984   *Nunca Más* is published by the
Argentine National Commission on "the
disappeared," which documents the
human rights abuses that occurred during military rule in Argentina. The report
contains numerous personal accounts of
abduction, torture, death, and disappearance. Prosecution of military officers for
these abuses also begins.

1985   The government launches the *Plan
Austral,* or Austral Plan, a heterodox
shock designed to combat inflation and
stabilize the economy—inflation falls to
some 80 percent by 1986. *La Historia
Oficial (The Official Story)*, a film dealing with the dirty war, wins the
Academy Award for Best Foreign
Language Film.

1986   Alfonsín approves the *Punto Final* legislation that blocks investigations of (and
indictments against) military officers
involved in the dirty war. The country
wins the 1986 Football World Cup with
a national team captained by world-
renowned superstar Diego Maradona.

1987   The Easter Rebellion, which is led by
a number of army units dubbed the

	carapintadas, directly challenges Alfonsín's presidential authority. Two more *carapintada* uprisings occur in 1988.
1989	Political support for Raúl Alfonsín's government plummets, reflecting a rapidly deteriorating economy (especially hyperinflation) and his handling of human rights cases related to the dirty war. After the UCR loses the national elections, Alfonsín negotiates an immediate transfer of power to the Peronist winner Carlos Saúl Menem.
1991	The Argentine peso is formally pegged to the U.S. dollar at a one-to-one ratio, leading to so-called convertibility. Argentina is the only Latin American country to participate in the Gulf War under a UN mandate. The country also joins Mercosur, a customs union including Argentina, Brazil, Uruguay, and Paraguay. News stories begin to appear alleging corruption at high levels of government.
1991–1994	Carlos Menem pushes the privatization of public companies as part of a larger program (typically dubbed neoliberal) to reduce public sector deficits and stabilize the economy. Often highly unpopular, Menem's policies also lead to a considerable number of strikes and protests.
1992	Terrorist attack on the Israeli Embassy in Buenos Aires kills twenty-nine people. Iran denies any role in the attack; Hezbollah is suspected of involvement, while Islamic Jihad claims responsibility.

1994	Menem and Alfonsín lead negotiations to produce a constitutional reform, leading to the *Pacto de Olivos*. The reformed constitution allows Menem to run for a second successive term in office (although part of the deal is to reduce the term from six years to four years). Menem wins the election and assumes a second term as president.
	Another terrorist attack in Buenos Aires, this time a car bomb detonated at the AMIA Jewish Community Center, kills 85 people and injures some 300. Iran is suspected of being behind the bombing.
1995	Carlos Menem wins a second term to the presidency. Inflation falls to 3 percent. Argentina accedes to the Nuclear Non-Proliferation Treaty.
1997	The Radical Party joins with left-leaning FREPASO and others to form the *Alianza,* an electoral alliance designed to oppose Menem and the Peronists. The official rate of unemployment climbs to 17 percent, contributing to the dissatisfaction with Peronist rule.
1999	Fernando de la Rúa, as head of the center-left alliance of opposition parties, defeats the Peronist candidate Eduardo Duhalde in presidential elections. However, de la Rúa is confronted almost immediately by deteriorating economic conditions. The country enters a protracted recession.

2000	Millions of Argentines go on strike to protest economic austerity policies and the high unemployment rate. Vice-President Carlos Álvarez resigns in October in protest of a bribes scandal, causing a crisis in the somewhat fragile ruling alliance.
2001	In March, the remaining FREPASO ministers resign from the government to protest labor and economic reforms. The economy is in its third year of recession, and foreign debt reaches well above $100 billion. In November, the government responds to a run on the banks by limiting access to bank deposits, a move called the *corralito*. By December, Argentines take to the streets in protest, often banging pots and pans in the *cacerolazo*. Protests and violence grow.

President de la Rúa resigns from office on December 20. Adolfo Rodríguez Saá is appointed president by the Argentine congress on December 22. In his short tenure, Rodríguez Saá declares a debt moratorium. A few days later Argentina officially defaults on its near-$100 billion in external debt. Rodríguez Saá resigns after a week due to lack of political support.

After three interim presidents come and go during a tumultuous two-week period, Eduardo Duhalde, the losing candidate in the 1999 presidential

	elections, is appointed president with cross-party support.
2002	Eduardo Duhalde, sworn in as president on January 2, imposes a number of economic policy measures, including a move to convert dollar-denominated accounts into pesos and to end convertibility, or the one-to-one parity of the peso to the dollar. The Argentine peso loses 40 percent of its value on its first day of floating freely and declines considerably more in the months to follow.
2003	Ex-president Menem wins in a first-round presidential vote, but pulls out when he faces almost certain defeat by fellow Peronist Néstor Kirchner, who then wins the election. The maneuvering by Menem denies Kirchner a clear political mandate as he assumes the presidency on May 25 (becoming Argentina's sixth president in 18 months).
2004	President Kirchner pushes for a favorable restructuring of Argentina's defaulted external debt, much to the chagrin of international bondholders, who stand to lose huge sums of money in the inevitable "haircut." Economy Minister Roberto Lavagna unveils the restructuring plan that aims to give investors about 30 percent of their original capital. A deadly fire in a Buenos Aires nightclub kills 194 people.

2005

Argentina's Supreme Court overrules "Laws of Pardon" that were used to pardon military figures from the dirty war. Midterm elections in October see a big victory for Kirchner's wing of the Peronist party, boosting his political power. In December, Kirchner cancels Argentina's debt with the IMF with a single, final payment of $9.7 billion; popular politically, the move is designed to reduce the Fund's influence on domestic economic policies.

2007

Cristina Fernández de Kirchner wins the October 28 presidential election, succeeding her husband, Néstor Kirchner, to the nation's highest office. Critics suggest the move is little more than a ploy to create a sort of family dynasty in which the Kirchners alternate in the presidential office. Only time will tell whether Néstor Kirchner can return to the presidency, whether Christina Fernández de Kirchner assumes a second term in the presidency, or whether a third candidate manages to defeat the aspirations of both.

Significant People, Places, and Events

AAA *Alianza Argentina Anticomunista* (the Argentina Anti-communist Alliance, or Triple A) was formed during the short presidency of Isabel Perón and was used to wage war against real and suspected enemies of the state. The group's activities can be seen as foreshadowing the horrors of the dirty war.

Alberdi, Juan Bautista (1810–1884) Alberdi, born in Tucumán, was a political theorist, a diplomat, and one of Argentina's most influential liberals of his era. He was a member of the group known as the Generation of 1837, a literary and political circle of Argentine elites. Despite his importance to Argentine history, he lived much of his life in exile in Montevideo as well as in Chile. It was Alberdi's opposition to the dictatorship of caudillo Juan Manuel de Rosas that forced him into exile. Only after Rosas fell from power did Alberdi become a leading Argentine figure (although he chose to reside in Chile). Importantly, his work *Bases y puntos de partida para la organización política de la República Argentina* (*Bases and Points of Departure for the Political Organization of the Argentine Republic*) served as the basis of the national Constitution of 1853. His writings also encouraged European influences and immigration as a way to bring civilization and development to Argentina.

Alem, Leandro Nicebro (1842–1896) An important political figure in Argentine history, Alem became a supporter of the political interests of the city of Buenos Aires and then later, after 1893, a cofounder of the *Unión Cívica Radical* (Radical Civic Union, or Radical Party). The Radicals would later become Argentina's first national political party based on popular support.

Alfonsín, Raúl Ricardo (1926–) Alfonsín is an important Argentine politician, a leader of the *Unión Cívica Radical* (Radical Civic Union) and an ex-president of the country. (He was president from December 10, 1983, until July 9, 1989.) Alfonsín was elected president in 1983 and helped manage the country's transition from military to civilian rule, including efforts to bring members of the military to justice. Alfonsín's government suffered from a number of military rebellions, including the notable Easter Rebellion of the *carapintadas* in 1987. However, Alfonsín's downfall came as a result of the disastrous state of the economy. In 1989, Alfonsín left office six months before the end of his term as a result of rapidly deteriorating economic and political conditions, handing the reins over to president-elect Carlos Menem.

Ameghino, Florentino (1854–1911) An Argentinean scientist who gained fame for his geology, paleontology, and zoology, Ameghino was largely a self-taught naturalist and his work centered on the lands of the pampas. Together with his brother Carlos, Ameghino established a foundation dedicated to the physical sciences in Argentina. He also put together one of the world's largest collections of fossils at the time. The Ameghino crater on the moon was named after him.

Anti-Personalistas These were members of the *Unión Cívica Radical* who challenged Hipólito Yrigoyen's control of the party during the 1920s; this faction supported the *Concordancia* of the 1930s.

Aramburu, Pedro E. (1903–1970) An army general who rose through the ranks during Juan Perón's first presidency, Aramburu gained notoriety when he participated in the coup against

Perón in 1955. After the initial provisional president Eduardo Lonardi, Aramburu stepped in as the country's leader; he remained active in the country's political scene after turning over power to Arturo Frondizi in 1958. Aramburu's life came to a premature and violent end. In 1970, a group of Montonero guerrillas kidnapped and then assassinated the general in the first and one of the most notorious atrocities that culminated in the dirty war.

Asiento The term signifies "permission" and generally refers to a 1702 agreement that gave Great Britain control of the slave trade in Spanish America.

Avellaneda, Nicolás (1836–1885) Avellaneda was born in the province of Tucumán and helped lead the creation of Argentina's economic and political foundation after the fall of Juan Manuel de Rosas. He served as president (1874–1880) and was a leading figure in the conservative political party *Partido Autonomista Nacional* (National Autonomist Party, or PAN).

Azules Literally the term means "blues," but it refers to a faction within the military that supported civilian rule—so long as it was not under Peronist direction.

Belgrano, Manuel (1770–1820) Belgrano was born in Buenos Aires but was educated in Spain; he served as the secretary of the viceroyalty's Trade Council between 1794 and 1810. His numerous essays and reports helped build support for trade reforms. He also emerged as a key figure in the struggle for independence from Spain. After helping to set up a revolutionary government in 1810, Belgrano led a campaign against Asunción the following year. The defeat of his forces at the Battle of Tacuarí led to the separation of Paraguay from the United Provinces of the Río de la Plata.

Blandengues This term is used for the militia first formed during the colonial era that was used to protect against indigenous raiding parties in the pampas.

Borges, Jorge Luis (1889–1986) Borges was an Argentine writer known particularly for his short stories and poetry. He became the country's most famous modern author and is considered one of the most important literary figures of the twentieth century. Borges's writings are complex in structure and are considered by many experts to have contributed greatly to the spread of "magical realism" throughout Latin America. Although Borges never won the Nobel Prize in Literature, he is usually identified as the most important writer of fiction in Latin America.

Bureaucratic authoritarianism Often referred to as BA, the term has come to be synonymous with the repressive military regimes seen in Latin America in the 1960s and 1970s, notably in countries such as Argentina, Brazil, and Chile. In such regimes, bureaucrats from areas such as the military, civil service, and the private sector were commonly selected for public office. The working classes and popular sectors were tightly controlled and typically excluded from politics; solutions to political problems were deemed to be administrative or technical in nature. One critical focus of such regimes was economic growth, which was fostered through ties to the international economy and multinational corporations.

Cabildo The term signifies "town council." The term *cabildo abierto* signifies an "open council" and refers to the assemblies that directed political developments during the independence era between 1808 and 1825.

Calfucurá, Juan (d. 1873) Calfucurá was a great military and political leader of the Araucanian peoples in the period after independence. Specifically, Calfucurá worked to build links between the various tribal groups and, in the process, created a highly effective—and feared—military force. Juan Manuel de Rosas negotiated a number of treaties with Calfucurá in attempts to maintain a truce between the indigenous tribes and the growing number of settlers pushing into the pampas after independence. Following Calfucurá's death in June 1873, the system of alliances that he helped build fell apart, easing considerably the so-called Conquest of the Desert, the military conquest of the region by Argentine troops in 1878 and 1879.

Caudillos While in much of Latin America this term generally refers to a political boss, in Argentina it refers specifically to the political authorities of the early and mid-nineteenth century. These figures typically used military force and other forms of political violence to dominate regions and provinces prior to the period of national unification.

Cavallo, Domingo (1946–) Domingo Cavallo is an Argentine economist and politician who may be best-known for introducing the convertibility plan, which fixed the exchange rate between the Argentine peso and the U.S. dollar at 1:1 between 1991 and 2001. He also is known for the so-called *corralito,* which kept savers from withdrawing their funds from banks and contributed to widespread rioting and the downfall of President de la Rúa. After rising tensions with the Menem administration, Cavallo was asked to leave; he then founded a political party and was elected to the congress. (He ran for president in 1999, but lost.) Cavallo was asked to join President de la Rúa to help the country emerge from economic crisis. While Cavallo tried a number of adjustments to right the economy, it was simply too little too late. The *corralito,* an attempt to block massive capital flight, sparked angry protests by Argentines, forcing Cavallo and then de la Rúa to resign.

CGT *Confederación General del Trabajo,* or General Confederation of Labor, this group is an umbrella organization that is a leading player in Argentina's union movement.

Cimarones This term was used by authorities and ranchers to refer to wild cattle. It was also commonly used to designate escaped slaves.

Colonos In a literal sense, this term refers to colonists. It is commonly used to refer to grain farmers in the Pampas region.

Colorados Translating literally as the "Reds" (although it has no relation to communism), the term was first associated with Juan Manuel de Rosas and other powerful Federalists. It was later used to refer to hard-line anti-Peronists within the armed forces in the 1950s.

CONADEP The *Comisión Nacional Sobre la Desaparación de Personas,* or National Commission Concerning the Disappearance of Persons, took place in 1984. The Commission, which was led by Ernesto Sábato, conducted its own investigation of the human rights violations committed during the dirty war by government and government-sponsored forces.

Concordancia The term refers to a political pact between a number of important political parties that ruled Argentina between 1932 and 1943, often resorting to electoral fraud and political repression to sustain power. Considerable censorship of the media also was employed during the period.

Consulado The term refers to merchant councils that monopolized trade in the early colonial era from Cádiz in Spain in cooperation with allied merchant groups in Veracruz, Lima, and Mexico City in the New World. After trade reforms in the late eighteenth century, merchant councils in each colonial port worked with Crown officials to monitor trade.

Cordobazo The term refers to the popular protests that shook the provincial Argentine capital of Córdoba in May 1969. The revolt contributed to a decline in the power of dictator Onganía, who was ultimately driven from power by other factions of the military.

Cortázar, Julio (1914–1984) Julio Cortázar was an important Argentine writer and intellectual. In an act of opposition to the government of Juan Domingo Perón, Cortázar emigrated to France in 1951. While Cortázar would return to Argentina periodically (and stay in contact with Argentine writers and intellectuals), he resided in France until his death in 1984. In his later years, Cortázar became active in leftist political causes in Latin America. Cortázar is well known for his short stories, many of a fantastic nature. He published several well-known novels as well, including *Los Premios* (*The Winners,* 1965) and *Rayuela* (*Hopscotch,* 1966). Many consider *Hopscotch,* an experimental piece of sorts, to be one of the best novels of Spanish American literature of the twentieth century.

Criollo The term means "creole," an American-born male of Spanish (or European) descent. Creoles became the most important force calling for, and ultimately fighting for, independence from Spain in the early nineteenth century.

De la Rúa, Fernando (1937–) An important Argentine politician, de la Rúa emerged as a leader of the Radical Party in 1982 as the country's political parties selected candidates for political office following the end of the military dictatorship. De la Rúa lost out to Raúl Alfonsín for the nomination to represent the party in presidential elections; but over time, he managed to gain in national prominence through a number of political offices, including mayor of Buenos Aires in 1996. He became a candidate for the presidency in 1999, representing the *Alianza (Alianza para Trabajo, Justicia y Educación,* or Alliance for Work, Justice and Education). The *Alianza* was a coalition built by the Radicals and the FREPASO to defeat the Peronists. De la Rúa's presidency proved ill-fated and was plagued by economic crisis and weak political control; his own lack of charisma and apparent slow demeanor did not help matters. De la Rúa was forced out of the presidency in December 2001 by growing financial crisis and civil unrest.

Debt crisis This crisis, which hit Argentina and Latin America in the early 1980s, followed a dramatic run-up in overseas borrowing and accumulating foreign debt in the 1970s. When the U.S. credit-tightening policies led to higher debt service payments and global recession (and therefore lower demand and prices for Argentina's exports), a crisis became inevitable. Many countries went into default on their international obligations.

Descamisados Literally meaning the "shirtless ones," the *descamisados* was a term used by the Peronists to refer to the poor and working-class supporters of Juan Domingo Perón.

Echeverría, Esteban (1805–1851) Echeverría was a significant Argentine literary figure who played a very important role in the development of Argentine literature; he is generally considered one of the most important Latin American Romantic authors. As the leader of the Generation of 1837, he was one of the country's first great literary figures. In general, his fiction and poetry represented a mixture of European and local topics, perhaps a reflection of the fact that his studies took place in both regions. Echeverría argued for the creation of a unified Argentina, and his political work led him into confrontation with the Rosas dictatorship and ultimately into exile in Uruguay, where he remained until his death. His most important work is the story *El Matadero* (*The Slaughter-house*), considered a landmark in Latin American literature and one of the first to contrast the forces of "civilization" with those of "barbarism." Of course, this would emerge as an important theme in Argentine literature and cultural thinking. Another important work by Echeverría is *La Cautiva* (*The Captive*), also considered an important contribution to Latin American literature of the nineteenth century.

Encomienda One of the key institutions of Spain's New World colonies, the term referred initially to the responsibility that a person of authority took to act in the name of the Spanish Crown; the holder of the *encomienda,* the *encomendero,* had the right to use the labor and resources of a community for his own needs. The *encomendero* was then theoretically responsible to protect the communities under his charge, including the charge of Christianizing local inhabitants. In practice, the system led to the destruction of most Native American communities within a few generations.

ERP *Ejército Revolucionario del Pueblo,* or Revolutionary Army of the People, was originally based in Tucumán and became active throughout the country in the 1960s and 1970s. This was an important revolutionary group whose activities contributed to the unleashing of the dirty war.

Estancia The term refers to a cattle ranch; ranch owners are referred to as *estancieros.*

Fernández de Kirchner, Cristina (1955–) Cristina Fernández de Kirchner was elected to Argentina's highest office on October 28, 2007 and assumed the presidency on December 10 of the same year. Fernández is the nation's second woman president, and the first to be democratically elected to the office. Fernández is also noteworthy in that her husband preceded her in the presidency. While Fernández undoubtedly grew in national stature as the nation's first lady during the Kirchner presidency, she has had a noteworthy political career in her own right, having served a number of times in the national legislature. Her most prominent victory came in 2005, in which she defeated the wife of Eduardo Duhalde, Hilda Gonzalez de Duhalde, for a seat in the Senate representing the Province of Buenos Aires. Many point to this contest as a tipping point in Peronist politics, representing the ascendancy of the Kirchners and the decline of Duhalde and his allies. Observers of Argentine politics will be watching the current administration closely to see if Kirchner retains significant power in his wife's administration and whether Fernández deviates meaningfully from the path taken by her husband.

Frondizi, Arturo (1908–1995) The president of Argentina between May 1958 and March 1962, Frondizi also was a lawyer, a university lecturer, and an outspoken critic of the Peronists during the 1950s. His role as a critic of the regime led him to become a leader in the anti-Peronist opposition and ultimately a successful candidate for the presidency in 1958, representing the *Unión Cívica Radical Intransigente* (an offshoot of the Radical Party). Frondizi pushed a set of policies often dubbed *desarrollismo,* which aimed to accelerate economic development and industrialization (in good part by encouraging foreign investment); he also managed to gain support from the middle class. However, his moves to lift the ban on the Peronists lost him the support of the military. (His meetings with Fidel Castro and Che Guevara did not help either.) Ultimately, as Argentina faced a mounting political crisis in 1966, Frondizi was deposed by a military coup d'état.

Galtieri, Leopoldo Fortunato (1926–2003) Galtieri was a career military officer, a general, and the de facto president of Argentina from December 1981 to June 1982; he also was an important member of the upper echelon of the military that planned and executed the dirty war. After four months in office and with popularity for the regime quite low, Galtieri implemented an invasion of the British-held Falkland Islands, known in Argentina as the Malvinas. For a very brief period, the invasion proved popular; and antiregime demonstrations were replaced by patriotic demonstrations. However, British retribution was swift and Argentina succumbed quickly to a humiliating defeat in the Falklands War. Within days, Galtieri was removed from power. Following the return to civilian rule, Galtieri was forced to face charges for human rights violations as well as for mismanagement of the Falklands War. He was cleared of the former but found guilty of the latter and sentenced to jail in 1986. He ultimately served five years in jail before being pardoned by President Menem in 1991. New charges were brought in 2002 relating to crimes of the dirty war; while Galtieri was placed under house arrest, he died of a heart attack before facing further trials or prison.

Garay, Juan de (1528–1583) Garay was a Spanish conquistador and a veteran of numerous military campaigns in South America that included expeditions to establish and fortify a number of cities, including Santa Fe (1573) and Buenos Aires (1580). The latter was the second founding of Buenos Aires. De Garay was killed in an ambush in 1583.

Gardel, Carlos (1890–1935) Carlos Gardel is Argentina's most famous musician of the tango; in fact, for most people, Gardel's name is nearly synonymous with the tango. He became famous for his frequent radio broadcasts and films and went on tour throughout the world. In 1935, at a relatively young age, Gardel died tragically in a plane crash in Medellín, Colombia. Fans throughout Latin America went into mourning. His recordings remain popular in Argentina as well as around the world.

Gaucho This term is used to refer to Argentina's rural population, especially those working for ranching interests. While the term was originally an insult, it became a nationalist symbol by the late nineteenth century.

GDP Gross domestic product is the total value of a country's production of final goods and services, not counting those directly transformed into other goods and services. GDP per capita divides this figure by the total population, allowing comparison with other economies.

GOU The *Grupo de Oficiales Unidos* was a secret military group aimed at advancing nationalist political objectives at the expense of civilian rule. Members of the group, which included Juan Domingo Perón, were central figures in the coup of 1943.

Guaraní This term refers to a group of native Argentineans residing in the northeastern portion of the country.

Guerra Sucia The *Guerra Sucia,* or dirty war, was declared against "subversives" but escalated to include state-sponsored terror against innocent civilians. The dirty war took place between 1975 and 1983 and is believed to have killed between 20,000 and 40,000 people.

Guerrilla Translated literally into "little war," this term has been used in Argentina to refer to the armed conflict between revolutionary groups and government security forces in the 1960s and 1970s. The culmination of the guerrilla was the dirty war.

Hernández, José (1834–1886) An Argentine journalist and poet, Hernández is best known as the author of the epic poem *Martín Fierro* (1872) and its sequel *La Vuelta de Martín Fierro.* Both works tend to romanticize Argentina's gauchos and their rural lives in the years before the country's rapid economic development irrevocably changed the countryside. The author's work represents an important contribution to

Argentine literature and has played a key role in the ongoing attempt to define Argentine culture and history. It represents the pinnacle of gaucho literature.

IAPI Created in 1946, the *Instituto Argentino de Promoción del Intercambio,* or Argentine Institute of Growth and Trade, was designed to control prices and exports of agricultural goods. The profits derived from such operations were funneled into the government's projects in industrialization and social welfare.

Illia, Arturo Umberto (1900–1983) Illia, born in the province of Buenos Aires to Italian immigrant parents, was a physician who became the democratically elected president of Argentina in 1963. He represented the *Unión Cívica Radical del Pueblo.* His administration suffered from a lack of popular support; and the combination of union strikes, political polarization, and economic instability made it more and more difficult for Illia to govern. The deepening political crisis led to a military coup in which he was deposed from the presidency.

IMF International Monetary Fund. The IMF is an international organization, based in Washington, D.C., that oversees the global financial system, observing exchange rates and balance of payments. It also offers financial and technical assistance.

Industrialization This occurs when industry becomes the leading sector of the economy—the real driver of growth— and it reflects dramatic structural change in an economy. It is typically preceded by a period of industrial growth in which an economy still depends primarily on the expansion of agricultural exports.

Inflation The persistent and substantial increase in the general level of prices in an economy, this has been a common phenomenon in Latin America in general and in Argentina specifically. The debate about the origins of inflation in Latin America typically has been between monetarists and structuralists. The monetarists blame inflation largely on the lack of control over government spending; the structuralists suggest that inflation's origins are more structural in nature.

Inflation financing This term refers to the common practice of covering public sector deficits by printing money. The inevitable result is a surge in inflation. Historically, this has been a problem in Argentina.

Informal sector This is the segment of the economy that operates outside the official taxed economy; transactions in the informal economy typically take place in cash. Informal workers pursue a multitude of occupations, from selling goods on the streets to working in households as maids, gardeners, nannies, and the like.

ISI Import substitution industrialization was a development strategy common in post-war Latin America that closed economies to imports in an attempt to bolster domestic production, especially industrial goods. While the strategy was effective in jump-starting the industrialization process, it also left a legacy of inefficient industries and high-cost, often low-quality goods. In good part, the strategy was scrapped as more liberal policies followed the region's debt crisis.

JP *Juventud Peronista,* or Peronist Youth, was formed as a youth component of the PJ, or *Partido Justicialista*. The JP became a key faction in the struggle between guerrillas and the government in the 1960s and 1970s.

Juárez Celman, Miguel (1844–1909) A politician, Juárez Celman was an ally of Julio Roca and was Argentina's president from 1886 to 1890. He was dedicated to the development and settlement of the country's interior, but his administration was known for its corruption and other abuses of power. The administration was known, at least by its opponents, as the *Unicato* for its one-man, one-party rule and autocratic style. Juárez Celman's regime faced crisis with the Baring Crisis of 1890, in which a collapse of foreign loans led to recession and popular protest. Under pressure from Roca and his supporters, Juárez Celman resigned the presidency; the subsequent political crisis led to the Sáenz Peña Reform Law (1912) and the decline of the National Autonomist Party (PAN) as the dominant political force in the country.

Justicialismo This term refers to the extensive, rather diverse ideological program of the Peronist movement.

Justo, Agustín P. (1878–1943) President of Argentina from 1932 until 1938, Justo was a career military man, a diplomat, and a politician. He was president during the so-called *decada infame,* or infamous decade, which lasted from the early 1930s until 1943. After serving as minister of war for President Marcelo T. de Alvear, Justo joined the 1930 coup against Hipólito Yrigoyen and then served briefly as part of General José de Uriburu's authoritarian government. Justo led the formation of the *Concordancia* and became president in 1932 in a fraud-ridden election.

Kirchner, Néstor (1950–) Néstor Carlos Kirchner served as Argentina's president from 2003 to 2007. Born in Argentina's desolate and sparsely populated south, Kirchner rose to political prominence as the Peronist governor of the Patagonian province of Santa Cruz. After an unusual first-round presidential election in 2003, in which former president Carlos Menem narrowly defeated Kirchner but failed to win the presidency outright, Menem withdrew from the second round contest, making Kirchner president by default. These conditions led to concerns about the strength of Kirchner's mandate; however, his mandate was strengthened considerably after mid-term elections which saw widespread victories by Kirchner allies. Kirchner's administration was noteworthy for a number of reasons, including the strong recovery from the nation's economic crisis, the active rejection of "automatic alignment" with the United States, and the aggressive restructuring of the nation's foreign debt. Kirchner is also the first Argentine president to be succeeded by his wife through national elections.

Lanusse, Alejandro Agustín (1918–1996) Lanusse was the military president of Argentina between March 1971 and May 1973. His successful military career was interrupted in 1951 when he was sentenced to life imprisonment for his part in an attempted coup against Juan Perón. He was released from prison in 1955 but was involved in further attempts to overthrow Argentine presidents (Arturo Frondizi in 1962 and Arturo Umberto Illia in 1966). Following Juan Carlos Onganía's successful seizure of power, Lanusse became commander-in-chief of the Argentine army in 1968. Following a coup in 1971, he then became president. Lanusse called elections in 1973, in which the Peronist Héctor Cámpora was elected president as a stand-in for the "old man" Perón.

Liniers y Brémond, Santiago de (1753–1810) A French officer in the Spanish military, he commanded the navy that guarded Buenos Aires during the final decades of the Spanish colonial era. The British invaded in 1806, causing the Spanish viceroy to flee the city; de Liniers helped organize local defensive militias that successfully defeated the invaders. He was then named acting viceroy and given full military command, which he used to defend Buenos Aires against another British invasion in 1807. He was officially appointed viceroy in 1808 and served until 1809.

Lost decade The term is used to describe the environment of the 1980s for much of Latin America as it suffered the impact of the debt crisis. Most countries used some combination of recession and devaluation to service debt, which was often accompanied by plummeting investment and rising inflation (quite often the result of inflation financing). In general, the lost decade saw a decline in living standards, an increase in inflation, reduced investment, and stagnant growth.

Mármol, José (1817–1871) A well-known Argentine writer, Mármol spent much of his productive time in exile, notably for his opposition to the dictator Juan Manuel de Rosas. His exile in Montevideo was interrupted by an attack on the city by a Rosas ally, and Mármol fled to Brazil. He was able to return to Argentina in 1852 following the defeat of Rosas at the Battle of Caseros, at which time he entered politics. Famous for his romantic novels and poetry, among his most important works are the poem *"El Peregrino"* and the novel *Amalia.*

Mazorca This word literally refers to an ear of corn, but it was used specifically to refer to the police force that Juan Manuel de Rosas used to rule the province of Buenos Aires after 1829.

Mendoza, Pedro de (1487–1537) Mendoza founded the *Puerto de Nuestra Señora del Buen Aire* in 1536 (later to become known as Buenos Aires) after he was given the right to lead an exploration and the settlement of the Río de la Plata region. The settlement was relatively isolated; this isolation coupled with indigenous attacks on settlers caused the site to be abandoned in 1541—only later would the site become permanently inhabited.

Menem, Carlos Saúl (1930–) The child of Syrian Muslims born in a small town in the province of La Rioja, Menem rose to become the Peronist president of Argentina from 1989–1999. Menem was elected governor of La Rioja in 1973, but he lost the post and was imprisoned after the overthrow of Isabel Martínez de Perón in 1976. He was imprisoned until 1981; with the fall of military rule, he was again elected governor of the province of La Rioja. He was then elected president in 1989, succeeding Radical Raúl Alfonsín. While elected on vague promises made to working-class supporters, Menem faced hyperinflation and recession and responded with "neoliberal" reforms, including Domingo Cavallo's plan to peg the Argentine peso to the U.S. dollar. (Other plans included instituting a major privatization program, creating Mercosur, and opening the country to foreign investment.)

In 1995, Menem was elected to a second term by a large majority. Still, his second term was plagued by growing economic difficulties, not to mention increasing allegations of high-level corruption. His pardon of high-level officials of the 1976–1983 military dictatorship has been heavily criticized. Menem's attempt to run for a third term in 1999 was unsuccessful. (It was ruled unconstitutional.) He ran again in 2003, winning the greatest number of votes but failing to achieve an overall majority. Certain of a loss in the run-off vote with Néstor Kirchner, Menem withdrew his candidacy, making Kirchner the new president. Menem has faced a number of legal charges following his presidency, but seems to have emerged victorious; he maintains that he will run again for the presidency in 2007.

Mercosur The *Mercado Común del Sur,* or Common Market of the South, this common market—technically, a customs union—is a trading zone that was created in 1991 and updated in 1994. It includes Argentina, Brazil, Uruguay, and Paraguay. Venezuela joined in 2006; a number of additional South American countries are associate members.

Mestizo The term is used to refer to people of mixed ancestry, typically descendants of European and Native Americans. This term is used commonly throughout Latin America.

Mitre, Bartolomé (1821–1906) Mitre was a liberal who served in the militias that fought against Rosas in the 1840s; he was forced into exile until the defeat of Rosas. He fought against the federal system and was appointed to a number of government posts when Buenos Aires seceded from the Confederation. He was then defeated by Urquiza, and Buenos Aires reentered the Confederation. (Mitre helped forge a compromise solution.) He was elected president of the republic in 1862; the period of national political unity ushered in considerable progress and reform. Mitre also was the founder of *La Nación,* one of Latin America's leading newspapers.

Montoneros This term was first used to designate cavalry forces retained by the caudillos of the nineteenth century. The term was adopted in the 1960s by a guerrilla group that eventually became one of the key revolutionary factions in Argentina in the 1970s.

Moreno, Mariano (1778–1811) The son of a Spanish colonial official, Moreno became an important advocate of liberal reform in activities associated with the *cabildo* of Buenos Aires. He was the author in 1809 of the *Representación de los hacendados,* a tract that became a rallying point for the forces seeking a break with Spain. Moreno was a key figure in the early years of the independence struggle, calling for the creation of a new liberal government.

Newton, Ricardo B. (d. 1868) An immigrant from Great Britain, Newton became a highly influential rancher, a great example of a generation of Europeans in Argentina that became wealthy from ownership of cattle and sheep ranches. Historians generally credit Newton with the introduction of barbed wire fencing, which, in turn, allowed selective breeding of cattle and sheep. He also was a founding member of the Argentine Rural Society.

Onganía, Juan Carlos (1914–1995) Onganía was the military president of Argentina from 1966 until 1970, reaching the post after participating in a coup d'état against democratically elected president Arturo Illia. Onganía then directed the "Argentine Revolution," which attempted a conservative restructuring of the country. Onganía's government was weakened by a popular uprising known as the *Cordobazo,* which took place in the city of Córdoba in 1969. A faction of the military led by General Alejandro Lanusse forced Onganía to resign in 1970.

Pampa Derived from the Quechua word *bamba,* which refers to an upland meadow, the pampas constitute the main physical feature of the central region of Argentina. It is a broad plain extending in an arc to the west of Buenos Aires that represents the core of the country in terms of population, political power, economic output, and the like.

PAN *Partido Autonomista Nacional,* or National Autonomist Party, this party was formed in the 1870s, in large part to represent opposition to Bartolomé Mitre and his supporters. The PAN was a major force in the country's golden age between 1880 and 1910.

Pellegrini, Carlos (1846–1906) Pellegrini was an important leader of the PAN, or *Partido Autonomista Nacional,* starting in the 1870s. He began a career in politics with a seat in the national congress and various ministerial posts. He then became Argentina's president following the resignation of President Miguel Juárez Celman in 1890. Following the widespread use of fraud and force in the election of Luis Sáenz Peña, Pellegrini became an important supporter of fundamental electoral reform.

Periphery A term used in economic analysis to distinguish between countries of the industrialized "center" and those of the nonindustrialized, or industrializing, "periphery." Often an argument is made that the fortunes of peripheral economies depend on events and conditions in the center.

Perón, Eva María Duarte de (1919–1952) Known as Evita, Juan Domingo Perón's second wife, Eva Duarte, was originally a radio actress. She married Perón in 1945, working closely with him to build the support of organized labor during and after his election to the presidency. Evita held no formal position within the Perón administration, but she wielded considerable power, mainly through her ability to direct public funds through the *Fundacion María Eva Duarte de Perón*. Evita also played a very important role in the movement to achieve women's suffrage, which was accomplished in 1947. Evita died at a relatively young age of cancer, becoming even more important to Argentina as a symbol for the Peronist party and its commitment to the poor and working classes.

Perón, Juan Domingo (1895–1974) Juan Domingo Perón was the son of poor European immigrants who became a soldier and a politician and eventually the country's most famous and controversial political figure of the twentieth century. Perón served as president from 1946 to 1955 and from 1973 to 1974 (the year he died). After starting his career in the military in 1911, Perón participated in the coup against Hipólito Yrigoyen in 1930. He also helped put together the GOU, a key political force that pushed for a nationalist revolution during the so-called *Concordancia* and helped lead the 1943 coup. Perón quickly became a leading figure in the military government that followed the coup, working to build political support for the military regime. He was elected president in 1946 and then reelected in 1952.

Perón managed to reshape Argentine politics, relying on a wide range of supporters including labor unions, the military, industrialists, and the Church. One of his main goals was the industrialization of Argentina. Perón was immensely popular with a portion of the Argentine population (as was his second wife, Eva), but his detractors labeled him a demagogue as well as a dictator. Ultimately, the latter group grew in importance, in part as a reflection of Perón's failed policies; and in 1955, Perón was forced into exile by a military coup. Having started a political movement known conventionally as Peronism, Perón worked from exile to maintain his control over the movement. While Perón managed to return to Argentina in 1972 and be reelected president in 1973, he died in office, leaving his third wife and the country's vice-president, Isabel, to assume the office.

Petrodollars A term generally associated with a period in the 1970s characterized by easy credit, in part a reflection of the vast sums of money that oil exporters recycled into the global financial system via multinational banks. At the time, countries such as Argentina vastly increased their foreign debt to speed up development plans. This action would prove shortsighted when global economic conditions deteriorated in the early 1980s.

PJ The *Partido Justicialista,* or Peronist party, was a major force in Argentine political history, not to mention the party of the current president of Argentina, Néstor Kirchner. It was formed to support Juan Domingo Perón in the years after World War II.

Porteños This term is commonly used to refer to a person from the city of Buenos Aires (and refers specifically to the city's status as a port).

Privatization A key component of liberal economic reforms, the term refers to the selling of state-owned enterprises to private sector investors. Proponents argue that the process brings resources to the state, reduces budget deficits, and improves economic efficiency. Critics suggest the process is riddled with corruption and amounts to a giveaway of the national patrimony, among other problems.

Processo Referring to the *Processo de Reorganización Nacional,* or Process of National Reorganization, the term was coined to refer to the military dictatorship's political program during the period from 1976 until the transition to democracy in 1983.

Pueyrredón, Juan Martín de (1777–1850) An important figure in the independence movement, Pueyrredón is perhaps best known for his participation in the local defense against British military invasions in 1806 and 1807. He served as supreme director of the United Provinces of the Río de la Plata between 1816 and 1819.

Renovadores The "Renewal" faction within the PJ, or Peronist party, the group was instrumental in Peronists' return to national leadership after electoral losses in 1983 and 1985.

Rivadavia, Bernardino (1780–1845) Rivadavia is one of the most important figures from Argentina's independence movement; he was a leader within the *Unitario* cause and became a cabinet member before ultimately becoming president of the United Provinces of the Río de la Plata. Rivadavia was a key leader of the Constitutional Convention of 1826. He also was a key proponent in the attempt to hold together the territories that once made up the Viceroyalty of the Río de la Plata following independence. However, his efforts to promote the national project at the expense of powerful local interests helped rally the Federalists, who eventually succeeded in removing Rivadavia from power.

Roca, Julio Argentino (1843–1914) Roca was a general in the Argentine army and a dominant figure in Argentina's political arena; he served as president of the country from 1880 until 1886 as well as from 1898 until 1904. Roca is perhaps best known as the leader of the so-called Conquest of the Wilderness that eliminated resistance of Native Argentines to central authority and led to the widespread settlement and development of the pampas in 1879. As president and as a major political figure, Roca worked to maintain elite control of the system during Argentina's golden age.

Rosas, Juan Manuel de (1793–1877) A conservative political figure who ruled Argentina from 1829 until 1852, Rosas is the country's most famous caudillo. Raised on a cattle ranch, Rosas ascended to power as an important cattle rancher, emerging as a leader in battles against the British and against native groups. He became governor of Buenos Aires in 1829; in 1851, he became Supreme Chief of the Argentine Confederation—effectively, the dictator of the nation. Rosas cultivated an image of a "man of the people," but he also resorted to considerable violence to sustain his rule. A confederation of rivals led by Justo José de Urquiza finally forced Rosas from power in 1852. Rosas spent the rest of his life in exile in the United Kingdom.

Sábato, Ernesto (1911–) Ernesto Sábato is one of Argentina's most famous and most important literary figures. After an early career in the sciences (he earned a PhD in physics and worked at the Curie Institute in France), Sábato turned his energies to writing. His first major novel was *El Tunel,* or *The Tunnel.* At the request of Argentine president Raúl Alfonsín, Sábato directed the *Comisión Nacional Sobre la Desaparación de Personas* (National Commission on Missing Persons, or CONADEP), which investigated the human rights abuses that took place during the dirty war. Sábato has remained active in Argentine society, commenting frequently on the country's political, economic, and cultural experiences.

Saladero This typically rural operation slaughtered cattle and then produced dried and salted beef for sale domestically and often internationally.

San Martín, José de (1778–1850) A general and a leading figure in the southern part of South America's successful struggle for independence, San Martín is regarded in Argentina as a national hero and the country's most celebrated military leader. After receiving training in Spain and fighting for the Spanish army, San Martín returned to his home to fight against the mother country, helping to organize the forces fighting for independence. San Martín planned and directed invasions of Chile in 1817 and Peru in 1820; his heroic crossing of the Andes has been compared to feats of Hannibal and Napoleon crossing the Alps. The victory in Peru secured the independence of South America. Conflict with Simón Bolívar, the leader of independence forces from Venezuela, Colombia, and Peru, as well as disillusionment with growing internal strife within the United Provinces of the Río de la Plata in the 1820s, led San Martín to move to France in 1824; the national hero of Argentina lived the rest of his life in self-imposed European exile. The nature of San Martín's meeting with Bolívar, which precipitated San Martín's resignation of the command of his army and ultimately his departure to Europe, remains a subject of debate among historians.

Sarmiento, Domingo Faustino (1811–1888) Sarmiento was an important Argentine statesman, educator, and author; he also was the president of Argentina from 1868 to 1874. Born in San Juan, Argentina, Sarmiento lived in exile in Chile in the 1830s and 1840s due to his support of the *Unitario* cause. It was in Chile in 1845 that he wrote his most famous work, known as *Facundo,* which deals with the issues of personalism and *caudillismo* in politics. The work is the most well-known writing to contrast the supposed barbarity of Argentina's interior with the progressive civilization of its cities, especially Buenos Aires. Sarmiento became well known as a staunch critic of the Rosas dictatorship, of which *Facundo* is a thinly veiled critique. The work is regarded as a classic of Latin American literature.

Following the fall of the Rosas regime, Sarmiento participated in the construction of the Argentine Republic. He was a supporter of modernization following North American and European models; public education was, in his view, one of the principal vehicles to achieve modernization (as was European immigration). Among many public roles, Sarmiento served as the governor of two provinces; as secretary of education; as ambassador to the United States; and in 1868, as president of Argentina. Latin American Teacher's Day was established in 1943 in Sarmiento's honor.

Solís, Juan Díaz de (1470–1516) After voyages to the Yucatan and Brazil, Díaz de Solís led an expedition, which left Spain in 1515, to explore the southern part of South America. Following the east coast to the mouth of the Rio de la Plata in 1516, he then sailed up the estuary to the confluence of the Uruguay and Paraná rivers. His party was attacked by indigenous groups, and survivors reported that Díaz de Solís and most of his men were killed and cannibalized. Some sources suggest that Díaz de Solís was actually killed in a mutiny, with the alternative story invented by his crew. Díaz de Solís's brother-in-law, Francisco de Torres, assumed control of what was left of the expedition and returned to Spain.

SRA *Sociedad Rural Argentina,* or Argentine Rural Society. Formed in the nineteenth century, the association has over 10,000 members. Its function is to serve, and celebrate, Argentina's rural traditions and history. It was founded on the slogan "to cultivate the soil is to serve the country."

Stabilization This term refers to an attempt to control inflation; and it typically involves economic pain as wages fall, credit is tightened, and the economy moves into recession. Argentina's debate about inflation has led to both orthodox and heterodox plans to reduce inflation. A heterodox plan attempts to minimize economic pain by using political consensus to control wages and prices.

Torre, Lisandro de la (1868–1939) An important Argentine lawyer and politician, de la Torre played an important role in the founding of the *Unión Cívica Radical* (Radical Party) in 1890. Following a dispute with Hipólito Yrigoyen, de la Torre founded the *Partido Progresiva Democratica* (Progressive Democratic Party), which became an important political force in his home state of Santa Fe. As a member of congress supported by a strong provincial base, de la Torre played an important role in national politics.

UCR The *Unión Cívica Radical,* the official name for the Radical Party, was formed in 1890 and remains one of Argentina's most important political parties.

UIA *Unión Industrial Argentina,* or Argentine Industrial Union, is an important group representing business interests in Argentine politics that is made up of business and factory owners.

Unitario This term refers to those interested in controlling the central government in the city of Buenos Aires and, by extension, the United Provinces of the Río de la Plata between 1816 and 1829. The term was then used to designate the enemies of Juan Manuel de Rosas that aimed to unite the provinces into a single country.

Urquiza, Justo José de (1801–1870) Urquiza was an Argentine general and politician, as well as president of the

Argentine Confederation from 1854 to 1860. Acting as the leading caudillo of Entre Rios, Urquiza supported Juan Manuel de Rosas. However, he broke with Rosas in 1851 and led the forces that eventually defeated Rosas in 1852 at the Battle of Caseros. Urquiza's work toward national organization was hindered by Buenos Aires, which seceded from the Confederation. Urquiza then defeated the provincial army headed by Bartolomé Mitre in 1859, leading Buenos Aires to reenter the Confederation. Urquiza was assassinated in Entre Ríos at the age of 69 by a political rival.

Vaquería This term refers to the expeditions taking place during the colonial era to gather and slaughter wild cattle.

Videla, Jorge Rafael (1925–) Videla was Argentina's de facto president from 1976 to 1981, assuming power after a coup d'état deposed Isabel Martínez de Perón. Ironically, as the country descended into a near permanent state of violence and terrorism, he rose to a position of power working for Perón, supervising the dirty war against real and suspected enemies of the state. Videla, a leader of the Process of National Reorganization, was ultimately convicted of crimes against humanity in 1984 and sentenced to life imprisonment. After serving five years, he was granted a presidential pardon by Carlos Menem. Charged with crimes again in 2000, he remains under house arrest. On September 6, 2006, an Argentine judge ruled that Menem's pardon was unconstitutional, making a new trial possible. During Videla's regime, Argentina came to the brink of open war with Chile in a dispute surrounding three islands in the Beagle Channel; only intervention by the pope prevented war.

War of the Triple Alliance This conflict, also called the Paraguayan War in neighboring Brazil, lasted from 1865 to 1870 and pitted Argentina, Brazil, and Uruguay against

Paraguay. Argentina, Brazil, and Uruguay triumphed, decimating Paraguay.

Yerba mate A plant from which dried leaves are used to make *mate*. This highly popular drink, which is like tea and is caffeinated, can be found throughout Argentina, not to mention other South American countries such as Brazil, Paraguay, and Uruguay.

YPF *Yacimientos Petrolíferos Fiscales* was Argentina's state-run petroleum company until it was privatized in 1991 by the government of Carlos Menem. The company was then purchased by the Spanish multinational firm Repsol to form Repsol YPF.

Yrigoyen, Hipólito (1852–1933) A founding figure of the *Unión Cívica Radical* (Radical Party, UCR), Yrigoyen became the leading politician of his generation. He also became the first political leader to benefit from the Sáenz Peña Law of 1912, which called for a secret ballot and universal male suffrage. In 1916, Yrigoyen and the Radical Party capitalized on the newly enfranchised population to take control of the national government. He blended paternalism with nationalism in his attempts to control the party and the country; divisions within his party weakened his hold, but he managed to win reelection in 1928. However, the Great Depression left him weak and isolated; and he quickly succumbed to a military coup that forced him from office in 1930.

Argentina-Related Organizations

BUSINESS AND ECONOMIC RESOURCES

Argentine-American Chamber of Commerce, Inc.
630 Fifth Avenue, 25th Floor
Rockefeller Center
New York, NY 10111
Phone: (212) 698-2238
Fax: (212) 698-2239
Web site: http://www.argentinechamber.com
E-mail: info@argentinechamber.com

The Argentine-American Chamber of Commerce, Inc., is an independent, not-for-profit business organization that aims to promote trade and investment flows between Argentina and the United States. In the process, it also tries to promote closer ties between the business communities in both countries.

World Trade Organization (WTO)
Rue de Lausanne 154, CH-1211
Geneva 21, Switzerland
Phone: (41-22) 739-51-11
Fax: (41-22) 731-42-06
Web site: http://www.wto.org
E-mail: enquiries@wto.org

The WTO is an important international organization that deals with the rules of international trade. It supports free trade in general and specifically promotes free trade among its member nations. Argentina has been a member of the WTO since January 1, 1995.

CULTURAL EXCHANGES AND EDUCATIONAL RESOURCES

American Field Services—U.S.A. (AFS-USA)
71 West 23rd Street, 17th Floor
New York, NY 10010
Phone: (212) 807-8686
Fax: (212) 807-1001
Web site: http://www.afs.org/usa
E-mail: info.centers@afs.org

AFS is an international, nonprofit, voluntary organization that provides international and intercultural learning opportunities. The organization's goal is to help people develop knowledge, skills, and understanding to help create a more peaceful and just world. AFS sponsors an impressive international exchange program with thousands of students participating annually. Each year American students participate by living, studying, and volunteering in a multitude of countries overseas, including Argentina.

The Americas Society
680 Park Avenue
New York, NY 10021
Phone: (212) 249-8950
Web site: http://www.americas-society.org
E-mail: inforequest@a-coa.org

The Americas Society, started in 1965 by a group of businessmen led by David Rockefeller, is a not-for-profit institution that promotes an understanding of the political, economic, and cultural issues facing the nations of the Americas today. An understanding of the people and societies of the region is essential to the Americas Society agenda, which includes promoting democracy, the rule of law, and free trade.

Fulbright Program for U.S. Students—Sponsored by U.S. State Department
Institute of International Education/Headquarters
809 United Nations Plaza
New York, NY 10017-3580
Phone: (212) 984-5330
Web site: http://www.iie.org
General Inquiries: Walter Jackson, Program Manager, wjackson@iie.org
South America, Mexico, and Canada: Jody Dudderar, Program Manager, jdudderar@iie.org

The Fulbright Program is the largest U.S. international exchange program, offering students, scholars, and professionals opportunities to undertake international graduate study, advanced research, university teaching, and teaching in elementary and secondary schools worldwide. In 2004 alone, the program awarded some 6,000 grants to U.S. students, teachers, scholars, and professionals to study, teach, lecture, and conduct research in more than 150 foreign countries around the world. The Fulbright Program's main source of funding is an annual appropriation from the U.S. Congress to the Department of State.

GOVERNMENT RESOURCES

Argentine Embassy in Washington, DC
1600 New Hampshire Avenue, NW
Washington, DC 20009-2512
Phone: (202) 238-6401
Fax: (202) 332-3171
Web site: http://www.embassyofargentina.us
E-mail: embajadaargentinaeeuu.org

This is an important resource for anyone interested in Argentina, from tourists wanting to visit Argentina to those wanting information on trade and investment to those needing basic consular services. The site provides information on various events sponsored by the Argentine government as well as by the country's consulates located throughout the United States.

Embassy of the United States, Buenos Aires, Argentina
Information Resource Center
U.S. Embassy
Av. Colombia 4300
(C1425CGM) - Buenos Aires
Argentina
Phone: (54-11) 5777-4533
Fax: (54-11) 5777-4236
Web site: http://buenosaires.usembassy.gov/general_information9
       .html
E-mail: BuenosAiresIRC@state.gov

Like U.S. embassies around the world, the U.S. Embassy in Buenos Aires, Argentina, represents the U.S. government in Argentina, provides services to Americans traveling and doing business abroad, and processes visa applications for Argentines wanting to visit the United States. Information and services provided by the embassy include tax and voting information, handling of passports, and birth registration. The general Web site is an important resource and includes considerable information. Note that e-mails regarding visas or consular affairs should be sent to BNS-Visas@state.gov.

NEWS RESOURCES

There is no shortage of sources for obtaining news about Argentina; anyone who is interested just needs access to a computer—an incredible wealth of sources is just a few clicks away. One way to start is to conduct an online search on *Argentina* or *Argentina news*. Another resource is the Argentine Embassy's Web site listed previously, which is a valuable source of information. Another good resource is the University of Texas's Argentina-LANIC Web site, which is listed in the annotated bibliography. This is a wonderful source for all sorts of information on Argentina.

AllYouCanRead.com is a helpful resource for people looking to access current news or to remain up to date with central issues relating to Argentina. The site is http://www.all youcanread.com/news/argentina_news.asp. While some of the information is free, other information requires a fee.

Argentina News is a comprehensive source available on topix.net. The site is a great place to get news about Argentina from the whole world. The full site for Argentina is http://www.topix.net/world/argentina. Interested readers also can access Argentina Forums, which contains an archive of months' worth of important news stories.

Finally, *The World Factbook: Argentina,* provided by the CIA, is a great place to find important economic and political facts about Argentina, along with a variety of maps. This information can be found at https://www.cia.gov/library/publications/the-world-factbook/geos/ar.html.

TOURISM RESOURCES

Fodor's

Web site: http://www.fodors.com

Fodor's Web site provides one-stop shopping for anyone interested in visiting Argentina. The site is easy to use, providing everything from miniguides to major cities to travel tips, restaurant/hotel recommendations, and maps. This is a great place to start planning a trip to Argentina. A simple online search inputting *Argentina travel* will yield a large number of additional sources.

Lonely Planet

Web site: http://www.lonelyplanet.com

Like Fodor's, Lonely Planet is a great place to begin planning a visit to Argentina. The site is easy to navigate; from the main site, you simply type *Argentina* to get started. From this point, you can begin looking for flights, hotel recommendations, possible sites to visit, etc. You also can find overviews on history, religion, culture, and the like; a resource section provides additional Web links. Finally, helpful hints from other travelers may come in handy for first-time visitors to Argentina.

Annotated Bibliography

The sources discussed in this section are organized according to the chapters of the book, with a few important works mentioned first. The works are primarily general sources that can help you begin to understand modern Argentina. Likewise, all sources are written in English. A multitude of great sources are available on Argentina; the following bibliography is meant to serve simply as a starting point. Similarly, while there are countless articles on the country in popular magazines as well as in academic periodicals, this section focuses primarily on books. These books have been of tremendous help in putting together this text; and they are, for the most part, recognized as "industry standards" among Argentina experts. Any reader wanting to find more detailed or specialized sources should start with the Reference section at the end of each chapter and the bibliographies listed within each of the following sources.

GENERAL WORKS

A great place to start with nearly all of the subjects in this book is the University of Texas's Web site dedicated to Latin American Studies (Lanic), which has separate sites for most of the region's countries. Once in the site, interested readers can narrow their search by selecting one of the many topics. For Argentina specifically, the site is http://lanic.utexas .edu/la/argentina. The site contains a wealth of information on subjects ranging from Argentina's wines to its financial sector; general areas such as education, history, the arts, and contemporary culture also are covered. This site can serve as an excellent companion to the more scholarly sources listed next.

Burns, E. Bradford, and Julie A. Charlip. *Latin America: A Concise Interpretive History,* 7th ed. Upper Saddle River, NJ: Prentice Hall, 2002.

This volume deals with all of Latin America, not just Argentina. It is a unique book that attempts to present the major thematic issues concerning this complex region in one coherent history. Importantly, one major goal of the book is to present these themes along with one of the sobering realities of Latin America—the existence of large numbers of poor people inhabiting seemingly rich lands. This is an important contribution to the literature and a very good place to start building a foundation of knowledge about Latin America, knowledge that is critical to understanding the specific historical trajectory of Argentina.

Lewis, Colin M. *Argentina: A Short History.* Oxford: Oneworld Publications, 2002.

This is a great source to use to build a deeper understanding of both historical and modern Argentina. While the work is nominally a history of Argentina from its nineteenth-century independence to the present era, it is also a valuable introduction to key social, economic, and political issues. The work is particularly valuable in examining the "Argentine paradox," the reasons a country so rich in resources has encountered such difficulties in its path to development.

Nouzeilles, Gabriela, and Graciela Montaldo, eds. *The Argentina Reader: History, Culture and Politics.* Durham, NC: Duke University Press, 2002.

This is another great volume for interested readers to begin building a broad-based knowledge of Argentina. While the book contains a number of entries relating to the country's history, it moves well beyond that topic into areas such as politics and culture. Likewise, the volume spans Argentine history from early colonial days to the present and includes diverse sources such as poems, comic strips, photographs, and scholarly writings. Importantly, while many historical texts deal primarily with the country's elites, this source also deals with many of the country's forgotten groups, such as indigenous peoples, blacks, and women. Finally, this collection provides a fairly comprehensive list of suggested readings.

Skidmore, Thomas E., and Peter H. Smith. *Modern Latin America,* 5th ed. Oxford: Oxford University Press, 2001.

This volume should be an important source for introductory readers for two reasons. First, it contains an interesting chapter dedicated specifically to Argentina entitled "Argentina: Prosperity, Deadlock, and Change." This is a great introductory piece covering the country's history from the struggle for nationhood to the transition to democracy. Second, the book contains two important general chapters on Latin America and its history—from colonial foundations to the region's most recent return to democracy. These chapters provide an excellent framework for understanding Argentina's unique position within the region. Together the introductory chapters and the specific piece on Argentina can provide the broad foundation needed to tackle more detailed sources.

GEOGRAPHY AND HISTORY

Bethell, Leslie, ed. *The Cambridge History of Latin America, Vols. I–X.* Cambridge: Cambridge University Press, 1984–1995.

The Cambridge volumes begin with colonial times, including an examination of the existing indigenous cultures in Argentina, and move up through the modern era. This a very important source of articles on Argentine history. In addition, more general articles are available on the region, which can help build a conceptual framework for further analysis of Argentina and its place within Latin America.

Lewis, Colin M. *Argentina: A Short History.* Oxford: Oneworld Publications, 2002.

As mentioned previously, the Lewis book is an excellent starting point for delving into Argentina's history, covering in the process such issues as nation building, foreign relations, and economic crisis. This also is an excellent source for an introduction to the country's diverse geography. The book's introduction is a great place to start reading about the country's four main geographical areas and their roles in Argentina's history.

Rock, David. *Argentina, 1516–1982: From Spanish Colonization to the Falklands War.* London: I.B. Tauris, 1986.

Another interesting history of Argentina, this text is an important one for students of the country. The author is a leading authority on Argentina—those interested in more detailed examination of the country and its history should become familiar with this work.

Scobie, James R. *Argentina: A City and a Nation,* 2nd ed. New York: Oxford University Press, 1971.

As indicated by the publication date, this book is somewhat dated. However, it is one of the best single-book sources for an examination of the country's history, especially the often-overlooked colonial and early post-colonial periods. Likewise, it is excellent source for description and analysis of the country's diverse geography.

Shumway, Nicholas. *The Invention of Argentina.* Berkeley: University of California Press, 1991.

This is a very interesting book that focuses on Argentina's independence movement and its immediate aftermath. Shumway presents the ideas of Argentina's "founding fathers," helping to illuminate the gap between the regional caudillos and their followers and the country's more urban, intellectual leaders who wanted the country to pursue a European direction.

THE ECONOMY

The subject of the Argentine economy is a complex one, and the literature reflects this fact. Countless books and articles cover the economy as a whole and deal with specific problems facing the economy. It is suggested that beginning students, after reading this book's chapter on the economy, take three additional steps to dig deeper into economic issues. First, a simple online search for items about the Argentine economy can prove quite useful. Specifically, anyone looking for general information and descriptive statistics will find this the best starting point. As mentioned, one good place to start is with the University of Texas's Argentina Web site. A second step is to refer to the following list of sources. For the most part, these are general texts that can help build a broader foundation of knowledge about Argentina's economy. Finally, a look at the bibliographies of each of these texts, as well as those of the books listed at the end of the economics chapter, provides a much deeper body of economics literature.

Cardoso, Eliana, and Ann Helwege. *Latin America's Economy: Diversity, Trends, and Conflicts.* Cambridge, MA: MIT Press, 1995.

This book covers all of Latin America, not just Argentina; however, Argentine examples are used throughout the text. It is an excellent introduction to the economic challenges that face Argentina specifically and the region in general, from inflation and debt crises to poverty, inequality, and land reform. Argentina features prominently in the book, as the authors use the region's countries to illustrate their points. Any student wanting to delve deeper into the country's economy should use this book as a general companion volume to works dealing specifically with Argentina.

De la Balze, Felipe A. M. *Remaking the Argentine Economy.* New York: Council on Foreign Relations Press, 1995.

This is an interesting source dealing with the country's economic history as well as its more modern attempts at economic reform. Given the publication date, however, the book predates the collapse of convertibility and its aftermath—and thus the severe recession and the surprising economic recovery as well. Still, this is a good source for Argentina-specific economic analysis that covers the big picture in nonspecialist language.

Díaz Alejandro, Carlos F. *Essays on the Economic History of the Argentine Republic.* New Haven, CT: Yale University Press, 1970.

This book is a very important economic history of Argentina and, as such, should be one of the first economic sources that students of Argentina consult.

Di Tella, Guido, and Rudiger Dornbusch, eds. *The Political Economy of Argentina, 1946–1983.* London: Macmillan, 1989.

This is an interesting collection of pieces about the Argentine economy. The editors are well-known scholars of Argentina; and in general, the pieces contribute to an understanding of the dilemmas Argentina has faced in its volatile struggle for development.

POLITICS AND GOVERNMENT

Lewis, Paul W. *The Crisis of Argentine Capitalism.* Chapel Hill: University of North Carolina Press, 1990.

Lewis's book is an important examination of the interaction between politics and economics in Argentina, particularly as it relates to the increasingly frequent and intense economic and political crises the country has faced in the modern era. The author focuses on pressure groups to get to the root causes of what he calls "the country's politics of economic stagnation."

O'Donnell, Guillermo, Philippe C. Schmitter, and Laurence Whitehead. *Transitions from Authoritarian Rule: Latin America.* Baltimore: Johns Hopkins University Press, 1986.

This is an important text examining the critical period of transition from authoritarian rule to democracy. The book provides an introduction to the issue of transition in Latin America as well as a number of important case studies in which Argentina plays a prominent role.

Potash, Robert. *The Army and Politics in Argentina,* 3 vols. Palo Alto, CA: Stanford University Press, 1969–1996.

Clearly, the military has played a very important role in politics and political development in Argentina. Therefore, any student wanting to delve more deeply into politics must examine the historical evolution of this institution's role in Argentine politics. This book is a good source, but there is extensive literature examining the subject.

Rock, David. *Authoritarian Argentina: The Nationalist Movement, Its History, and Its Impact.* Berkeley: University of California Press, 1993.

As mentioned, David Rock is one of the leading experts on Argentina; and this is another good text by this important scholar. As the title suggests, this is a good source to get a deeper understanding of authoritarianism in Argentina and to examine the role nationalism has played in Argentine authoritarian government.

Wynia, Gary W. *Argentina in the Post-War Era: Politics and Economic Policy Making in a Divided Society.* Albuquerque: University of New Mexico Press, 1988.

While somewhat dated, this book fills in important detail necessarily left out of Wynia's chapter on Argentina (just mentioned). Likewise, as the title suggests, the book goes beyond an analysis of traditional party-based politics to look specifically at economic policymaking in Argentina—a helpful addition.

Wynia, Gary W. *The Politics of Latin American Development,* 3rd ed. Cambridge: Cambridge University Press, 1990.

Like Skidmore and Smith's *Modern Latin America,* Wynia's books deals with all of Latin America—although in this case, with politics rather than general history. The book provides an interesting general section on how to approach Latin American politics, which can serve as an excellent framework for more detailed analysis. The book also provides a good, short introductory analysis of Argentina and its politics.

SOCIETY AND CULTURE

Cubitt, Tessa. *Latin American Society.* Essex, England: Longman Group UK Limited, 1988.

This text is a general one, covering the whole of Latin America. It is a great place for students of Argentine society to start a deeper exploration of the issues discussed in the society and culture chapter, since the issues and problems facing Argentina today can be found throughout the whole of Latin America. The book provides an excellent introduction to a host of issues, such as poverty and unemployment, race relations, rural-urban migration, and education.

Elliot, David. *Art from Argentina.* Oxford: Museum of Modern Art, 1994.

Within the cultural realm, Argentina is perhaps best known for its rich literary tradition; however, it also has an important tradition of fine art. This is a good book for interested students to begin exploring this subject.

Foster, David William, Melissa Fitch Lockhart, and Darrell B. Lockhart. *Culture and Customs of Argentina.* Westport, CT: Greenwood Press, 1998.

This volume is a good place to start exploring the culture and society of Argentina; it provides considerable content as well as a large number of additional sources. The book covers diverse topics, from religion and social customs to literature and the performing arts. This is a great place to start exploring typical Argentine customs such as the tango and *mate* tea.

Foster, David William. *Contemporary Argentine Cinema.* Columbia: University of Missouri Press, 1992.

Argentina has a rich tradition of cinema, and this book provides a good introduction to contemporary Argentine cinema. Those wanting to review the topic can refer to the short chapter on cinema in *Culture and Customs of Argentina.*

King, John, ed. *On Modern Latin American Fiction.* New York: Noonday Press, 1987.

This text provides an excellent introduction to the considerable literature of Latin America, covering both the historical evolution of the region's literature and its best-known authors. Interested readers can find valuable essays on Argentina's most important authors, such as Jorge Luis Borges, Julio Cortázar, and Manuel Puig.

Nouzeilles, Gabriela, and Graciela Montaldo, eds. *The Argentina Reader: History, Culture and Politics.* Durham, NC: Duke University Press, 2002.

This book, discussed previously, is an excellent compilation of pieces dealing with the many facets of Argentina, spanning a broad range of time from the early colonial days to the present. It also provides a comprehensive bibliography for those students who want to dig deeper.

Index

About the Author

Todd L. Edwards is an independent writer, consultant, and investment strategist based in Fort Collins, Colorado. He received his PhD in Latin American studies from Tulane University in 1995, with concentrations in development economics, political science, and public policy. His dissertation research focused on political economy and institutional reform, using Mexico's stock market reform as a case study. He then pursued a career on Wall Street, working for firms such as U.S. investment bank Salomon Brothers and Spanish Banco Bilbao Vizcaya Argentaria (BBVA). On Wall Street, Edwards specialized as an investment strategist for Latin America. In this role, he combined political, economic, and financial analysis to assist major global investors (primarily American and European) operating in the region. Edwards also was the director of Latin American equity research for BBVA, leading a team of research analysts based in New York as well as in major financial capitals of Latin America such as Buenos Aires, Mexico City, and São Paulo.